Paradigm Shift

Paradigm Shift

The New Promise of
Information Technology

Don Tapscott

Art Caston

McGRAW-HILL, Inc.
New York San Francisco Washington D.C. Auckland Bogotá
Caracas Lisbon London Madrid Mexico Mexico City Milan
Montreal New Delhi San Juan Singapore
Sydney Tokyo Toronto

Library of Congress Cataloging-in-Publication Data

Tapscott, Don.
    Paradigm shift : the new promise of information technology / Don
Tapscott and Art Caston.
        p.   cm.
    Includes bibliographical references and index.
    ISBN 0-07-062857-2
    1. Information technology — Case studies.   2. Industrial
management — Case studies.   I. Caston, Art.   II. Title.
    HC79.I55T37   1993
    658.4'038 — dc20   92-17696
                                                                 CIP

        5 6 7 8 9 0   DOC/DOC   9 8 7 6 5 4 3

ISBN 0-07-062857-2

*The sponsoring editor for this book was Betsy Brown, the editing supervisor was
Ruth W. Mannino, and the production supervisor was Suzanne W. Babeuf. It
was set in Baskerville by McGraw-Hill's Professional Book Group composition
unit.*

Printed and bound by R. R. Donnelley & Sons Company.

To our children, Kim and David Caston and Nicole and Alexander Tapscott. It is our hope and ambition that the smaller, more open world they inherit will be a better one.

Contents

7. The Industrial Revolution in Software   165

Part 3. The Transition   181

8. Achieving a Shared, New Vision   185

9. Reengineering the Business   207

Preface

A fundamental change is taking place in the nature and application of technology in business. This change has profound and far-reaching implications for your organization and for you.

To date, no one has fully articulated this change. As a result, developments in technology often appear as a barrage of random, unrelated events. Further, most enterprises are having severe difficulties embracing the change, remaining constrained by traditional approaches to exploiting technology and by legacy technology investments and cultures.

A multimillion dollar research program conducted by DMR at the turn of the decade and early 1990s was launched to understand this problem and find some answers. Several thousand organizations in North America, Europe, and the Far East were studied to investigate the nature and impacts of changes in technology, including emerging applications, organizational benefits, and management implications.

The research came to a number of striking conclusions, which all center on one theme: Information technology is going through its first *paradigm shift*—driven by the demands of the new, competitive business environment on the one hand and profound changes in the nature of computers on the other. *The information age is evolving into a second era.*

The paradigm shift encompasses fundamental change in just about everything regarding the technology itself and its application to business. The old paradigm began in the 1950s. The late 1980s and the 1990s are a transition period to the new paradigm. Organizations that do not make this transition will fail. They will become irrelevant or cease to exist.

A paradigm shift is a fundamentally new way of looking at something. It is often necessitated by new developments in science, technology, art, or other areas of endeavor. Such shifts are necessary because important changes in reality demand a shift in conceptualization. For example, in the early twentieth century the march of science began to raise issues that were not easily explained by Newtonian physics. A new paradigm, in this case Einstein's special theory of relativity, emerged as a new and more comprehensive theory and framework to explain the new realities.

The concept of a paradigm shift was first introduced by philosopher and science historian Thomas Kuhn in his 1962 book, *The Structure of Scientific Revolutions.*[1] The notion of a paradigm has grown beyond the dictionary definition. Today the term is widely used to define a broad model, a framework, a way of thinking, or a scheme for understanding reality. Psychologists discuss a reinforcement paradigm; politicians speak of political paradigms; doctors discuss a paradigm shift in medicine; and so on.[2] The idea that the information age is going through its first paradigm shift was first elaborated by DMR Group in 1987.[3,4]

Four paradigm shifts impact business today. These are illustrated in the figure below.

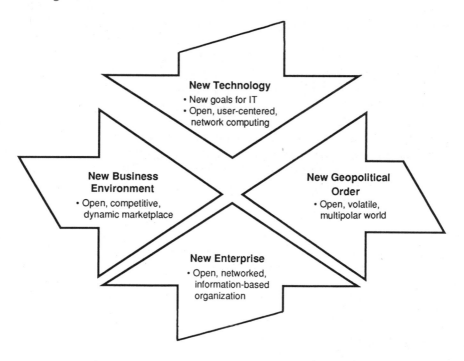

New Technology
- New goals for IT
- Open, user-centered, network computing

New Business Environment
- Open, competitive, dynamic marketplace

New Geopolitical Order
- Open, volatile, multipolar world

New Enterprise
- Open, networked, information-based organization

1. The change in the world economic and political order is quite apparent to anyone who reads newspapers. No one is really sure what that change is or where it is going, but the end of the post-World War II era has occurred. The world is opening and is volatile.

2. A related shift is occurring in the business environment and marketplace. The stable, postwar period of limited competition is over. Markets and national economics are being transformed. Old rules are disappearing, as are walls to competition.

3. A shift is occurring in the nature of organizations. The corporation of old simply does not work anymore. Business transformation enabled by information is required to succeed in the new environment. The new enterprise is dynamic and can respond quickly to changing market conditions. It has a different structure—flatter and team-oriented—eliminating bureaucratic hierarchy. It is based on commitment rather than control. Business processes are streamlined for productivity and quality. The new enterprise is open and networked.

4. The information age is entering a second era. The new technology paradigm parallels the other shifts. Like the new enterprise it is open and networked. It is modular and dynamic—based on interchangeable parts. It technologically empowers, distributing intelligence and decision making to users. Yet, through standards, it is integrated, moving enterprises beyond the system islands (and their organizational equivalents) of the first era. It works like people do, integrating data, text, voice, and image information in its various formats—and provides a backbone for team-oriented business structures. It blurs walls between enterprises, enabling the recasting of external relationships. Most important, it has matured to the point where it is achievable and affordable. In fact, the longer your organization waits to begin a transition, the more you have to spend, even in the short term.

This book is about the paradigm shift in information technology and how it relates to the other historic changes in our world. We believe this shift is the missing piece in the discussion of how to achieve the new enterprise. The computing platforms that exist in most organizations today are unable to deliver the goods for corporate rebirth. They are expensive, are limited in function, and seem to take forever to change. Worse, these old computing structures lock organizations into old corporate structures.

It is only through open network computing that the open networked enterprise can be achieved. Understanding the technology paradigm shift is therefore becoming a precondition for business success in the information age.

This book investigates the critical dimensions of the shift to help you uncover the new promise of IT in your organization, demystify the sometimes bewildering changes occurring in technology, and provide a framework for leading the transition to the new.

Don Tapscott
Art Caston

Acknowledgments

This book is a product of the collective work of a number of leading thinkers in DMR Group Inc. and other organizations.

A primary source is several large multiclient studies performed by DMR and others over the period of 1986 to 1992. These programs received more than $7 million in funding from more than 300 companies and government agencies in the United States, Canada, Australia, and several European countries, each of which contributed approximately $25,000. The programs were initiated by DMR to investigate critical issues of information technology direction and management. In total, more than 5000 organizations participated in these programs, providing information about their current technology, technology directions, key problems, successes, failures, attitudes, and perceptions on a wide range of issues. The people who contributed their time included *information systems* (IS) executives and professionals as well as a wide range of business people who have responsibilities for decision making regarding IS. As well, more than 100 DMR professionals were involved in the research and execution of these programs. We are deeply indebted to all. The main programs are:

- *The Integration of Data, Text, Voice, and Image.* This $2.5 million investigation examined the rise of integrated systems and their impact on both organizational effectiveness and the computer industry. The program was conducted by DMR and collected information from more than 1500 persons in 100 subscribers.

- *Unix in Canada.* This $500,000 effort was cosponsored by the

UniForum Canada association and involved research in more than 400 companies and government departments.

- *Strategies for Open Systems.* This multimillion dollar effort was launched by the UniForum association, X/Open consortium, and DMR and conducted by DMR. Funding came from more than 50 computer vendors and 90 government agencies and other companies. It was also sponsored by the U.S. government's National Institute of Standards and Technology, the Commission of European Communities, the Open Software Foundation, and the Unix International Consortium.

- *Aligning IS with the Business.* In partnership with Cognitech Services Corporation of Connecticut, this study investigated the issues of how to measure the contribution of IS to the business and how to better align IS with the business to maximize IS contribution.

A second key source of the conclusions reached in this book is the DMR consulting experience. We are deeply indebted to dozens of colleagues and clients who have worked with us around the world in various projects to help organizations compete more effectively through IT, reengineer their businesses, retool their technology architectures, and realign the IS functions to improve IS contribution.

Finally, we are indebted to a number of individuals who have made specific contributions to the manuscript. These include consultants Joe Arbuckle, who provided important insights on the challenges of reimaging and relearning for the new enterprise, and Alex Lowy, who provided essential information on the issues of building team-based work systems; Stephen Sieck of Link Resources, who provided valuable data on the new information markets; Lyle Anderson of Aetna for his insights on the issues of network computing, the transformation of IT architecture, and software development; consultant Michael Anderson for his thoughts on changing organizational structures and the role of the CIO, Stephen Caswell of Incomnet for his assistance on the issue of the extended enterprise; futurist Robin Macrae for his collaboration, years ago, in developing the concept of the IT paradigm shift; Tom Vassos for his review of the manuscript and for, along with Araldo Menegon and Ed Palmer, as executives of UniForum, being instrumental in launching the original syndicated research on open systems; Ben Porter of Anderson Consulting for his assistance on the issue of IS organizational structures; Tom Lodahl and Kay Redditt of Cognitech for their considerable insights on the issue of aligning IS with the business; Bob Tapscott, the visionary behind the initial Citibank workgroup implementation; Paul De Lottinville for his initial case study research for the paradigm shift; and Stephen Davies for his insights on the open networked enterprise. We are also endebted to Betsy Brown of McGraw-Hill for her collaboration throughout the project and to the production team managed by Ruth Mannino for helping to make the manuscript sing.

From DMR, David Ticoll, who was instrumental in the launching of our open systems research, gave us invaluable suggestions and comments throughout the process of writing the book. We are also indebted to Stan Rolland, Paul Martino, Jean-Marc Proulx, and Joe Deragon for their thoughts on the issue of software development; André Dubuque, Burnes Hollyman, and John Thorp for their insights in the area of IT strategy and architecture; Del Henderson-Langdon for sharing her considerable expertise in work-systems redesign; Andrew Lamb for his assistance on the issue of the extended organization; David Forrest and George Lysenko for advice on geographic information systems; Mike Lovell for his work on continuous improvement; and Rob Howie, Randy Russell, Colleen Radigan, Nancy Miller, Andrew Toller, Tamerey Camp, and Kim Hatton of DMR's Emerging Technologies consulting practice; and DMR's Australian team headed by Kim Fitzpatrick for its critical contribution to the research effort. Additional thanks to Tamerey, Kim, Helen Mroczkowski, Halyna Fenkanyn, Tim Warner, Catherine Colburn, and Ruby Densmore for their help in the production of the manuscript.

We would also like to thank other DMR executives, Pierre Ducros, Ron McCulloch, Pat McLagan, Serge Meilleur, Mike Power, and Alain Roy, for their encouragement and support for this project.

While we are grateful for the contributions of those mentioned above, final responsibility for the content and views expressed herein rests with ourselves.

Finally, we are most indebted to our partners and spouses Penny Caston and Ana P. Lopes, not just for their support in holding the fort while this book was in the making, but for invaluable collaboration throughout the project.

Paradigm Shift

1

Introduction

What on Earth Will Happen Next?

It happens to you at various points throughout the day—starting with reading the morning newspaper and ending with watching the late night news. The staggering changes taking place in the world and their implications for our professional and personal lives are relentless, changes unimagined just a few years, months, or weeks ago. There is a new openness and volatility that seem rich with opportunity and fraught with danger for humanity, your country, your organization, and you. As you read the headlines, you often find yourself shaking your head: What on earth will happen next!

When news of the collapse of the Berlin Wall reverberated around the globe at the end of the 1980s, even the most diehard cold warriors realized that the world was changing. The assumptions that had directed the economic and political events of the world since 1945 suddenly had to be questioned and reconsidered. The status quo of more than four decades was quickly disappearing. Authors of east-west espionage thrillers, such as John LeCarré, admitted that their work was quickly becoming dated.

The Berlin Wall, the physical and symbolic barrier that had separated two countries, two ideologies, and divided a continent, was dismantled and its pieces sold as souvenirs of another time. Its demise, to people all over the globe, was the beginning of a new decade and a new world. Its destruction symbolized the birth of an uncertain but exciting new era and a profound shift in the structure of world order.

The Berlin bulldozer engines were still warm when Saddam Hussein—freed of the constraints of a bygone, bipolar world—boldly set out to exploit the new world situation. He was followed, in turn, by

George Bush, who sought to define and establish a new world order. The United States and the Soviet Union stood side by side. Old rules and alliances were quickly swept away. New alliances and rules were forged. Six months and tens of thousands of deaths later the world had seen a first glimpse of the dark side of a new era.

Other dramatic changes continue as the twentieth century draws to a close. With the postwar era and its economic, political, and social barriers collapsing, changes in economic and political relations are affecting countries everywhere and challenging traditional ways of thinking. Whether they be concrete blocks in Berlin or tariff barriers in Europe and North America, physical, economic, cultural, and political barriers are tumbling. There is a growing awareness of the interdependency of nations, individual countries no longer operating as island states if they hope to survive, let alone prosper.

Countries, whether they be in southeast Asia, western Europe, North America, South America, Africa, or the Middle East, have become integral parts of a world trading market. Through economic necessity as well as political and social pressures, attitudes are rapidly changing. As the world prepares to enter the twenty-first century, there is a new openness among countries and cultures and a freer flow of information, goods, and ideas.

As more and more of the traditional postwar barriers fall, a new era bringing upheaval, unprecedented change, and major political and economic realignments continues to unfold. The stunning disintegration of Stalinism in eastern Europe and the breakup of the Soviet Union clearly constitute one of the most significant developments in the century (ranking with the "10 days that shook the world" in October 1917) and arguably in human history.

Information and information technology are at the center of this opening. Faxes provide students demonstrating in Tienanmen Square with information about what is happening in their own country and enable them to communicate their story with the world. People around the world view the Iraqi war from live television feeds in besieged Baghdad. Debates once restricted to the Soviet underground *samizdat* rage in the pages of Russian newspapers, presenting views that a few years ago would have qualified most authors for a one-way trip to a psychiatric hospital. Smart bombs enter 6 ft^2 windows, and thousands of networked personal computers become key battlefield weapons. Global telecommunications networks energize the metabolism of world commerce and move us inexorably toward Marshall McLuhan's global village.

There are new opportunities, but there are also potential perils for nations, cultures, economies, and people. The growth of political, economic, and technological openness and interdependence is occurring alongside rapidly growing nationalism, cultural reaffirmation, and radicalism which have both positive and negative dynamics. Witness the continually shifting relationship of forces between democratic, ultranationalist, neofascist, Islamic fundamentalist, Stalinist, and other factions in the countries of the former Soviet Union. Who will win out in each of these countries? What will become of the region and the continent?

The transformation of world economics has produced massive casualties, and these are not confined to eastern Europe or the countries of the former Soviet Union. Many countries are stalled economically. Canada continues to reel from an increasingly distorted economy and volatile national differences. Although buoyed by the 1992 European Community unification, many countries in western Europe are up and down or stalled. Even the Japanese industrial behemoth shows signs of weakness.

The heartland of free enterprise—the United States—is in serious trouble, by most accounts. Economic growth has been lackluster to say the least. It is estimated that 25 million Americans—20 percent of the work force—were unemployed at some point in 1991.[1] The United States has lost ground in key industrial sectors—for example, the loss of the consumer electronics and car manufacturing hegemony to the Japanese. Today, the United States imports over $30 billion per year in automobiles and parts and over $25 billion in consumer electronics. The federal debt tripled from $1.3 to $3.6 trillion during the 1970s and 1980s (in part a legacy of the cold war with its military buildup). The annual cost of servicing this debt is $360 billion—more than the cost of the war in Iraq. The United States was once the world's largest creditor. It now is the world's largest debtor.

Today's American children will be the first generation in U.S. history to experience a lower standard of living than their parents. Infant mortality ranks with some third world countries despite much higher per capita health care costs compared with other western economies. The infrastructure of roads, sewers, and the like is in serious decay. Homelessness is an international disgrace. Substantial numbers of people are socially and economically marginalized, as the growth of drug use and drug-oriented economies and subcultures indicates. The dream of home ownership is becoming just a dream for millions of young people. Productivity of knowledge and service workers is a huge problem.[2]

There is growing awareness of the seriousness of this situation. For example, Barlett and Steele's stunning indictment of the American decline entitled *America: What Went Wrong?* rose to the top of the nonfiction best-seller list in 1992. Among other things, the book documents the dismantling of the American middle class, leaving a two-class society of rich and poor.[3] The 1992 Los Angeles riots were a wake-up call to the nation, notwithstanding widely divergent interpretations of the origins and causes of unrest.

The New Business Environment

The titles of new management and business books by leading thinkers at the turn of the decade tell a story of changing business conditions linked to the global political and economic changes: *The Borderless World, Power and Strategy in the Interlinked Economy* by Kenichi Ohmae,[4] *The New Realities in Government and Politics/in Economics and Business/in Society and World View* by Peter F. Drucker,[5] *Megatrends 2000, Ten New Directions for the 1990s* by Patricia Aburdene and John Naisbitt,[6] *Cracking the Global Market, How to Do Business around the Corner and around the World* by Jack Nadel,[7] and *The Competitive Advantage of Nations* by Michael E. Porter.[8] All discuss the fundamental shifts in the world economic situation, the nature of business, and the need for a new paradigm—a fundamentally new approach and way of thinking to understand and deal with the new realities.

Businesses face a paradox. They have unprecedented opportunities to tap new markets. Meanwhile, traditional markets are changing dramatically, shrinking or becoming intensely competitive. Additionally, reduced profit margins along with rising customer demands for quality products and services are placing unrelenting pressures on many enterprises.

A pressing reality of the new global environment is the emergence of a new era of competition. Competition is arising not only from traditional adversaries in traditional markets, or from new entrants to a specific industry or economic sector, but also from the disintegration of barriers to previously insulated and protected markets. Enterprises no longer limit their growth to traditional customer bases. Bankers offer insurance and brokerage services. Credit card companies enter territory previously reserved for banks. Insurance companies market financial services. High-technology companies sell consumer goods. Even national postal services are becoming heavily involved in direct mail and retailing.

On the other hand, some other companies that had expanded into new markets have retrenched as the pressures of the early 1990s recession force them to "stick to their knitting." For example, American Express, which expanded aggressively into a wide range of financial and related businesses, has more recently refocused on its core credit card business.

The barriers that separated economic and vertical market sectors and the companies that operated within them are quickly falling. Competition can arise unexpectedly from anywhere. This means that enterprises can no longer be overconfident about their market shares and their competitive positions. For businesses faced with shrinking profit margins, the ability to lower unit operating costs and overheads in these highly competitive markets has become a key concern. No longer are the minor gains in efficiencies of a few percentage points experienced over the last two decades sufficient to meet the cost-containment demands of the 1990s.

The opening of world marketplaces has caused many corporations to reel — resulting in massive restructuring in virtually every business sector. According to its chairman, the General Motors of the mid- to late 1990s will be half the size of the General Motors of the mid- to late 1980s. IBM is becoming a network of autonomous businesses. Citibank is completely transforming its organization. All are restructuring their cost bases through severe downsizing.

The restructuring of national economies is relentless, largely driven by advances in information technology. Although there is a transition from the old industrial economy, the terms *service economy* and, to some extent, *information economy* are misleading. The planet, and even the Western world, still relies on agriculture and industrial production for the creation of wealth and the meeting of basic human needs. You can't eat or live on information. Humanity is a long way from an economic structure based on tourism, leisure, government services, software, and fast food. Just as industrial production was applied to the previous (agricultural) economy, *information technology* (IT) is being applied to all aspects of production, and in turn agriculture. Information, as a result, has become a capital good. It is becoming similar in value to labor, materials, and financial resources. Furthermore, the IT sector itself is undergoing explosive growth.

For example, in 1992 the IT and communications sector had grown to close to 10 percent of the gross domestic product in the United States. The computer equipment and services sector alone was larger than auto, steel, mining, petrochemical, and natural gas combined.

Information technology is also penetrating every other sector in ways that are stunning. If you purchase a new car this year, you'll find more computer power under the hood than Neil Armstrong had in his lunar lander.

With markets and their players constantly changing, the possibility of enterprises establishing a sustainable competitive advantage no longer exists. No organization can afford to rest on its laurels; each must constantly innovate to compete.

Seven Key Drivers of the New Business Environment

Since the 1990s will be a decade of major transition in the way business is conducted, this is a time to get serious about implementing strategic programs focused on business development and survivability and to begin building the future enterprise.

A number of recurring business themes are emerging in today's strategic plans as enterprises reengineer themselves for the new environment: Each of these is demanding a new technology paradigm.

Productivity of Knowledge and Service Workers

A critical business challenge facing our clients is the need to significantly improve the productivity of knowledge and service workers. Peter Drucker argues that the single greatest challenge facing managers in the west today is to raise the productivity of knowledge and service workers. He says that productivity will dominate management thinking for many decades. It will ultimately determine the competitive performance of companies, the quality of life in every industrialized nation, and the very fabric of society.[9]

Drucker goes on to compare and contrast this need for productivity in the information age with that of the industrial age. Productivity in manufacturing, farming, mining, construction, and transportation has improved at a combined annual rate of 3 to 4 percent, resulting in a phenomenal 45-fold improvement over the last 120 years! These improvements continue today; however, their impact on the economy is diminishing since their relative proportion of the economy is shrinking. These outstanding productivity gains were the result of the effective application of scientific methods, advanced engineering, and management sciences. The capital and technology of the industrial age focused on industrial productivity. The capital and technology of the information age is focused on knowledge and service worker productivity. Information technology is the foremost tool for making the substantial and ongoing productivity gains that will shape the leaders (individuals, companies, institutions, and countries) of the twenty-first century.

For many organizations this means a restructuring of their cost base. No longer are minor gains in efficiencies (of a few percentage points here and there) adequate to meet the cost-containment demands of the 1990s. The focus is now shifting to major business transformations where entire processes (both production and management) are streamlined. Paper-based systems, bureaucratic approval processes, labor-intensive clerical activities, batch processing cycles, and multilayered decision-making processes are being replaced by source data capture, integrated transaction processing, electronic data interchange, real-time systems, on-line decision support, document management systems, and expert systems.

Another important trend is a shift in the focus of productivity programs from cost cutting to improving organizational performance and effectiveness. This trend is occurring for two reasons. Many cost-restructuring programs have failed, permanently weakening a company in its market and compromising its chances for survival.[10] Moreover, the enabling effect of information technology is leading to completely new high-performance work-system models. Human energy is reinvested in new things as opposed to being eliminated through head-count reductions. You will read in subsequent chapters how this can be achieved.

Quality

In many manufacturing and production operations today, quality problems can back up an entire plant and cause a chain reaction along the supplier network. This is primarily due to the integrated nature of production processes, and can be exacerbated by such things as just-in-time inventory. Failures in shipped products often result in expensive outages for customers, costly repairs, and, most regrettably, dissatisfied customers.

Product and service quality programs have moved from manufacturing operations to knowledge and service work. Service industries are faced with similar client and competitive drivers for improved quality of services and means of delivery. Quality expectations continue to rise. By building a corporate culture around quality, many companies such as Federal Express have been able to achieve significant success. Quality has become a broad theme, encompassing the notions of consistency, predictability, employee motivation, supplier involvement, and performance measurement.

Responsiveness

The need to react to rapidly changing market conditions, competitive threats, and customer demands is another growing challenge to enterprises. The time from product/service innovation to delivery to the market is rapidly shrinking in most business and industrial sectors.

For example, programs for "mass customization" are beginning in several sectors. The clothing industry in the United States has implemented integrated solutions to capture purchasing trends by area at the point of sale and to feed back this information to the manufacturing and distribution operations.

The ability to react and the time to react are key considerations in setting strategies and enabling organizations to become more market-driven and opportunistic. In global markets there is a need to eliminate, or at least reduce, time and space dependencies.

The old saying "Better late than never" has been turned around to "Better never than late." It is often better not to have started to develop a product than to get to the market after a competitor, or after the market has changed.

Globalization

With the emphasis on the expansion of free trade zones and the removal of access barriers, another common strategic theme is the globalization of markets, operations, and competition. This often involves mergers, acquisitions, and alliances to gain market knowledge and presence.

Operations often extend to 24 hours a day with worldwide networks linking customers, suppliers, and the supporting business infrastructure (financial, customs, shippers, etc.).

Globalization also brings new competitive threats to the "home" market. Aggressive new entrants can seriously disrupt established markets and set new standards. The consumer electronics and automotive markets in North America are good illustrations of this factor.

Linked to this is an erosion in the ability of national governments to shelter inefficient industries. As world economies become more interdependent, protectionism will increasingly fail.

Outsourcing

There is a paradox occurring around the role of key suppliers to an organization. As the ability to integrate the production facilities and support resources of suppliers into our own production and management processes increases, the same infrastructures enable the off-loading of previously internal processes to outside suppliers.

We are experiencing a resurgence in interest for outsourcing certain aspects of production, distribution, sales, service, and support functions. The interest is on focusing the resources of an organization on key areas of value-added capability and not diluting attention to these areas by overloading the capabilities of the organization.

In the past, organizations attempted to be self-sufficient through vertical integration within the enterprise. The streamlined enterprise of the 1990s has shifted the focus to vertical and horizontal integration across organizations, including alliance partners, sales and distribution agencies, key suppliers, support organizations, and other divisions within their own company. As Joe Brophy, president of the Travelers Insurance company told us, "Outsourcing is ready to take off." The Travelers will focus on its unique competencies and partner with others to provide additional services.

Partnering

Companies that previously had little in common are merging or forming joint ventures to go after both new and traditional business opportunities. Many businesses are positioning themselves to function in the growing worldwide marketplace by establishing alliances and joint ventures with other key players in both similar and disparate markets. Others are forming strategic alliances with governments to meet specific market needs. These partnerships (which involve enterprises of all sizes) can involve the creation of research and development consortia, joint ventures, and cross-licensing arrangements. They are providing many of these organizations with the financial, human, and other resources required to compete in diverse and sometimes volatile markets.

The Japanese *keiretsu* — the association of a number of industries centered on a bank — has proved to be devastatingly effective in reducing time to market and creating long-term competitiveness. Variants of the keiretsu have now sprung up in North America and Europe as important companies such as Ford and IBM acquire equity positions in suppliers, participate in various consortia, and in other ways become partners with external organizations.

The enterprise is becoming "extended" — based on new kinds of relationships with suppliers, customers, affinity groups, and even competitors. Such relationships enable organizations to develop comprehensive approaches to markets, jointly fund large efforts in their common interests, respond quickly to new or ephemeral opportunities, get access to each other's customers without acquiring each other, create new markets, share information, combine as interest groups or lobbies, rapidly expand geographically, etc.

Social and Environmental
Responsibility

Due to changing and growing expectations by employees, business partners, and customers, today's enterprise must act responsibly in its relationships with others. The *sleaze* factor of the 1980s has resulted in a responsibility backlash. The 1990s have become the decency decade. Customers want to purchase goods from companies that are ethical, good corporate citizens, and green. The triumph of The Body Shop tells the story. The company presented itself convincingly as one that created healthy, environment-friendly products developed without animal testing and that championed various causes with corporate profits. The result was a huge international success.

In the new business environment, employees and groups must be empowered and motivated to cooperate for success. A prerequisite for such change is employer responsibility toward staff who expect fair treatment, some control over decision making, a stake in the success of the group and enterprise, and proper tools to do their jobs and collaborate effectively.

The New Enterprise

You can read about it everywhere. Management lecturers talk about it. Business schools debate it. But as Bob Dylan once wrote, "You don't need a weatherman to know which way the wind blows." The traditional, hierarchical organization is in deep trouble. The reason is that the old enterprise is poorly equipped to respond to the new business needs. The command-and-control hierarchy has its roots in the church and military bureaucracies of a previous time. It separates people into two groups—the governed and the governors. At one end of the chain of command is the supreme governor. At the other end are the supremely governed. In between there exists a chain of people who alternately act as governor or governed. These middle managers act as transmitters of the communications that come down from the top. Communication the other way is limited, except through formal labor–management relations. Communication either way can take the form of meetings, telephone calls, or memos.

You were an employee, nested somewhere in the hierarchy of an organization owned by someone else. Your goal was to move up the hierarchy and have more people reporting to you. You were motivated by material rewards and fear of punishment. Your work goals were determined by your boss, and his or her goals by his or her boss—all the way up to the top—where decisions were made. You were focused internally rather than on the customer. Innovation and creativity (for example, in giving better customer service or creating products) were typically not part of the picture. Often you found yourself taking credit for the work of those below you in the hierarchy, or in seemingly never-ending "turf" battles and organizational politics. You hung in with the company until you retired or were fired. You were the "organization man."

While this picture may seem stereotypical, especially given the changes occurring in organizations today, this was the traditional model of the enterprise. Today there is growing acceptance that this structure stifles creativity, self-motivation, commitment, and responsiveness to market demands, not to mention failing to meet the human needs for fulfilling work. Fundamental changes—in fact, the transformation of the nature of our organizations and the way business is undertaken—are required.

Just as walls are falling in the political and economic world, today's enterprise is opening up.

Many companies have begun a transition to the new enterprise. Others are struggling with what to do. Virtually none has actually achieved a comprehensive implementation of the new model. There is no handbook or guide for the new approach. There are also many dimensions of change, and organizations tend to move at different paces along some or all dimensions. Yet, conceptually, some strong themes are emerging. In total, these themes create an image of what we refer to as the open networked organization. These are illustrated in Fig. 1-1.

The structure of the new enterprise is shifting from a multilayered hierarchy to flatter networks or relatively autonomous businesses. The

	Closed Hierarchy	Open Networked Organization
Structure	Hierarchical ⟶	Networked
Scope	Internal/closed ⟶	External/open
Resource focus	Capital ⟶	Human, information
State	Static, stable ⟶	Dynamic, changing
Personnel/focus	Managers ⟶	Professionals
Key drivers	Reward and punishment ⟶	Commitment
Direction	Management commands ⟶	Self-management
Basis of action	Control ⟶	Empowerment to act
Individual motivation	Satisfy superiors ⟶	Achieve team goals
Learning	Specific skills ⟶	Broader competencies
Basis for compensation	Position in hierarchy ⟶	Accomplishment, competence level
Relationships	Competitive (my turf) ⟶	Cooperative (our challenge)
Employee attitude	Detachment (It's a job.) ⟶	Identification (It's my company.)
Dominant requirements	Sound management ⟶	Leadership

Figure 1-1. The open networked organization.

responsive, entrepreneurial business team is becoming a key organizational entity rather than the traditional department locked into a traditional organization chart.

The concept of the organization is being expanded to include links with external business partners—suppliers and customers. The resource focus is shifting from capital to human and information resources. Rather than remain static and stable, the enterprise must be dynamic and constantly changing. The professional, not the manager, is emerging as the central player—often working in multidisciplinary teams that cut across traditional organizational boundaries. Interpersonal commitment, rather than traditional reward and punishment mechanisms, is becoming the desired basis for organizational cohesion and stability.

The new team is self-managed. Team members are united by a common vision that cascades across the enterprise. Individuals are empowered to act, and do so responsibly and creatively. Freed from bureaucratic control, they take initiatives and even risks to get closer to customers and work more productively. They are motivated by one another to achieve team goals rather than to satisfy superiors. With common interests that are immediate and clear, cooperation flourishes.

This is a working-learning environment where individuals develop strong specialized expertise and broader competencies, not just specific skills. The notion of learning job skills that require periodic updating is replaced with the notion of life-long learning. Income is tied to level of competence and accomplishments rather than to position in the hierarchy. The enterprise holds a sense of social responsibility, and people identify with it. Rather than good management, leadership and vision are becoming the dominant requirements for success in a changing and volatile business environment.

It is generally accepted that all of this is achievable, because the new enterprise is becoming information-based. It is assumed that information technology provides the means whereby organizations that have remained fundamentally unchanged for decades, and arguably for centuries, can be transformed. The theory (and it is often just that) is that the new structure is possible when each member understands the team vision; has the competencies required; has the trust of others; and, very important, has access to the information and tools required for functioning and collaborating within the team in a broader context.[11]

Information technology has enabled a reduction of the middle layers of management who are "relays—human boosters for the faint, unfocused signals that pass for communication in the traditional pre-information organization."[12] The old organization also needed separate departments that housed specialized information and knowledge. This assumption can now be challenged. For example, it was unthinkable that a plant worker could (or should) be involved in any marketing activities. However, with technology able to provide information regarding production, shipping, warehousing, and sales along with tools for marketing such as telemarketing workstations—all within a plant—it is possible to build a different kind of organization structure. Perhaps a team approach could provide variety for plant workers, get them closer to the customer, reduce interpersonal friction, and build commitment. (See the case study in Chap. 9).

However, until recently, technology to deliver the new structure did not really exist.

The New Paradigm in Information Technology

Through what technology and by what means will this shift to the new enterprise occur? It is clear that a new paradigm in the *world geopolitical situation* is occurring. This is creating a new paradigm in the *international business environment*. The rise of the new open, networked enterprise constitutes a *new organizational paradigm.*

Just as the organizational structures, business environments, and old world order are being dramatically altered by ongoing global changes, the first era of information technology is experiencing a similar fate. Technology walls are falling. Old computing architectures are being overthrown. The nature and purpose of computing are being radically altered. Like traditional cold war thinking, the old approach to technology is proving to be inadequate to deal with the new world.

A series of DMR syndicated studies investigated a number of critical changes taking place in the use of technology and in the technology itself. The research confirmed that a paradigm shift is occurring. A new technology era is unfolding—an era that parallels and is inextricably linked to changes in organizations and to the broader world changes. We are entering a *second era of information technology* in which the business applications of computers, the nature of the technology itself, and the leadership for use of technology are all going through profound change. Organizations that cannot understand the new era and navigate a path through the transition are vulnerable and will be bypassed.

For its first few decades (1950s, 1960s, and 1970s) data processing was pursued primarily to reduce clerical costs. As one insurance company executive told us, "We were after clerical heads." Today, however, technology has moved to the front line in most organizations. It has become strategic in the sense that it is a necessary component in the execution of a business strategy. Countless books and articles discuss the innovative use of computers to achieve temporary competitive advantage or parity. For example, many banks felt the sting of losing customers to better information services such as Merrill Lynch's Cash Management Account. These banks and others in similar circumstances have scrambled to expand computing beyond back-room data processing to the front-line delivery of business services and products to customers.

A change has also occurred in terms of who uses computers. In the first era the focus was on technical specialists, professionals, and managers who designed, implemented, managed, controlled, and usually owned the computing infrastructure of the enterprise. With the transition to the new era, business users of technology have moved to the fore. They number in the tens of millions and are more sophisticated and more demanding. They are also no longer content to depend on management information systems departments to achieve the benefits that technology can bring. Users want to shape the technology that is implemented in their organizations. They want to control its use and determine the effect it will have on their own work. They are rapidly understanding that their effective use of technology coupled with a change in how they do business will determine their personal and organizational success. They have become the vanguard of an information technology revolution that is quickly altering the old ways of organizational computing.

Three Critical Shifts in the Application of Information Technology

There are three fundamental shifts now occurring in the application of computers in business, each affecting a different level of business opportunity. Information technology enables enterprises to have a *high-performance team structure*, to function as *integrated businesses* despite high business unit autonomy, and to reach out and develop *new relationships with external organizations*—to become an "extended enterprise." These levels are depicted in Fig. 1-2 and discussed in Chaps. 2, 3, and 4, respectively.

Shift 1: From Personal to Work-Group Computing

Personal computers (PCs) have percolated throughout organizations to touch almost every job. However, their impact can rarely be described

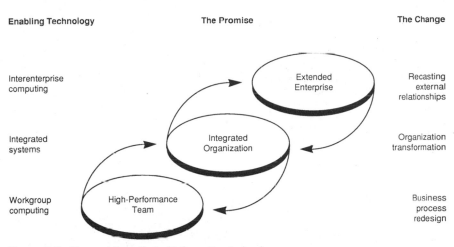

Enabling Technology   The Promise   The Change

Interenterprise computing — Extended Enterprise — Recasting external relationships

Integrated systems — Integrated Organization — Organization transformation

Workgroup computing — High-Performance Team — Business process redesign

Figure 1-2. The enabling effect of information technology.

as strategic. The main limiting factor is that the stand-alone PC does not work the way that people do—in communication with others, especially within a work group. The new thrust appreciates the importance of the business team as the cornerstone organizational unit and the huge opportunities to support teams within the execution of business functions.

Work-group computing provides personal and work-group tools, information, and capabilities to directly support all categories of people in the information sector of the economy. If well-conceived and implemented, work-group systems can be a focal point for the redesign of business processes and jobs. This can result in spectacular improvements in productivity and responsiveness. Rather than improving the efficiency of a task such as writing a report or preparing a budget, the goal is to improve the effectiveness and performance of the group.

Work-group systems enable users to streamline a work process and change the nature of jobs in a business unit. The results are typically a reduction in the turnaround time for creating work products. Staff are also able to save time, which can be reinvested in doing more important activities. For example, a West Coast electric utility's process to complete a customer order had a 7-week cycle time. An investigation revealed this was completely unrelated to the actual work time required to execute the process. A reengineering program, enabled by information technology, reduced the cycle time to several hours.

As another example, Citibank Corporate Real Estate marketing personnel were able to save hours a day, freeing them to spend more time in direct customer contact. This was achieved through redesign of work processes, the implementation of work-group computing, and the building of high-performance work teams. The result was a dramatic increase in revenue and profit, and, interestingly, quality of work life for employees.

Shift 2: From System Islands to Integrated Systems

Traditionally, information technology was used to help manage and control costs of three resources: physical assets, financial resources, and people. As a result, separate system islands sprung up through the organization in three areas.

1. *Management and control of physical assets and facilities.* These included a broad range of sensor-based or real-time control systems associated with production and process control; systems involved with more efficient storage and movement of raw materials and intermediate or finished goods; and systems dealing with improved management, operation, and protection of facilities and equipment that included plant sites, sales and distribution points, vehicles, and offices.

2. *Financial management and control systems.* These systems formed the origins of the data-processing department and dealt with the automation of the bookkeeping end of business transactions. They were oriented toward reducing clerical overhead and increasing the efficiency of processing business transactions. Data-processing systems grew beyond financial applications to address broader information such as customers and insurance policies.

3. *Technologies to manage and support the human resource.* These technologies were intended to support management and other employees in fulfilling their various job functions. They included administrative technologies such as photocopiers, office automation systems such as word processing, records management and library systems, and office communications including telephone, telex, electronic mail and facsimile, and human resource applications such as benefits administration and skills inventories.

In the first era of information technology, organizations were forced to keep these areas separate and independent, because of the immaturity of the technology and our ability to exploit it. This strategy resulted in the creation of isolated islands of technology. Separate areas of the organization (engineering departments, the information systems function, and the administrative function) took responsibility for these three different types of systems applications. Unfortunately, the result was often systems that were not integrated, that were highly fragmented, that overlapped in function and content, and that were costly to maintain.

Because of the maturity of technology standards, it is now possible to plan an entire enterprise architecture, rather than to continue to add another room on the farmhouse as required.

Enterprise architectures provide the backbone for the new open, networked enterprise; in fact, they are a key prerequisite. They enable moving beyond the organizational hierarchy, as layers of management are not required when information is instantly available electronically. Such architectures can enable the enterprise to function better as a cohesive organization, providing corporatewide information for decision making and new competitive enterprise applications that transcend autonomous business units.

A good example is Federal Express (FEDEX), which has built an integrated, and very competitive, company on an enterprise architecture. Integrated systems at FEDEX enable tracking of a parcel in *real time* and provide detailed information regarding minute-by-minute parcel movements for the management of quality. The architecture integrates systems capabilities to manage the three resources — physical, financial, and human.

At the same time, such architectures provide a platform for entrepreneurial innovation in the use of computers by business teams — while maintaining an enterprise capability. As a transitional step, many companies are building links between various systems to enable an enterprise capability. For example, Phillips Petroleum, Frito-Lay, and Northern Telecom have implemented management support systems to provide information from a variety of disparate systems for executive decision making.

Shift 3: From Internal to Interenterprise Computing

In the first era, systems were viewed as being internal to the organization — reflecting the walls that existed between enterprises. Computer systems are now extending the reach of organizations outward to link enterprises with their suppliers, distribution channels, and consumers. Insurance companies and airlines link with agents. Governments provide information kiosks for the public. Banks provide on-line access to customers. Manufacturers tie in to terminals in the trucks of a distributor. The research found that such systems can strengthen customer loyalty, lock out competitors, speed up distribution of goods and customer service, and save money (to name just a few examples).

Technology is becoming a vehicle for creating links between business partners — both suppliers and consumers of products and services. Early systems, such as American Airlines SABRE reservation system and the American Hospital Supply customer order system, have become legends in how to use technology to link with customers to defeat the competition. However, they were really the tip of the iceberg.

The new technology of *extended reach* enables the recasting of relationships with external organizations. Computer systems between enterprises are beginning to talk to each other. The manual value chain from suppliers to consumers is becoming an *electronic value network* that also links to affinity groups (such as business partners) and even competitors. Corporate computing is becoming interenterprise computing, enabling the rise of the "interenterprise."

The emerging technologies include interenterprise databases, voice response systems, electronic messaging, and new point-of-sale technologies. Standards such as electronic data interchange (EDI)—the computer-to-computer interchange of business documents between companies—is transforming the ways companies work together. For example, when large auto manufacturers demand that their suppliers communicate with them using EDI, one of the objectives is to make suppliers more productive, profitable, and therefore stable. Auto manufacturers acquire an interest in the profitability of their suppliers and can contribute through EDI. New extended enterprises are being born.

Overall then, information technology can be viewed as classes of systems from the personal level to interenterprise systems. *Personal* applications directly support and are controlled by the end user. *Work-group* applications are shared by a team or function that may be centrally located or widely dispersed throughout the enterprise. *Corporate* or *enterprise applications* support a broad range of users across the enterprise and may involve many divisions or departments. *Public* or *interenterprise* applications involve interaction with users and systems that are external to the organization.

Eight Critical Technology Shifts

The DMR research shows that the computing environments of the last few decades are now failing to deliver the goods required for success in the new business environment. The high-performance business team, the integrated organization, and the extended enterprise cannot be achieved with first-era technology. The old technology cannot respond to the main requirements of today's world—globalization, quality, productivity, responsiveness, partnering, outsourcing, and cost control (all discussed in Chap. 5).

Simultaneously with the demand pull for a new kind of technology, the maturation of computing and telecommunications is creating a technology push for a paradigm shift. Rather than attempting to extend their current platforms, leading organizations are setting out on a course of migration to fundamentally new and different IT infrastructure.

The problem is that today's enterprises are locked into the technology of the past—isolated systems based on outmoded host computers. These systems are costly, poorly integrated, hard to maintain, and difficult to learn and use. Such system islands are also self-perpetuating as new software applications are built on the old platform. The need to address this problem is urgent, for the longer an enterprise waits, the greater are the inertia and investment in its legacy systems.

What are the themes of the new paradigm? Following are eight shifts that are revolutionizing information technology today (depicted in Fig. 1-3).

Network Computing

Shift 1: From Traditional Semiconductors to Microprocessor-Based Systems. The microprocessor—computer on a chip—is at the center of the new paradigm. Traditional semiconductor technology, which fills the massive cabinets of the mainframe and minicomputers in your corporate data centers, is going the way of the dinosaur. Microprocessors are beginning to dominate leading-edge computers of every size. Since

	Era I	Era II
Network Computing		
Processing	Traditional semiconductor ⟶	Microprocessors
System	Host-based ⟶	Network-based
Open Systems		
Software standards	Vendor-proprietary ⟶	Vendor-neutral
Information forms	Separate data, text, voice, image ⟶	Multimedia
Vendor–customer relationships	Account control ⟶	Multivendor partnerships
Industrial Revolution in Software		
Software development	Craft ⟶	Engineered
User interface	Alphanumeric character set ⟶	Graphical
Applications	Stand-alone ⟶	Integrated

Figure 1-3. Eight critical technology shifts.

1988, desktop machines costing under $20,000 have outperformed the multimillion dollar mainframes that preceded them. Similarly, when comparing the speed of computers today, a unit of performance costs hundreds of dollars on a microprocessor-based system compared with tens of thousands of dollars on mainframe systems. Systems that combine many microprocessors into a single large computer can dramatically outperform mainframes in sheer power.

The advantage of the microprocessor will continue to grow. The capacity of traditional semiconductor computers is growing at around 20 percent per year. The number of transistors on a microprocessor chip, however, has grown from around 30,000 in 1980 to an anticipated 100 million by 1999 — a compound annual growth rate of over 150 percent. In addition, we can anticipate that well before the end of the 1990s, a single microprocessor chip will pass today's mainframe in raw power.

The microprocessor is the precondition for a new approach to computing, which (like organizational empowerment) moves intelligence out into the enterprise where the action is (for example, at the point of sale, customer service, research and development laboratory, or marketing department). It enables organizations to have *empowered architectures* that exploit the superior price/performance of microprocessor technology. Even IBM has recognized this shift, announcing a development effort to build a supercomputer based on *massively parallel* microprocessors.

Shift 2: From Host-Based to Network-Based Systems. Era I systems were based on large host mainframe or minicomputers each supporting an attached network of local or remote terminals. These hosts were optimized for efficiency given the high cost of traditional semiconductor technology. The terminals were typically "dumb" with a cryptic user interface. Only data-processing specialists (often viewed as "gurus") could make changes to the system. New applications that made their way to the front of the queue seemed to take forever to build. Systems from different manufacturers and often those from within one manufacturer did not talk to one another.

By the early 1980s, two forces were at work to dislodge the degree of centralized control implicit in era I architectures. The first was distributed computing — the concept of moving some of the computing resources closer to the operational areas of the business. This typically involved departmental computing using various sizes of low-end mainframes or minicomputers usually incompatible with the central mainframe environment. There was often great resistance to these approaches by the data-processing department, resulting in many renegade user departments going their own way. Minicomputers and distributed computing became a force to be reckoned with.

The second force was the arrival of the personal computer. This brought distributed computing down to the desktop and ultimately the briefcase. More important, the relatively low cost of PCs opened up many new application areas, especially for knowledge workers, who had not been well served by era I applications. The rapid proliferation of PCs could not be constrained by the centralized data-processing department. When host attachment and networking requirements emerged, some of the underlying architecture issues and opportunities became apparent. The transition to the second era was on.

Now, because of the spectacular power of the microprocessor and the maturity of networking technology and standards, a fundamentally different style of computing is emerging. It goes by different names, such as network computing, cooperative processing, and client/server architectures. Regardless of the name, the new approach provides the potential for users to access a wide range of data, applications, and computing resources without worrying about where they are or how they are connected.

Most important, software is processed not only on a host but wherever it makes most sense. It does not even have to be limited to one machine, but can be processed cooperatively on various computers on the network. The computer becomes the network, and the network becomes the computer. To use a human analogy, thoughts are processed in the minds of many people in an office—not just in the mind of the person with the biggest brain. And the results are communicated as required to meet the requirements of the collective process.

The advantages of this shift are huge. Network computing exploits the inherent power of the microprocessor. It more efficiently uses computing power as unused devices on the network can be brought to bear on a problem as required. It enables information and applications to be processed where they should be—close to the user, such as in the case of a work-group application.

Open Systems

Shift 3: From Vendor Proprietary Software to Open Software Standards.   In the early days, computers used software created specifically for that computer—*one computer, one vendor*. When a larger computer was needed, the software had to be re-created at huge cost to the customer. In the 1960s vendors introduced the concept of *scalability* with software that would work on different-sized computers—*one vendor,* *multiple computers.* However, each vendor had a unique product architecture. Software, whether purchased from that vendor or developed in house, worked only on the hardware of that vendor. Consequently, the organization was locked in to that vendor, as it was too costly to move the software to another vendor's equipment.

Now the computer industry (like the construction industry of seventeenth-century Boston, the railroad industry of the nineteenth century, and the electric bulb and automobile industries of the twentieth century) has matured to the point where it is consolidating around standards. Open systems, based on industry standards that are not controlled by any one vendor, are transforming the computer industry and presenting a monumental challenge to commercial organizations. Standards are arising in all areas of computing including communications, databases, user interfaces, computer operating systems, and software development tools. By 1992, every major computer vendor had adopted open systems as its main approach to technology.

Open systems result in information and software being portable, that is, run on hardware regardless of size or brand. Such standards also enable systems of different sizes and brands to interoperate, that is, communicate with one another.

DMR's research showed that open systems have far-reaching advantages over the traditional approach. They are significantly less expensive as a result of their exploitation of microprocessors, lower vendor margins due to customer freedom, and use of shrink-wrapped, as opposed to home-grown, software—to name a few. More important, the leading organizations had concluded that industry standards were necessary to enable them to adopt the new computing paradigm. Standards in general, and open systems in particular, do not simply provide benefits. They are becoming imperative in order to create the kind of modular, flexible, powerful, networked computing architectures required by the new business environment.

Shift 4: From Single to Multimedia—Data, Text, Voice, and Image. In the first era, the immaturity of technology and the absence of open standards meant that these four forms of information were separate, each with separate technologies to manage them. Data-processing systems handled data. Word-processing systems and telex handled text. Telephone and dictation systems handled voice. Photocopiers and microform systems handled image. As the information contained in these systems becomes digitized, and as standards grow, the opportunity unfolds to integrate them. Today, for example, two professionals in different parts of the globe can exchange (at the speed of light) computerized or *digital* documents that contain all four forms of information. A document on a workstation screen may have text surrounding a digitized photograph and a so-called live spreadsheet with another's voice (requesting clarification from the recipient) attached to certain parts of the document. This compound document can be filed electronically, retrieved, altered, and communicated as appropriate without ever being transformed into paper. Again, the research showed that the benefits can be striking.

An example extension of such integration which is getting a lot of press these days is virtual reality. This technology creates an artificial reality for the integration of not only visual and audio information but also information from other senses in three-dimensional, interactive real time. The foreshadow of such systems was the Spatial Data Management System developed at MIT in the 1970s, in which a user sat in a chair and, through touching small screens on the side, "navigated" around through "dataland" on a giant color screen facing the chair. The next step was flight simulation systems that enable pilots to lose all their engines in a training situation without losing their lives. With virtual reality the user actually wears some kind of clothing such as a glove (Nintendo already has a commercial product), goggles, and headset. The user sits in hyperspace, experiencing a simulated world.

Sound like science fiction? Entertainment applications will make a critical mass of users—leading to commercial viability for commercial applications in the mid-1990s. Petroleum engineers will penetrate the earth. Doctors will navigate through your cardiovascular system. Researchers will browse through a library. Students will go for a stroll on the moon. Auto designers will sit in the back seat of a car they are creating to see how it feels and examine the external view. By the end of this decade, the home computer, television, and telephone will have converged into multimedia devices delivering a vast array of applications that currently are provided by separate telecommunications, entertainment, publishing, computing, and home electronics industries.

Shift 5: From Account Control to Computer Vendor–Customer Partnerships Based on Free Will.   In the first era, customers were locked in to a given vendor's products. This allowed the vendor to have account control over the customer. The good news was that vendors typically provided reasonable service and support. However, there were problems. The vendor could also charge high margins for products because the customer in the account relationship didn't really have a lot of choice. Customers also lacked the freedom to take advantage of new technology coming from unpredictable sources. They just hoped that they had chosen the right vendor.

When asked to describe their IT architecture, customers would typically respond, "We're a System 370 architecture," or "We've adopted the VAX VMS architecture." Both of these architectures are product architectures, rather than a disciplined organization of the IT resource to achieve a business vision.

More recently when we asked Dave Carlson, the chief information officer at Kmart to describe his company's architecture, he responded: "We have the Kmart architecture." It is based on vendor-neutral standards. "We say to vendors 'don't tell me how good your products are. Tell me how you comply with my architecture or how you could make it better.'"

In the open systems market, the account relationship breaks down. Vendors must now work to seek partnerships with their customers based on customer choice. Although this is a difficult transition for many vendors to face, in the long run it will benefit everyone.

The Industrial Revolution in Software

Shift 6: Software Development—From Craft to Factory. Like the preindustrial creation of guns, software development in the first era was a craft. The quality and cost of software was a function of the skills and creativity of the professionals developing it. Typically, programs from within the same organization—even running on the same computer and developed by individuals within a team—were as different in style, utility, and cost as the weapons of early America. When a gun broke, a craftsman had to fix it, as there were no interchangeable parts.

As significant as the move to the industrial design and production of rifles, software is going through a fundamental transformation. It is becoming an engineered profession using factory-of-the-future production techniques. This is an important issue given the huge investment in software made by any medium or large organization.

Because computers are now the basic delivery systems for products and services, companies need new computer applications in days or weeks, rather than months or years. For example, some financial products in the banking industry have a competitive life span of a few weeks. Leading enterprises have concluded that the traditional model of custom software development on traditional computing platforms was too expensive and too slow.

Developers use and reuse modules or parts that are standardized and that work together. *Computer-aided software engineering* (CASE) tools (after much ballyhoo and delay) are finally showing their potential to radically improve the way software is created—not unlike the automated industrial production line.

Interestingly, it is wrong to conjure up images of Orwellian servitude for programmers. DMR research showed that programmers working in this production environment tend to love it. They are freed from the alienating work of reinventing the wheel every time they create a program. They also have better collaboration with other team members. Developer workbenches facilitate the management of projects and communication among team members. Repositories of information about the software being developed give programmers a better handle on what they are doing, enabling large complex processes to be undertaken in a more managed and coordinated fashion. This also facilitates the reuse of previously developed modules.

Shift 7: From Alphanumeric to Graphical, Multiform User Interface. To describe the user interfaces of the first era as unfriendly is to be charitable. Terse cryptic interfaces using numbers and letters were, more often than not, "user-vicious." Semantics and user feedback told the tale; "system dead," "illegal entry" (a felony), "abort," "fatal error," "kill," and "execute," were the vocabulary of a time when systems were designed by computer specialists to be used by computer specialists.

The personal computer, standards, and network computing are changing all this. With computing power on the desktop and with industry standards for software developers, the alphanumeric user interface is disappearing. In its place is the *graphical user interface,* known affectionately by programmers as the GUI (pronounced "gooey"). This technology was popularized by Apple. Users work with the computer by manipulating graphical images or icons on the screen. Various files or tools are contained in windows on the screen which can be changed in size or closed. Activities on the computer can be performed by pointing to them. Images can be captured, displaced, and processed on the screen, as can voice information.

Again the research showed huge advantages of GUIs over traditional alphanumeric interfaces. People learn to use computers much more easily and quickly. They retain capabilities longer. They can perform computer functions faster, and they choose to use the computer for longer proportions of the business day. For the first time, computers are becoming usable by the general population.

Shift 8: From Stand-Alone to Integrated Software Applications. A number of changes now make it possible to integrate the system islands of the first era. Software programs are becoming more modular, like Lego blocks, built to standards that make them more interchangeable and integratable. For example, a standard GUI facilitates the creation of a similar look and feel for software applications. Open systems means that software programs can be moved to different vendors' hardware, again undermining the isolation of systems. DMR's research showed that the integration of these technology islands was being driven by business needs for new classes of information and new types of applications demanded by the competitive business environment.

The New Challenges

The fundamental changes in today's business environment coupled with the rise of the new technology paradigm are beginning to present a major challenge to organizations. While many complex and significant technical issues must be overcome, the research showed that the main difficulties were not in the area of technology. Rather, the organizational structures for managing computing, along with the knowledge, skills, resource base, approaches to systems planning, and even organizational culture, were being challenged by the new era. Moreover, the basic nature of business operations which have been essentially unchanged for decades needed to be questioned.

The challenge is one of managing change. Back in 1976, Marilyn Ferguson, in her book *The Aquarian Conspiracy—Personal and Social Transformation in Our Time,* was one of the first to popularize the notion of a paradigm shift.[13] She wrote that a paradigm shift involves dislocation, conflict, confusion, uncertainty. New paradigms are nearly always received with coolness, even mockery or hostility. Those with vested interests fight the change. The shift demands such a different view of things that established leaders are often the last to be won over, if at all.

How Will This Shift Occur?

How will the shift to the second era of information technology occur within your organization?

The research undertaken by DMR produced another very striking finding. Today's enterprise is typically faced with a crisis of leadership. Many traditional *information systems* (IS) professionals and managers are so buried in fighting the brushfires of the old IS world that they are unable to lead in the creation of the new. For example, three-quarters of the IS managers surveyed in one of the DMR studies frankly admitted that their organizations did not have the knowledge to understand and evaluate the relative merits of moving to open systems. Those IS executives who appreciate the change required are typically struck by the enormity of the challenge as they survey their legacy investments in outmoded technology and their armies of IS professionals whose entire experience, skills, and knowledge rest with the old paradigm.

Leadership is often not forthcoming from the technology vendors either. In the past, as part of the traditional account relationship, they shaped the evolution of first-era technology in customer organizations, providing leadership, complete support, and a safety net. The enterprise of today has relationships with multiple vendors. Today, technology standards mean that the providers of hardware are often commodity suppliers who deliver the best box for the cheapest price. Customers who want their cake (commodity price/performance) and want to eat it too (account relationship support and leadership) are typically a disappointed lot.

Nor is leadership forthcoming from third parties such as consultants, value-added resellers, and the like. Old approaches, knowledge, methods, and attitudes die hard, even (and perhaps especially) among the leaders of the old view. And leadership is a challenge for the CEO, the business unit executives, and the user community who traditionally have been cynical about the claims, arcane language, and perceived territorial motives of IS professionals. Many business managers have, until relatively recently, left technology to the technologists and feel that they lack the confidence and knowledge to engineer a change of this magnitude.

The premise of this book is that leadership is your personal challenge, whatever your organizational role. The research showed that critical leadership to manage change and achieve the spectacular results that have been identified came from every conceivable place in every conceivable type of organization. From secretaries to the chairman of the board, across every industry sector, from line business units to the central IS function, from both IT vendors and commercial enterprises, leaders are beginning to appear.

Paradigm Shift: The New Promise of Information Technology was written to provide nascent leaders with a framework for understanding the transition facing them. Rather than seeking to exploit a shopping list of opportunities and avoid a field of random mines, it will be helpful to know that you are setting out to lead a transition to a new way of doing business. This book synthesizes some lessons from those who have been most successful and others who have failed. Their experiences are worth heeding.

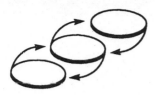

PART 1

The Promise

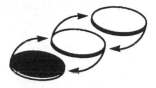

2
The High-Performance Business Team

A business team that markets a complex set of products examines its sales process. It discovers that most people spend a tiny proportion of the day in contact with actual customers. Most of the day involves indirect marketing activities such as completing forms or reports and documenting the steps in the process. A work-system reengineering process is undertaken. Everyone in the group receives multifunction workstations networked with the rest of the corporate technology infrastructure. Jobs, procedures, and the sales process are all redesigned.

The result? The turnaround time to negotiate a contract is reduced by 80 percent. Many activities are eliminated, automated, or performed in a mechanized fashion through the work-group system. The jobs of administrative personnel are transformed as they take on many of the activities previously performed by professionals. Senior marketing professionals save over 3 hours per day, which they reinvest in customer contact. As a result, sales increase by over 200 percent over the 1-year period after the reengineering occurs. Quality of work life, as measured by a job diagnostic index, increases dramatically. The group has become a high-performance team (see Fig. 2-1).

Unbelievable? An aberration? Actually, the fact that stories like this are becoming commonplace testifies to the profound ineffectiveness of many pre-era II organizations and the far-reaching impacts of a new class of systems called work-group computing.

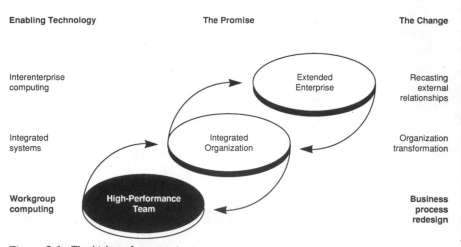

Figure 2-1. The high-performance team.

The advent of work-group computing is precipitated by two factors:

- A *demand pull* for a new kind of organization — the business team — growing from the new business environment.

- A *technology push,* resulting from the arrival of work-group technology that can enable new forms of work.

The Business Team and the Open Networked Organization

Nothing less than a transformation is occurring in the way business functions are executed and organizations are structured. An important theme is the shift in focus from the traditional highly structured, hierarchical organization to the business team, which cuts across traditional organizational boundaries.

The old model worked well in the less competitive, more stable and expansive market environments of the first era. It worked well for GM, before Honda; for AT&T, before deregulation; for GE, before Sony; for Siemens, before German unification; for Xerox, before Canon; for IBM, before Fujitsu and Microsoft. The hierarchical model had a vertical flow of information. It focused on efficiency, control, and the avoidance of failure.

Traditional hierarchical organizations are characterized by a centralized approach to information flow and multiple layers of management, accountability, and bureaucracy. Advances in technology are allowing growing numbers of companies to transform their hierarchical structures. Organizations are establishing new forms of corporate structures and, at the same time, are dramatically changing the way people work. The corporate pyramid that has been part of the business culture for decades is being replaced by a new organizational form. In both white- and blue-collar sectors, personnel are being organized into laterally based work teams with new accountabilities and responsibilities.

The *open networked organization* is based on cooperative, multidisciplinary teams and businesses networked together across the enterprise. Rather than a rigid structure, it is a modular organizational architecture in which business teams operate as a network of what we call *client* and *server* functions.

Teams are both clients and servers for other teams, who are both internal and external to the organization. As servers, they receive requests or directions from clients, make requests on other server functions, and add value for the purpose of serving these clients. The new model is derived from Michael Porter's concept of the value chain, but extended into the notion of a *value network*—reflecting the rise of the open networked enterprise presented in this book. The provision of value is not something chained in a linear way, but rather something generated through an ever-changing open network. It is a model designed to encourage flexibility, innovation, entrepreneurship, and responsiveness.

The new organization has many other names, and there are different angles on the topic. However, just about everyone agrees that a shift from the traditional hierarchy is needed and coming. Peter Drucker calls it the networked organization.[1] For Rosabeth Moss Kanter it's dancing elephants.[2] For Peter Keen it's the relational organization.[3] For Tom Peters it's life without hierarchy.[4] For D. Quinn Mills it's the cluster organization.[5] Charles Savage calls it human networking.[6]

The basic problem is that the turbulent open market requires organizational structures that are more open than the traditional organization. Business teams provide better responsiveness and flexibility than hierarchical organizations. The increasing and often unpredictable competition from local and international sources means organizations have to be ready to change their strategies and objectives. They also have to be sure that these changes will occur quickly and efficiently. Business teams can enable faster responses to changes in the business environment and to increasing customer demands. They can help bring the right people together at the right time to meet business demands. Business teams can help organizations dramatically change their cost structure through the elimination of traditional bureaucracies and also prevent the creation of new ones.

Moreover, changing market, industry, and regulatory forces, combined with the increasing geographical spread of organizations across regional, national, and international borders, have led enterprises to search for a more decentralized work structure. The structuring of business teams enables them to be closer to and to take advantage of local developments, new opportunities, and selected markets to achieve their corporate objectives.

As Peter Drucker explained some years ago: "Traditional departments will serve as guardians of standards, as centers for training, and the assignment of specialists; they won't be where the work gets done. That will happen largely in task-focused teams."[7]

In *Groupware: Computer Support for Business Teams*—one of the best discussions of the topic—Bob Johansen points out that many team-oriented companies are providing models for others and stimulating the move to a team approach. These models include both the Hollywood approach created for film making and the Silicon Valley companies that use teams to bring products to market quickly.[8]

One of the best-known examples is the team approach to designing automobiles used in Japan. Each new car project is treated as a project in which the project leader has genuine power. The team consists of people from all necessary disciplines—power train engineering, body design, purchasing, marketing, finance, and others. In the old North American approach, each department had a reporting stovepipe in which those at the top made important decisions. This bureaucracy inhibits effective collaboration and teamwork. It is a source of delay, and it creates many unnecessary costs and miscommunications. In Japan, the project manager is more than a coordinator who must go to various departments to get decisions made. The result has been better, faster, cheaper designs, and the devastation of the competitive dominance of the American "big three."[9]

Team thinking affects all levels of an organization. For example, managerial work is undergoing such an enormous change that according to Harvard's Rosabeth Moss Kanter, "Many managers are re-inventing the profession as they go. With little precedent to guide them, they are watching hierarchy fade away and the clear distinctions of title, task, department and even corporation blur."[10]

Teams are even being implemented as an alternative to the senior executive. After a challenge to overcome the intensely competitive history of mahogany row, many companies are focusing on team leadership at the top. One example is Xerox Corp., which in 1992 eliminated the role of president, substituting a six-member *corporate office,* consisting of Paul Allaire, Chairman and Chief Executive Officer, three operations executives, and the heads of corporate research and technology and of corporate strategic services. The move is part of a broader restructuring and shift to flatter, team-oriented networked structures.

In Praise of Hierarchy?

The team approach is not without its detractors. In a controversial *Harvard Business Review* article, "In Praise of Hierarchy," Elliott Jacques notes that hierarchy may seem difficult to praise—that bureaucracy is a dirty word even among bureaucrats. "Yet 35 years of research have convinced me that managerial hierarchy is the most efficient, the hardiest and in fact the most natural structure ever devised for large organizations."[11]

Clearly, many efforts to implement new models of organization have been fraught with dislocation, confusion, threatened managers, lack of clarity regarding emerging roles, and the like. Moreover, some aspects of traditional hierarchy are required for control and accountability even in an open networked enterprise. For example, Jacques makes a strong case for the "requisite structure" with a focus on accountability.

In our opinion, accountability as well as planning, coordination, and performance management can also be achieved in a networked structure. Such responsibilities can be built into individual jobs—making us all part managers and professionals—or can be assigned to business teams. Such teams can focus on strategic or tactical improvements in operations and develop new directions in collaboration with operational business units.

A good example is the new Shell Brockville Lubricants plant, which has significantly reduced hierarchy both in number and in functional definition. The plant is operated by three self-managed teams—bulk processing, packaging, and warehousing. Activities are coordinated by additional teams. Employees rotate among teams, and most have responsibility not only for plant operations, but for other activities including administration and even marketing. All of this is enabled by information technology. The elimination of traditional hierarchical distinctions has resulted in a uniquely productive operation run by committed employees who grow in a working-learning environment. (See Chap. 9 for a more detailed discussion.)

The praisers of hierarchy argue that only individuals can be accountable, not teams. We believe that the central issue is accomplishment, not accountability. This difference reflects a fundamental underlying difference in the two approaches. If you want to control, you design organizations for accountability. If you want to accomplish, you design for commitment.[12]

Moreover, it is simply untrue that teams cannot take actions for which they are, as a team, accountable. Teams can earn rewards and suffer losses — every hockey player knows that. And teams can be empowered to act — as the Shell Brockville plant shows.

Overall, it is becoming hard to defend the control-oriented, hierarchy model. The writing is on the wall for the traditional, multilevel structure with its boss-subordinate, command-control orientation. The new business environment is shaking hierarchy to its roots. New commitment-oriented models are needed to free up the human creativity and motivation required throughout an enterprise.

Overall, the shift is one from the hierarchical to the open networked enterprise in which the business team is the dominant vehicle for the execution of business functions. This shift requires a rethinking of the business processes that are associated with the traditional organizational structure.

The DMR research showed that important changes in information technology enable companies to redesign their business processes and to remove many of the vertical barriers associated with traditional hierarchical organizations. In a growing number of organizations, business teams supported by technology have become the basis of enterprise operations. Establishing effective work groups and building high-performance teams have become strategic corporate objectives.

How People Used Computers in the First Era

During the 1960s, 1970s, and early 1980s, "host" mainframe and minicomputer-based systems were essentially the only game in town. The people who had direct access to these computers and computer systems were part of an isolated and highly specialized minority, commonly known as the *management information systems* (MIS) department. Technology was used primarily by technical specialists or clerical personnel such as data entry or inquiry clerks. Applications of technology were focused on the reduction of clerical costs, and the resulting computer systems tended to be unintegrated islands of technology.

Systems were usually so cumbersome, complicated, and cryptic that only computer specialists could use them — often required to work around the clock to keep them running. Employees outside data-processing departments had little or no access to technology other than seeing piles of batch printouts on company sales, inventory, and finances, while the people who worked in data-processing departments were often too immersed in technology. The majority of company employees, including senior executives, usually felt that while computer technology was useful, it had little relevance to the real day-to-day operations of the organizations.

The personal computer was the beginning of the end for the old view. The microcomputer allowed all employees, from secretaries and sales agents to professionals and senior executives, to work directly with technology and take advantage of the many benefits it could bring. Standard software packages that supported the PC hardware made the technology easy to use. By making computers accessible to everyone in an organization, the microcomputer revolution gave technology an entirely new reputation and presence in the enterprise. The personal computer gave people direct access to technology tools that enabled them to be more productive in their day-to-day activities. People who previously had little contact with computers were now seeing how they could use them to meet their individual work objectives.

While these new PC users and the traditional mainframe-dominated data-processing departments had widely divergent objectives in using technology, they did have something in common. Both used technology in an isolated environment. The data-processing department operated in sealed premises within the company's headquarters, detached from corporate operations and other divisions in the corporation. PC users were also detached, using their own programs on their own machines in their own offices. How other employees were using their microcomputers and what hardware and software they preferred was irrelevant. The choice of personal computer was personal. Local office equipment budgets provided funding for purchasing PCs, a trend that quickly became evident as organizations began to fill up with a myriad of different machines. PC users became dots of automation throughout the enterprise.

Stand-alone PCs enabled many managers and other professionals to break free of the centralized control of the data-processing department, but they had severe limitations. They created a systems environment where there was no effective information exchange. As stand-alone devices, PCs had a major flaw. They couldn't work the way people do—communicating with each other.

The Transition to Era II

It is said that the paperless office is as probable as the paperless bathroom. The recent introduction of paperless toilets and smart bathrooms by Japanese manufacturers should serve as warning that significant change is coming in the office as well.

A change in the way personal computers were used marked the transition to era II. The growing number of stand-alone devices made organizations aware of the need for communications. The communications capability of *local area network* (LAN) technology and the growing demands and sophistication of the individual user came together at the same time. A new awareness began to emerge. If more information, memory, computing power, and other computing resources could be shared, users would benefit. The result was the rise of the local area network. Although the original motivation for LANs was to reduce costs through sharing technology resources, such as software, printers, and other peripherals, LANs enabled people to begin functioning more effectively as groups within their departments. Rather than simply sharing technology, people began to share information and end-user functions such as electronic mail or the coauthoring of documents. Existing procedures, business processes, job types, and even organizational structures were called into question. The work group was in transition.

What was left unchanged was the business processes and the organization itself, which continued, for the most part, to be a hierarchical structure. Information and accountability flowed up and down, and senior management remained insulated from its work force by layers of management and established corporate procedures.

In particular, the maturing of technology provided the technological precondition for the redesign of business processes that were becoming a critical obstacle to organizational performance. As an early DMR multiclient study pointed out:

> Experience has shown that the biggest gains from systems that involve users are made through changes in the way people work, not simply through the installation of technology. Strategic impacts are achieved through broader changes in the worksystem, that is how we work together to create products or services and how we interact with our suppliers and consumers. A theme of this study is that integrated systems provide completely new ways of working and doing business. Redesigning these worksystems is a new challenge.[13]

Work Reengineering

If there was an IS buzzword olympics, the term *work reengineering* would have likely won the gold or silver during the early 1990s. Other terms addressing the same issue of technology-enabled redesign of work include *work-systems redesign, business process redesign,* and *the new industrial engineering*. In general, all refer to the analysis and (re)design of work flows and business processes, in some cases including procedures and jobs.[14] (In fact, the word *reengineering* has the potential to be misleading when applied to creating the new organization, in that it may imply that the product has a higher degree of structure and rigidity than is desirable. *Rearchitecting* is perhaps more appropriate. However, because of the widespread acceptance of the word *reengineering,* it is used here.)

Business processes are a set of work activities that are logically related and executed to create a business outcome such as producing a product, delivering a service, negotiating a contract, or processing an order. They occur when an individual or group takes inputs from support and supply groups and adds value—creating outputs to be consumed by clients or customers.[15] Examples of a business process include developing a business plan, negotiating a complex contract, processing a health insurance claim, responding to an RFP (request for proposal), and registering reservations. Processes can be highly structured and open to procedurization (e.g., ordering supplies) or less structured (e.g., generating new product ideas).[16,17]

Work systems result from combining business processes to achieve broader business objectives. In the era I enterprise, work systems tended to align with formal organizational structures. In the new enterprise they tend to involve multidisciplinary groups that transcend organizational boundaries.

Opportunities exist to improve business processes within individual work groups. There are also opportunities that transcend work groups because processes are common across broader components of an enterprise, the enterprise itself, or even *between* enterprises.

Endeavors to engineer work systems have been around for some time—actually dating back to Frederick Taylor's 1887 theory of scientific management. Taylor aimed to improve organizational productivity by applying principles of technical engineering to human work systems. Taylor symbolized what has become known as *scientific management* or *industrial engineering*.

"Speedy" Taylor, as he became known, was vilified for decades as the progenitor of anti-human, piecework approaches to human labor. It is true that Taylor's techniques—often known as time and motion studies—involved stopwatches, time measurement, and examination of the actions of individual workers. And his techniques included the analysis of a work system into its constituent components and subsequent assignment of an individual person to a component.

However, recent attempts to rehabilitate Taylor have shown another side of the story.[18,19] Taylor was in fact a social reformer of his day. He was driven by a strong morality (Quaker, pacifist) and by goals to improve cooperation between workers and management. In doing so, he hoped to increase not only the productivity but the standard of living and the quality of life of workers. The evidence is strong that when Taylor got involved in an actual industrial engineering project, both occurred. Some have even viewed his thinking as the precursor to today's quality-of-work-life approaches and even human resource management in general.[20] To those who argued that Taylor was simply a management flunky out to improve corporate profits, he replied: "It would seem to me a farce to devote one's whole life and money merely to secure an increase in dividends for a whole lot of manufacturing companies."[21]

However, notwithstanding Taylor's intentions, many disciples and others over the years began to use his techniques in the absence of lofty morality. Further, such techniques have spilled over from the industrial environment to the office.

What's wrong with existing work systems? Many work systems today are based on the Taylor model. Others are based on no model. They just happened. In both cases they have become obviated by the demands of the new business environment and the capabilities of second-era technology which enable new forms of work organization.

The industrial engineering piecework, or single-task, orientation to knowledge and service work typically creates work environments that are repetitive, alienating for staff, prone to errors, and characterized by extensive management and management controls. Limited worker and management visibility over the entire process leads to individual-unit optimization at the expense of the overall process and goals. Accountability for end results is often not explicit because of functional overlaps and the lack of whole jobs. Atomization and overspecialization often cause unnecessary delays, bureaucracy, and turf battles. Technology, when applied, tends to be suboptimal, eliminating bits of the process or mechanizing inefficiencies. Even worse, it regiments the inappropriate processes!

The dominant alternative to latter-day Taylorism—the laissez faire approach—has resulted in the truly bizarre procedures that exist in every medium or large organization. No one is really sure "why we do it that way." But typically, "we've been doing it that way as long as everyone around here can remember." This becomes the stuff of legends, such as the new employee who asked her manager what would happen if a weekly report that had been sent out for years were eliminated. The manager replied that he honestly didn't know, suggesting she try not producing it for a week. Months later there had not been one complaint, and the report—which consumed 30 percent of her job—was eliminated. Stories like this point to the tip of an iceberg. Most business processes today have just happened.

Work-Group Computing

What is the technology that enables us to go beyond traditional time and motion studies to reengineer business processes and refocus organizations around the business team? One is work-group computing, addressing opportunities to create the new high-performance business teams. (Other technologies addressing *the enterprise as a whole* as well as *its link to other enterprises* are discussed in Chaps. 3 and 4, respectively.)

Work-group computing has a variety of names. It has been referred to as *computer-supported cooperative work* (CSCW), *groupware, computer-supported groups* (CSG), *coordination technology,* and *decision conferences.*

What Is Work-Group Computing?

Elements
- Technology—networked multifunction workstations
- Work redesign—jobs, work processes, organizational structures

Typical Objectives
- Streamline communications, business processes
- Eliminate unproductive activities in the business process
- Improve collaborative creation of work products such as documents, specifications, designs, and code
- Exercise more efficient division of labor, timely contribution to work process
- Strengthen brainstorming, synergy
- Alert group members to important events, changes
- Improve decision making

The technology push to work-group computing comes from several sources. One is the growing power of desktop workstations. This has given the desktop user access to the equivalent computing power of former corporate mainframes, and it is a power that continues to grow. The growth of this desktop capability has meant that more and more enterprise information technology functions revolve around individual workstations.

A second factor has been the maturity of networking. Local and external network facilities allow these workstations to link to file servers, large databases, and other workstations throughout the organization. The growing capacity (referred to as *bandwidth*) of local and wide area networks has allowed more information and corporate data exchanges and led to more sophisticated technology applications.

Another factor has been the maturity of user interfaces — specifically the rise of the GUI and the integration of data, text, voice, and image. These have made technology more useful and usable by lay people, rather than just technocrats.

Additionally, in the past, the functionality of personal computers was severely limited by the fact that they were personal. It is true that spreadsheets, word processing, presentation graphics, simple databases, and the like provided adequate utility to create the PC explosion. But it could hardly be said that the PCs delivering such capabilities were strategic technology. However, as this functionality becomes combined with the ability to communicate, new workstation capabilities are emerging.

Ironically, work-group computing had its genesis decades ago. Its progenitor was Douglas Englebart, who in 1962 described a vision of the augmented knowledge workshop in a Stanford Research Institute paper entitled "Augmenting Human Intellect, a Conceptual Framework." By 1967, Englebart and his team had implemented a work-group environment that foreshadowed the sophisticated computing environments of today. It has taken almost three decades for the technological preconditions and the capacity of organizations to embrace such an innovation to mature to the point where the business case is both compelling and able to be communicated with credibility.[22]

Work-Group Computing Scenario: Yield Management in the Airline Industry

One of the great opportunities and challenges of the airline industry is to maximize yield. This is achieved through not only filling up airplanes but filling them with maximum-yield fares. Airlines need the flexibility to set fares and prices thousands of times a day as the situation warrants. This can involve discounting for an individual or for classes or groups of potential customers.

An airline may have a yield management team for coordinating such activities. The team is supported by a work-group system involving networked workstations tied with the rest of the airline technology infrastructure including travel agents. It also has a defined set of procedures and jobs which constitute a business process. Typically, the team would function as shown in Fig. 2-2 and as described in the scenario below.

One day a prospective customer walks into a travel agency and explains that he wants to fly 100 colleagues to a business meeting in Tokyo, preferring business class on September 20, returning October 1. The travel agent makes an inquiry to the airline in question through a text messaging system, asking "What can you do for these people?" Because of the size of the opportunity the airline sales manager gets involved and from her workstation accesses a flexible marketing database to identify the appropriate procedure to follow in this case. She also accesses the travel agent database to learn about the agent, the agent's record, and the kind of relationship the agent has with the airline. The reservations database enables her to determine the competitive position—what can other airlines do, and what kind of capacity and fares do they have? Then, using an *electronic mail* (Email) form, she creates an application for a discount which is sent to the yield management team located on another continent. This message is sent via direct communications link rather than through the post office.

The yield management officer receives the request and searches the "events" database for events that week in Tokyo that might affect the proposal, availability of hotels, etc. Using a modeling tool, he analyzes

Person	Activity	Technology
Travel agent	Messages airline—what to do?	Email
Airline sales manager	Accesses procedure for flexible marketing Accesses sales agent profile Determines competitive position Creates application for discount	Document database Agent database Reservation database Email
Yield management officer	Searches for important relevant events Analyzes capacity, outlook Requests further information from sales manager Initiates yield management group discussion Requests meeting Accesses during meeting Proposes deal to sales manager Assigns follow-up items	Events database Modeling tool Email Computer conference Meeting scheduling Reservation database Email Tickler
Airline sales manager	Reviews proposal and forwards to travel agent	Email
Travel agent	Books customer	Reservation database
Travel agent	Automatically generates invoice	Document creation

Figure 2-2. Work-group computing scenario—yield management in the airline industry.

the capacity and outlook of the airline to respond (what planes will be in the appropriate locations on the required days, etc.).

Further information is requested from the sales manager using electronic mail, and when tricky issues arise, a computer conference is requested within the yield management group. It turns out that the Tokyo meeting will be an annual event, and the yield officer decides to hold a face-to-face meeting with her colleagues to discuss arranging this meeting with an on-line scheduling tool. During the meeting, various databases are accessed, and the model is projected on a screen for each of the team to review and alter. A deal is formulated and then proposed to the sales manager by electronic mail, and a tickler file is created for the assignment of follow-up items. The sales manager then reviews the proposal, and she forwards it to the travel agent with voice annotation on the document, which adds some marketing flair.

The travel agent advises the customer of the proposal and, when it is accepted, accesses the reservations database to book the customer. The invoice and supporting documentation for the deal are sent to the customer using *electronic data interchange* (EDI).

Without information technology this business process, indeed this business function (yield management), is not possible.

Work-Group Computing Scenario: A Sales Team in Manufacturing

Selling in the new environment requires understanding the customer's needs and being able to customize orders and, in many cases, products and services to meet those needs. The following scenario (outlined in Fig. 2-3) is about a sales representative of a company that manufactures sailboats. The customer (a dealer) requires boats for showroom display and also for specific customer orders. Competitiveness in this market is not just a function of features and quality, but of price, customizability, delivery, and relationship (between the vendor and the dealer, and in turn between the dealer and his or her customers). All these factors can be improved by utilizing a high-performance sales team.

In this scenario the sales agent sitting in the dealer's office configures various proposals on his portable workstation. These are presented to the client on the screen, including color images or products, selected video clips, performance models, and competitive cost comparisons. The salesperson checks inventory through a telephone data linkup and develops quotes for pricing and delivery. The client suggests alterations that are required to close the deal, and the agent provides alternative proposals. The customer writes her signature using a digitized pad.

Various databases of the vendor are therefore updated, such as product levels, parts, inventories, accounts receivable, and payroll (for sales

Person	Action	Technology
Sales person	Configures order Checks inventory Gets price quote	Portable PC
Client	Signs order	Digitizing pad
Client	Updates order levels by product, parts, inventories, AR, AP, payroll (for commissions)	Database
Client	Sends message to sales person's secretary, manager, marketing, shipping, accounting, and production	Email
Secretary	Sends letter to customer	Document creation
Manager	Notes that employee has hit target	Email
Shipping	Requests additional support	Email
Finance	Does a credit check and issues invoice	Database
Production	Advised that inventories are below threshold Orders new parts	Database EDI
Salesperson	Reviews the month's achievements	Workstation

Figure 2-3. Work-group computing scenario—a sales team.

commissions). Messages are also sent automatically to the salesperson's secretary, to his manager, and to marketing, shipping, accounting, and production. Each of these takes an appropriate action, as defined in an appropriately designed procedure. For example, the secretary automatically sends a letter to the customer, documenting the arrangement and thanking her for her business. The manager notes that the salesperson is achieving his sales targets. Finance does a check of the customer's credit and issues an electronic authorization to production and shipping. Production is advised by a database entry that inventories on certain parts are low and through EDI automatically places orders with suppliers. Shipping requests additional support via electronic mail. In the airplane on the way home the salesperson reviews this month's achievements on his workstation and prepares his schedule for the next week.

In this scenario a sales team uses information technology and a defined set of procedures to work effectively with other business teams, with a goal of providing effective marketing and good customer service.

The Impact of Work-Group Computing

While such scenarios, based on actual organizations, sound impressive, what is the broader evidence that such work-group systems are having significant impacts? This question was investigated in the $2.5 million syndicated study conducted by DMR Group and entitled, "The Integration of Data, Text, Voice and Image." The program examined the experiences of the 100 sponsoring organizations and came up with a number of conclusions centering on the theme: *Cooperative work-group computing can be a central part of a process of business transformation at the level of the work group, which can, if managed, achieve spectacular benefits. To achieve such benefits, business processes must be redesigned, organizational change managed, and benefits harvested.*

Benefits were divided into two categories. The first was "bottom-line," or "direct," benefits. It was found that work-group computing can improve the efficiency and productivity of a team by directly reducing or avoiding administrative, communications, personnel, and redundancy costs. Work-group computing environments can also add value — enabling greater production of output and generation of revenue.

A second class was called *indirect,* or *enabling,* benefits. Work-group computing can improve many aspects of an organization that may not directly translate into cost savings or increased revenue but can contribute to the enterprise's success. Work-group implementations, for example, typically save people time — an indirect or enabling benefit. Time savings can be reinvested (resulting in direct benefits such as more sales revenue) or divested (also resulting in direct benefits such as reduced personnel costs). If indirect benefits are left to materialize just through some kind of magic cosmic event, Parkinson's law usually prevails: "Work expands to fill the time available." The problem is that it is usually the wrong kind of work. Benefits accrue when:

- Time savings are applied or "reinvested" in building the capacity to handle a larger volume of business and work while maintaining present staff levels.

- Time savings are reinvested in improving the quality of existing work and outputs, such as product or customer service quality.

- Time savings are reinvested in spending more time with the "customer" to expand business and revenues (for example, marketing managers having more time to spend with prospective clients).

- Time savings are reinvested in doing new things such as providing new services or developing new products or outputs (for example, a marketing campaign) that previously did not exist.

Another type of enabling benefit is "qualitative benefits." For example, implementations can result in an improvement in the quality of the workplace and work life by encouraging cooperation and offering individuals more personal work satisfaction and support. The ideas and innovations that arise from the sharing of resources and the enhanced exchange of information and expertise can result in innovative, improved product or service quality, strengthened customer loyalty, or labor stability, all of which can lead to direct benefits.

Our experience indicates that initial head-count redirection goals may be superficial and even misleading. For example, one large defense contractor undertook a reengineering project in its purchasing group with the goals of improving quality and reducing cost. Cost savings were an important objective because of the shrinking post-cold war market. The work-systems redesign showed opportunities to reduce by 42 percent the actual work performed through moving to a high-performance work-group computing platform. Although the initial focus was cost savings — implying head-count reductions — the analysis indicated that greater cost savings could be achieved by keeping head count flat. The strategy adopted was to reduce the number of suppliers from 1500 to 700, from which the company could negotiate larger discounts (due to larger volumes) as well as improved levels of quality, delivery, and timing. This was achieved through reinvesting the time saved in building supplier relations, in particular building joint quality programs with suppliers. In the end, both quality and cost reduction goals were surpassed considerably.

One key to unlocking the productivity opportunities among service and knowledge workers is to empower those workers with the skills, tools, information, and motivation so that they can maximize their individual contributions. By reengineering the work to remove unnecessary tasks and procedures and simplifying business processes, service workers become more involved in completing transactions, rather than just being a part of the process.

In most cases, the scope of activities also broadens. The contribution of knowledge and service workers is greatly expanded by developing common procedures, providing consistent user interfaces to tools and applications, incorporating network access to electronically stored information in appropriate forms, using decision-assist applications and expert systems to support the work activities, and providing effective communications with support and coaching resources.

One government organization we investigated uncovered an opportunity for empowering its service workers for such results. Under increasing pressure to deliver more services for less cost (an apparent contradiction), the organization discovered opportunities to combine operations such as field service offices. It did this by empowering government employees to deal with customer transactions for multiple departments and services at the same location. This resulted in expanding the number of service access points, combining services for customers' convenience, and saving real dollars. Obviously this is an exciting solution—given the willingness to remove old barriers between departments.

External users, including customers, suppliers, other business partners, and stakeholders, are also candidates for empowerment. By allowing direct access to external users, many routine requests for information or common business transactions can be handled directly by the technology.

In summary, direct and enabling benefits were found to have been achieved through improvements in various aspects of the work process. To understand how these benefits are being achieved, it is important to understand the functionality provided by the emerging workstation.

Work-Group Computing Functionality

In each of the above scenarios, and in the wider group of organizations investigated which had successfully implemented work-group systems, a powerful set of computer functions was integrated into a workstation to directly support various classes of personnel. Such functionality is a far cry from the limited spreadsheets and word-processing packages of the early personal computer. As communications capability is being added to PC functionality, a new array of functions is growing. (See Fig. 2-4.)

Information Exchange

The new work-group workstations contain access to a wide range of tools for communicating information in various combinations of data, text, voice, and image. The new functionality embraces all these forms and includes electronic data interchange across the system within an organization and, in growing instances, to suppliers and customers (structured information exchange). It also includes electronic messaging, computer conferencing and electronic document distribution (person-to-person store and forward technologies for documents), teleconferencing, slow-scan teleconferencing, and video conferencing (interactive information exchange technologies). One of the exciting new concepts awaiting full commercialization is group telepresence, which seeks to eliminate distance as a barrier to work-group functioning. The "offices" of various group members, distributed across multiple locations, are

Stand-Alone Personal Computer	Work-Group Systems

1. NIL	Information exchange
	  Email document distribution
	  Computer conferencing
	  Teleconferencing

2. Stand-alone word processing and presentation graphics	Shared document creation
	  Coauthoring (hypermedia thinking tools)
	  Shared work space/multiuser idea processing

3. Desktop database	Shared information handling
	  Access to information resource (data, text, voice, image)
	  Application sharing

4. Spreadsheet	Multiuser decision support
	  Modeling environments
	  Flags, threshold indicators
	  Knowledge bases

5. Diaries	Time and Resource Management
	  Scheduling
	  Meeting management
	  Procedure automation
	  Process management
	  Group project management

6. Tutorials	Computer-aided learning

Figure 2-4. The shift from personal to work-group computing.

linked using multimedia workstations, video cameras, and multiple display screens. The knowledge worker in one location has a full sense of the presence of other locations, even as far as the ability to look out the window of another location. When the office door is closed, it closes the video signal to indicate a desire for privacy.

As a result of information exchange functions, work groups may exist within a single department or be widely dispersed across the organization and the globe. As Christine Bullen and John Bennett point out, the work-group environment can be such that "people co-located in an office area do not necessarily work together as a group, and people geographically separated may form a team focused on achieving a common work result. Through the power of electronic media, these groups are dynamic and fluid; this is true for both formal and informal organizational units."[23] In work-group computing environments the walls of the office and barriers to information flow in the organization can disappear. The office becomes an interactive system rather than a place.

■ *Tool impact: Work-group computing can improve and positively transform communication.* This is accomplished by enabling more effective exchanges of information among those involved in a business function or project and beyond. Enhanced communications technologies can reduce costs in areas such as long-distance and courier usage, in employee travel, in the preparation and distribution of memos, and in the reduction of media transformations. Enabling benefits include significant time savings, better synergy through effective brainstorming, and improved quality of work life (for example, through the reduction of miscommunications or shadow functions like telephone tag).

Document Creation

Rather than the simple word-processing tools of the PC, communications tools are enabling new document creation and production capabilities. For example, coauthoring and shared work-space tools enable two or more persons to create and work with material over remote distances. Idea-processing tools enable authors to structure complex documents by creating layered outlines and viewing the structure of documents graphically in a multiuser context. The variations for different knowledge worker types are limitless. Software developers, as a unique case of knowledge workers, use a repository of all information regarding the components and activities undertaken to create a piece of software (a document). Musicians use music workstations to create and chart (document) compositions. Radiologists speak key words into a microphone when examining an x-ray. The key words automatically create sentences in a document with text and graphics (in one case changing the turnaround time for x-rays from 48 hours to 2 minutes).

■ *Tool impact: Document creation is faster and easier, and quality is better.* Using tools such as integrated word and graphics processors to create documents, users are able to shorten the time taken on individual work tasks and to increase enterprise responsiveness to unexpected changes. By being directly involved in document creation applications, users can reduce shadow functions, retyping, and media transformations and reuse common templates to shorten turnaround time. The direct author involvement, combined with the multiple author support that is part of the work-group computing environment, also improves both the content and the appearance of the documents that are created.

Information Storage and Retrieval

Simple PC filing and retrieval capabilities such as desktop databases are being transformed by communications into powerful, shared information-handling tools. Members of a work group can better access the information resource within the group or beyond. New multiuser applications based on personal computers are proliferating across organizations and threatening the traditional hegemony of the mainframe computer. The information that is stored can be any combination of data, text, voice, and image — as in the case of a hospital medical team that has interactive access to patient information in the form of charts, video, and voice-annotated x-rays.

Information gateways can provide access to a myriad of external databases — both those sold by information providers (ranging from stock prices to the news in today's paper) and those provided by other external organizations such as government agencies, suppliers, and customers. One internal application is the *executive information system* (EIS), which consolidates information from a variety of sources and presents it in graphical form for senior managers. When such capabilities are combined with broader workstation tools and access is provided to broader user communities, the result is the management support system.

- *Tool impact: Better access to information opens new doors.*   Information is available immediately on-line at the workstation, requiring less effort to find and retrieve it as well as enabling reuse of appropriate recaptured work. In physical terms, there is often a reduction in overhead and space costs for filing, improved access to archived information, and a reduction in document inventory. Improved access to information also means that the decisions that govern the work group activities and help to establish organizational strategies and objectives are more accurate, timely, and comprehensive. Better information is found to correlate with better decisions on a wide range of topics.

Decision Support: Analytical and Modeling Tools

Communications takes the user beyond the realm of the simple spreadsheet into the world of cooperative decision support. Teams with members in many locations can build powerful models of business situations or problems ranging from financial plans to market models and integrate them into a decision process. Decision rooms, available in many organizations, provide networked workstations around a boardroom table. Real-time alarms or threshold indicators can advise the user when an important event happens—for example, when a stock reaches a certain volume of trading. Expert systems contain knowledge bases and can aid human decision making in a growing range of applications. For example, they can diagnose what's wrong with everything from a locomotive to a patient.

- *Tool Impact: Better, faster decisions can transform the business.* Using processing, modeling, and simulation tools to develop forecasts, compare alternatives, and analyze results, a work-group computing approach enables enterprises to reduce error rates and therefore risk. The mechanization of business functions that are part of the work-group computing environment can also improve decision making as measured in a number of ways, helping to ensure that decisions made have the highest probability of being optimal.

Time and Resource Management

The simple diaries and scheduling applications of the PC become powerful tools for managing time and resources when combined with communications. Scheduling tools are proving valuable in getting the right people and/or resources to the right place at the right time. Face-to-face meetings have proved considerably more productive when on-line information is available, displayed, and manipulated by attendees or when group thinking tools are used to support and document the meeting. The processes and procedures of a business team can be streamlined and managed more effectively using various management tools. For example, a team member can be advised that lack of completion of an activity is holding up the process of negotiating an agreement with a customer.

- *Tool impact: Utilization of human and physical resources is enhanced.* Work-group computing environments were found to reduce the professional time required to administer and manage projects. They also allow workers to apply scheduling and planning tools to a greater variety of activities within the organization—as a new focus on teams enables and requires more extensive application of project management disciplines and techniques to business problems outside the purview of the traditional project. Other benefits can include reduction of clerical and professional efforts in scheduling meetings, higher attendance of key persons at meetings, improved tracking of project resources and costs, more productive employee interaction and division of labor in project activities, risk reduction through improved project costing, and actual improvements in the quality and turnaround time of work-group deliverables.

Educational and Entertainment Tools

Simple tutorials of PC software become powerful tools for computer-aided learning. A good example is the business team that learns a new skill through a new computer-based course that involves the interaction with others in the group. The program becomes much more dynamic, and in a more formal educational setting, students can be given ongoing comparative feedback regarding how they are doing. These programs have also merged with entertainment capabilities such as computer games, which legitimately have a role to play in education and motivation programs.

■ *Tool impact: Faster and more effective evolution of skill set, expertise, and culture occurs.* Work-group computing enables enterprises to develop approaches to integrate learning directly into the use of the systems and tools, which, in turn, results in more personalized education and training delivery. In an effectively implemented work-group computing environment, less effort is required to teach and learn end-user systems and new job skills. And a corresponding improvement in the quality of corporate education and training occurs as capabilities cascade across work groups. The benefits to the corporation are improved consistency, skills, and attitudes among its employees. This has many obvious ramifications. For example, the improvements in customer service that result from a more appropriately trained and educated work force can lead to higher levels of customer loyalty and satisfaction and to reduced customer support costs.

Citicorp: Building the High-Performance Team

Citicorp is one of the best examples of a company that reflects the impact of work-group computing. At Citicorp:

■ Implementations have been under way since the mid-1980s

- Implementations often involve a controlled measurement program so that the impact of the system is identifiable.

- The approach taken is to redesign work systems enabled through work-group technology, so the actual impact has been significant.

As a result, the company's experience is rich with lessons.

The New York–based company has a strong commitment to technological innovation. The corporation spends hundreds of millions of dollars annually on new technology acquisitions. Like any other enterprise, a key corporate objective is to secure and maintain a significant presence in its market. For Citicorp, that market is one where financial institutions around the world are fiercely competing to offer global electronic banking products and services. These services include automated delivery vehicles, on-line cash management, financial information database services, electronic funds transfer, letters of credit, and foreign exchange.

Citicorp adopted work-group computing because it found that traditional approaches to computing were inadequate for the new-generation end-user requirements. Too many corporate systems solutions that had been developed in the past were isolated from both the day-to-day and strategic operations of the bank. Senior bank executives recognized that systems planning and business planning were converging and that information technology was becoming more and more important to the business strategy of the corporation. Linking the two strategies meant bringing systems tools and databases directly to the end users at the desktop. Departments could then use the technology to establish and implement their own competitive and productivity objectives.

Citicorp first began developing a work-group computing environment in its Canadian subsidiary. Several business divisions were involved in the work-group computing implementation. They included Leasing, Capital Markets, Corporate Real Estate, Retail and Institutional Banking, and Operations. Initially, almost every employee of the Corporate Real Estate Group at Citibank Canada received a multi-function workstation. Employees were able to access from their workstations a wide range of information throughout the company. The work-group computing implementation meant that technology resided locally at the desktop, and also at work-group, departmental, establishment (Citibank), and enterprise (Citicorp) levels. Employees also had access to databases outside the enterprise. The implementation of these work-system changes altered the way the bank conducted its activities.

The bank was able to achieve dramatic results by streamlining processes, through a work-group computing approach, by delegating activities from account executives to market support and administration, and by using automated tools to do work faster and eliminate redundancies. Most of these were "enabling" benefits that were translated into direct or bottom-line benefits.

Work-group computing enabled marketing managers and other marketing professionals at the bank to reduce routine administrative and information-gathering activities and to direct their attention toward other activities. Instead of spending valuable time on administrative tasks, account representatives were able to focus their efforts on more productive and profitable tasks such as direct marketing, sales, customer service, and product development. Executive managers, professionals, and support personnel worked as business teams, focused on their respective marketplaces. An important success factor was that redesign of business processes was participative, involving all key stakeholders.

In the case of Citicorp's Real Estate Group implementation, detailed presystem and postsystem implementation measures were taken. This group markets, negotiates, and manages large corporate loans to customers who, for example, are building an office tower. An initial examination of the group showed weak financial performance, a slow cumbersome process of doing business, and vast portions of time spent by group members in what they considered to be unproductive activities.

Two years after the system implementation and business process redesign, profit center earnings more than doubled. The amount of time to process loans (all in the millions of dollars) was reduced by almost 50 percent. Executive management time spent on "administrative activities" dropped from 70 to 25 percent of the day. The number of customers managed per account executive rose by 170 percent, while the percentage of account representatives exceeding their targets increased from less than 6 to 75 percent. These and other improvements resulted in striking increases in business revenues. At the same time the bank was able to contain its operating costs.

Other indirect benefits resulted from the work-group computing implementation. Electronic mail streamlined communications, modeling tools helped with decision making, while automation made document creation more responsive to customer needs. The work-group computing system also helped bank personnel expedite, track, and document various tasks in negotiating large loans with corporate customers. The turnaround time to negotiate a loan was reduced by 75 percent, resulting in improved competitiveness. The group was often able to close a deal before the competition could get its act together.

One of the most significant changes was in the nature of the business team itself. In addition to business processes and procedures, the jobs of all Corporate Real Estate personnel were redesigned. For example, administrative personnel who were freed of any previous activities by the implementation undertook a program to reinvest their saved time in paraprofessional activities assisting with the loan process. Many aspects of their jobs changed, including their titles. Reflecting their new responsibilities, they became customer service representatives with a focus on the customer rather than internal administration. Over time some customer service representatives moved into another new role as relationship officers. As such, they provided analysis support, documentation, market research, and other support activities. From clerical staff, they had grown into paraprofessional and ultimately professional roles with a resulting increase in value to the organization. Similarly, marketing managers became relationship managers—reflecting the profound shift in their jobs from administering sales and sales support activities to building relationships through information technology. The Corporate Real Estate organization had built a high-performance business team.

Summary: Work-Group Computing—The Shifts

- Organizational hierarchy   →   Organizational network based on business teams

- Personal computing   →   Work-group computing

- Emphasis on the individual   →   Emphasis on the group

- Designing technology   →   (Re)designing the entire work system

- Taylorism   →   The new work reengineering

- Technical users   →   Direct support to all classes of personnel

- Installing technology   →   Leadership for changing ways of working

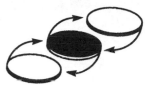

3

The Integrated Organization

- A courier company storms to number one in its industry—taking over half of the marketplace and becoming the largest freight airline in the world—by focusing on quality and basing its entire business on second-era technology.

- A U.S. insurance company changes its business from being a provider of indemnity insurance to providing a complete health care delivery system based on information technology.

- A Japanese soft drink bottler transforms the effectiveness of its customer service and distribution operations through an IT infrastructure in which, for example, vending machines are part of the system—phoning in when they run short of certain brands.

- An airline uses an imaging system to redesign its entire sales and marketing operations—eliminating all sorts of tedious tasks and allowing management to monitor and direct operations as they are being performed rather than waiting for after-the-fact status reports.

- A regional government integrates information from previously separate sources—maps, aerial photographs, demographic statistics, land titles, corporate records, and others—into a geographic information system (GIS) to sharply reduce costs and improve the effectiveness of public information required by various stakeholders.

- An elevator company revolutionizes its customer support and field service operations through a comprehensive network and redesign of business processes, resulting in lower costs and a uniquely competitive support operation.

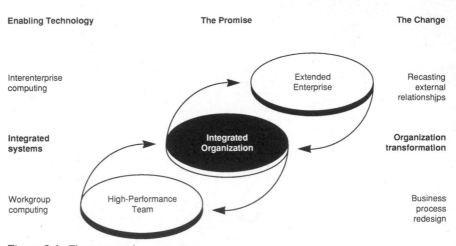

Figure 3-1. The integrated organization.

■ A large manufacturer goes beyond executive information systems to implement a management support system that integrates information from various systems across the enterprise—changing the way the company is managed.

All these are examples of the transformation, not only of work groups, but of entire enterprises enabled by the new technology paradigm (see Fig. 3-1). The rise of business teams and work-group computing is part of a broader change in information flow, organizational authority, and accountability within the corporation. The business pull and technology push are giving rise to something new—enterprise integration—which affects the entire breadth of an organization's operations and resources. In this new environment, corporate systems that differ dramatically in a multitude of ways from their predecessors are emerging.

Despite often rocky early implementations, new integrated technologies, combined with organization and business process redesign, are dramatically altering the effectiveness of enterprises and their ability to navigate in new competitive waters.

Era I Systems: Islands of Technology

Typical systems in era I were isolated islands, reflecting the structure of the era I organization. A system was implemented when a technology solution (such as a software package for a given industry application need) matured to the point where it could be cost-justified and when an organization matured in its understanding of systems to the point where the solution could be exploited.

Technology was implemented to help business units manage or reduce the costs of three fundamental resources: *physical assets, human resources,* and *financial assets.*

In the manufacturing, distribution, transportation, and retail industries, physical assets usually constitute the primary business of the organization. They may be raw materials, goods in production or transit, or items in inventory. They may also include the process and production facilities and equipment of an organization and the utilities required to operate them. For service industries they include the office or working space, vehicles, and the supplies required to operate the businesses.

The human resources of an enterprise include people in all types of job functions, from production workers to administrative support, professional staff, and management. These people vary by job function and the degree of manual labor versus mindpower involved in conducting their work activities.

The third area, financial assets, includes the management of cash, credit, receivables, expenditures, liabilities, and the like.

In the first era, systems that supported the three resource areas were separate and isolated, reflecting the typical lack of business integration. Various types of systems were designed to reduce costs or improve utilization of physical resources, financial resources, and human resources.

Systems Addressing Physical Resource Management

These systems consisted of real-time systems to monitor and control plant and production processes, culminating in totally automated process plants and factories. Physical systems directly interfaced with the physical environment and extracted information for monitoring and controlling the production and manufacturing processes of the enterprise. Examples of these systems include:

- Process control, such as refinery management systems and power utility management systems
- Production control and robotics, such as shop floor and assembly-line systems
- Security and surveillance systems for access control and site protection
- Air traffic control and similar real-time routing and scheduling applications in transportation and distribution

- Automated warehouses for mechanized storage and selection of inventoried items

- Heating, ventilating, and air conditioning (HVAC) systems for the climate control of buildings.

Systems Addressing Human Resource Effectiveness

An array of facilities, ranging from the telephone system to word processing, were implemented to support the needs of various classes of end users. These end-user systems included:

Telephone networks	Time management tools
Paging systems	Decision support systems
Telex networks	Computer-aided drawing
Facsimile transmission	Automated teller machines
Word-processing systems	Audio and video systems
Dictation systems	Computer-based learning systems

Systems Addressing Financial Resource Management

Financial resource management systems focused initially on reducing the administrative costs of functions such as accounts payable, accounts receivable, payroll, and general ledger. They evolved into systems for processing a wide range of business transactions and reporting on the results of these in the form of management information. Database-processing systems dominated this class, evolving from early batch processing to on-line and database management systems. Systems development professionals developed corporate and departmental information-processing applications, building upon the power of database management software and inquiry languages. Examples of these systems include:

- accounting and payroll systems
- customer information systems
- on-line banking systems
- insurance policy management systems

As a result of the growth of technologies in these three areas, it became common to discuss the rise and management of a fourth resource — information — which was in part a by-product of these classes of systems and overlaps them all.

The Problem of the Unintegrated Enterprise

Many of these islands of technology met the needs of specific business operations, but they also resulted in the fragmentation of systems applications and the organizational functions responsible for them. Their limited and specialized functions had nothing to do with the overall business objectives and strategies of the corporation. There was no such thing as enterprise computing. These systems were almost always balkanized. In most instances, formidable physical and organizational barriers existed between the data-processing departments, engineering and production, and administrative support areas of the organizations.

While these systems were an improvement over manual systems, the walls between systems and thereby between business units had many drawbacks. Overlaps in function and systems components occurred regularly, resulting in redundancies and inefficiencies. Two systems would be fulfilling similar or overlapping functions. There was limited systems use because few people in the organization had access to the technology. This latter factor often meant that there was limited access to useful corporate operational data. The information that would have enhanced the quality of decisions affecting the enterprise and its success in meeting its goals was simply not available. Lack of integration and gaps between systems islands also caused miscommunications and missed opportunities to achieve business value, for example by taking information collected for one purpose and using it for another purpose.

Operations and customer service were restricted and even governed by such isolated organizational and technological systems and structures. A person was not a customer of a bank, for example, but a customer of the savings department, the mortgage department, the loans department, or the credit card division. Anyone who dealt with multiple services within the bank had the experience of filling out the same personal information over and over again.

We recently encountered a glaring example of this redundancy in a government department where 22 systems collected the same information. This isolation of systems also made public access to government information difficult if not, in some cases, impossible, as government departments had no way of sharing and collecting data outside their specific areas. Inquiries for information on such areas as the environment or occupational health and safety, which may be required as part of an industrial accident investigation, for example, had to be collected separately.

The islands of automation were also internally focused, further contributing to their isolation. In the first era the notion of linking to systems of suppliers and customers was even more unthinkable than linking to those within one's own enterprise.

The approach to technology was much like the traditional western approach to medicine. If there was a problem with back pain, doctors treated the pain and not how it related to other areas of the body. Similarly, if there was a problem with a specific enterprise operation, a system solution was developed exclusively for that operation.

An additional problem is that for each of these three classes of systems, organizational functions were formed to take responsibility for them. The data-processing or MIS group evolved to build systems that had their origin addressing the financial resource. Various engineering groups evolved to build process control and other systems addressing physical resources and assets. And an administrative group evolved to plan for and manage administrative technologies such as photocopiers, the telephone system, micrographics, and so on. With the rise of the PC everyone got involved. The result has often been organizational conflict, turf wars, and lack of cooperation between those responsible for systems planning and implementation across the enterprise.

The Integrated Organization and Integrated Systems

Just as work-group computing enables the new business team, the integration of systems enables the integrated organization.

The demands of the new business environments are forcing a "reinvention" of the corporation.[1] Rather than being a collection of business units, organizations need to function as a *single enterprise,* often a global one. Yet at the same time, the new enterprise is moving to a client/server model—based on *empowered business teams* that have a high degree of autonomy. To address this seeming paradox, the new enterprise must also be *integrated*—with an overall strategy and architecture for the business, work organization, information, and technology.

Second-era enterprises are adopting a perspective that resembles the holistic approach to medicine. The individual parts of the body are regarded as part of an integrated whole (see Fig. 3-2).

It is information technology, more than any other factor, that enables the new integrated organization. Well-conceived applications of tech-

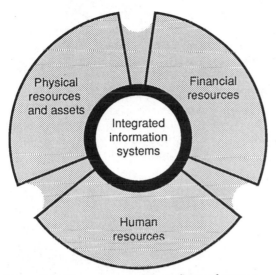

Figure 3-2. Three resources—three classes of systems.

nology can enable organizations to flatten by eliminating the management layers. It is information technology that can enable reengineering, not only of business processes, but of the enterprise, in ways that traditional organization development specialists could not imagine. (Many still have difficulty, and constitute a significant impediment to progress.)

The isolated technology applications of an earlier time are no longer adequate. Companies are discovering that they have to establish enterprise capabilities that will create new opportunities for sharing and reusing information and information technology resources at all levels. More and more organizations are becoming aware that the technical and structural barriers that have previously prevented or hindered internal communication and the sharing of resources must be dismantled. There is a growing need for direct links between the sources of information and the people who use it and for ways of sharing this information throughout the organization.

This in no way implies centralized systems or the centralization of systems planning. Rather, systems thinking and consistent strategy are required at every level of an enterprise, from the individual and business team to the enterprise level. Effective coordination through an ongoing user-driven process is often the way organizations can establish a high degree of autonomy combined with unity. Likewise, as we shall see in later chapters, this does not mean throwing out current systems. Rather, an enterprisewide IT architecture is required to incorporate the legacy of past investments as well as to ensure the integration of new ones.

DMR research shows that when an enterprise achieves appropriate integration between the three classes of systems, it can achieve significant improvements in organizational synergy, the quality of products and services, market responsiveness, management decision making, and a number of other variables that are linked to competitiveness and productivity.

For example, in manufacturing, integrated organizations are enhancing inventory control and distribution management systems. This results in improved delivery service levels by tracking goods through tools such as production management systems and distribution tracking services. Applying technology to production control and testing processes through robotics and sensor-based systems can also improve quality levels. Some companies are reducing service requirements through computer-based diagnostics embedded in the products themselves. Through the use of on-line database inquiries, on-line access to document filing, and records management systems, these integrated businesses are improving access to business records and customer information and, as a result, increasing their responsiveness and support capability.

In the integrated enterprise, information flows both within and between the three resource areas. Employees have access to information pertaining to the day-to-day operations of the enterprise, whether this information is sourced directly from the physical environment or obtained indirectly from stored information resources. In short, electronic information exchange occurs throughout the organization.

In integrated enterprises, information-processing systems are increasingly going to the source to capture information — which in turn is used by financial and other systems and databases. Often this information capture involves interfaces with physical systems in which a sensor is monitoring a physical process or activity. Pricing and inventory systems that use point-of-sale scanners and automated teller machines with cash dispensers are two early examples.

By reaching out to end users, information-processing systems are becoming a repository of current and historical information to support the operation and management of the business. The establishment of direct interfaces between end-user systems and the information resource is a key result. In these integrated organizations, users are able to access text and image-based documents as well as audio and video recordings or computer-based training courses. In addition to data-oriented business transaction records, this information is available in many other forms (data, text, voice, image).

In many of the organizations that have made the transition, information gathered from inventory, production, marketing, and other departments is being used to schedule the most efficient production of their products and services. This information also forms the basis for strategic production and inventory management.

One example of this is the Procter & Gamble Company (P&G), where an optimized production scheduling system is being used in concert with the company's inventory control and other corporate databases to meet a number of corporate objectives. These objectives are to improve production plans, to achieve significant inventory reductions, to improve manufacturing costs, and to increase the ability to respond more quickly to production disruptions and sudden changes in product demand. The system incorporates capacity constraints such as staff availability, material inventories, and production capability, and is linked to other corporate systems that order materials and plan deliveries. The system is also integrated with other components of P&G's corporate database which is used to support manufacturing decision making throughout the organization. The integration of the scheduling system with other corporate operational systems is part of the company's move to integrated logistics management, a strategic step that P&G is taking to ensure that it remains competitive in both current and future markets.

Many of the benefits of integration are complex. The research showed that objectives for integration fall in a number of areas. Objectives that were found to be achievable include:

- Establishing new service levels for increased customer satisfaction and loyalty
- Creating new business opportunities through the extension of existing product and service offerings or the development of new ones
- Streamlining organizational procedures and achieving of synergy through logical application integration
- Lowering unit costs of computer and communication systems through the sharing of common architectures and delivery systems
- Leveraging experience from all areas of systems applications to address common needs
- Developing an infrastructure to support increased decentralization and autonomy
- Establishing a basis for quickly reacting to changing customer demands and business developments.

Location, Location, Location

"Location, location, location" is the real estate agents' explanation of what determines property value. Keeping track of geographic data can be vital to business success.

A good example of the type of capability that results from integration and the considerable implications for how business can be conducted is a geographic information system (GIS). According to the United Nations, 1 percent of gross domestic product is spent collecting and maintaining geographic data! The challenge, for many years, has been to coordinate and combine this information into an integrated environment usable by various government and business organizations.

Until recently, it was either impossible or extremely expensive to combine geographically dispersed data. The emergence of the GIS, however, has enabled businesses to integrate and analyze information from multiple sources and locations. Such systems also combine information from all three classes of system types and all four forms (data, text, image, and sometimes voice) to provide powerful new capabilities.

Although a comprehensive definition of the technology is not shared by experts, GISs are generally regarded as systems that use a combination of digitized image and advanced database technologies to allow the user to store information against the geographic features of a "map."

Regional and municipal governments have demonstrated a strong interest in these systems to support planning, engineering operations, and all facets of land-use administration, including electoral rolls and tax base analysis. Telephone, water, electric, cable television, and other utility companies are using the technology to design and operate their distribution networks. Digital street maps are now commonly used to dispatch fire, police, and ambulance services.

Businesses are also adopting these systems or actively looking at the advantages they offer. Information captured at point of sale, for example, can be mapped to show customer purchasing patterns and preferences by geographic area. Advertising and marketing strategies can be designed more effectively based on the results. The siting of businesses and corporate services can be evaluated based on a combination of demographic data and other geographic information. Maps can be produced showing candidate locations that take into account target populations, transportation routes, availability of critical supplies, and location of competitors.

A growing number of companies are implementing GIS technology. Pizza Hut, a major fast-food company that operates a central ordering service for home delivery in major cities across the United States and Canada, uses mapping software to assign orders to the nearest restaurant. The *Los Angeles Times* uses GIS to manage its distribution and define geographic markets for its special editions. Transportation companies are implementing GIS applications that include navigation devices to provide drivers with a map display showing their current position and best route to a desired destination. Central displays can also be used to locate the positions of vehicles in a fleet. Courier companies use GIS for dispatching, planning routes, and tracking the location of parcels.

Needless to say, with such capabilities it is possible to (re)design a competitive enterprise or effective government agency around an integrated technology platform.

Multimedia Customer Support

Leading service industry companies are using integrated systems to provide better service and simultaneously handle more customers in less time. Through workstations that integrate data, text, voice, and image, the customer support function in many of these companies has been transformed.

Typically, such systems significantly decrease the average time spent handling telephone calls. When a customer calls in to initiate a transaction, the system obtains the caller's phone number directly from the telephone network and uses it to locate the customer's associated computer file. Appropriate customer information is displayed on the computer screen of the company representative as the voice call is being answered. This process eliminates the need for the representative to ask for and reenter customer information required to locate the customer's account. If the call needs to be referred to someone else, both the voice and the other information are transferred simultaneously.

An example of a company that has benefited from this technology is American Home Shield (AHS)—the oldest and largest home warranty company in the United States. The company conducts repair or replacement of residential heating, cooling, plumbing, and electrical systems under home service contracts. The national service center in Carrol, Iowa, generates more than 80,000 calls per month in addition to handling company sales and service activities.

As part of implementation, business processes were redesigned, resulting in considerable increases in productivity. For example, real estate professionals call in to purchase a warranty for a home buyer or seller. It was found that the system cuts the time to handle such calls by 27 seconds—enabling an additional 75,000 calls per year.

Other companies that have reported significant benefits from the same technology used by AHS are DIRECTEL Inc., Quartermaster, and Fidelity Investments. DIRECTEL provides complete product fulfillment services (order entry and returns processing, merchandise warehousing, inventory control, customer service) to the direct marketing industry. The company was able to handle almost 4000 additional calls per day through its integrated environment.

Quartermaster, a retail and mail-order company specializing in military and outdoor clothing, can process an additional 20,000 orders per year with no increase in staff. When a repeat customer calls Quartermaster's 800 number, the caller's profile appears on an operator's order entry screen as the call arrives, among other things avoiding duplication of customer profiles.

Similarly, Fidelity Investments customers can telephone their orders into any one of three regional service centers. Service representatives have immediate access to their files and histories and can execute the transactions they request. If there is a telephone system failure or overload, the call is automatically routed to another center for service.

Smart Card, Smart Key, Smart Customer

It seems that every time you rent a car these days, some new technology makes it easier and faster. National is a good example of the power of integration to improve customer service and competitiveness. In 1967, National built the industry's first centralized billing system, and two years later it had created the first nationwide reservation system. A recent innovation is Emerald Aisle, which eliminates the lengthy, time-consuming, multicarboned rental agreement. Emerald Club members provide detailed personal and billing information once; this is encoded onto a smart credit card. This and all subsequent transactions go into an enterprise database, providing a powerful marketing tool.

Club members proceed from the airport gate to the National lot and then choose any car they want, driving directly to a booth where an attendant passes their Emerald Club card through a reader and checks their license. After this, they simply drive away. Other "frequent drivers" can also use Smart Key. This involves the use of a terminal that allows them to select cars from a touch screen. Smart Key guides the renter through a number of questions, prints a contract, and then releases the car keys from a dispenser right on the spot.

Integration has delivered excellent customer service for other companies. For example, when a frequent renter exits the airport and steps on the Hertz bus, the driver enters the person's name into a terminal on the bus. Minutes later upon arrival at the Hertz lot the renter is dropped off at his or her car, which is gassed up, running, and ready to go. Upon returning to the lot, the renter provides mileage to an attendant right at the car, and a receipt is printed out at the car through a hand-held printer. All such transactions are part of the enterprise database usable for administrative and marketing purposes.

These programs are bellwethers of more to come in this industry. Expect light readers that scan cars as they enter and exit the rental lot, fleet management capabilities to track all cars' whereabouts and determine if they are due for maintenance, systems that integrate with broader reservations systems including air and hotel, and the elimination of forms completion and related airport lineups for all customers as data capture is done once for any customer (preferably at the time of reservation). With such powerful integrated systems environments, expect that, as with your local pizza chain, "You'll be driving within 15 minutes of walking out the airport door or the rental's free!"

Diet Coke—Phone Home

When Coke machines in Tokyo get low on Diet Coke, they phone home for more. A radio wave transmission system called Teleterminal is used to monitor 62,000 vending machines and speed up the ordering process. The system is part of a broader integrated systems strategy. The goal of this implementation is to overcome a labor shortage, raise operational efficiency, and improve services to retailers.

Soft drinks sold through vending machines are typically subject to considerable seasonal fluctuations and unpredictable buying patterns. As a result, dispatching trucks to check the stock and refill each machine is a guessing game and an inefficient business process. Because Teleterminal machines advise the system when a particular brand needs replenishing, machines are stocked when they need to be—just-in-time soda. The data from these machines are also used in rationalizing production and tracking the impact of marketing programs.

The strategy is also designed to give Coke a significant lead over its competitors in service to retailers. More than 200 Coke salespeople use portable terminals to transmit orders from a retail outlet (such as a food store) directly to the main system. The order is then processed immediately and a delivery schedule determined. This allows next-day delivery, which enables retailers to cut their inventories in half. It also reduces the need for the company's 29 branch offices which used to act as a clearinghouse for orders. Integrated systems are enabling the reengineering of an enterprise.

Artificial Intelligence Gets Integrated

Often thought of as the stuff for the new millennium, artificial intelligence (AI) is becoming a reality for many enterprises in the 1990s. And rather than being independent technologies, applications such as expert systems are becoming part of an integrated strategy. Expert systems capture important knowledge, not just data, and enable the application of rules to assist in decision making — ranging from diagnosing patients to evaluating business risk. A powerful application area pioneered by American Express (AMEX) is credit approval. AMEX has reengineered its credit approval process by providing employees with an expert system that helps them make the more difficult credit granting decisions. The expert system is based on the knowledge and expertise of the company's senior credit grantors and has dramatically reduced loan losses and expedited the approval process.

A striking example of the use of AI as part of enterprise computing is Phoenix Continental. This North American property and casualty insurance company depends on brokers to sell its policies to the customers. From the company's perspective, its brokers are its direct customers. It is the responsibility of Phoenix Continental's underwriters to provide ongoing customer service by managing the relationship with these brokers on a day-to-day basis. These responsibilities include determining policy risk levels, quoting a final price on policies, and identifying policy exceptions, monitoring the overall book of business of each broker, identifying high-performance brokers and assigning them discounts, and entering policy information into the company's corporate database.

Phoenix Continental wanted to develop a system that would support an underwriter's responsibilities and use technology to screen policies by exception rather than on a case-by-case basis. In doing so, the company wanted to establish more effective and productive business operations. It also wanted to transfer the task and cost of policy data entry to the brokers. As part of the implementation, the company would provide automated facilities for screening broker-entered policy data.

The company implemented a computing environment consisting of intelligent workstations and attached terminals at corporate headquarters as well as resident terminals at each broker location. Policy implementation in the new environment involves several steps: the broker keys in the policy application using a terminal provided by the company; the company's main computer processes and files the policy; the policy information is transmitted to the underwriter's workstation for screening; and the results are put on files with predefined views for the underwriter. Only questionable policies are brought to the attention of the underwriter.

Underwriters now use an expert system to evaluate applications. Screening that used to be a laborious file-by-file process that took months to complete is now done overnight. As a result, the entire approach to underwriting has changed. Instead of making underwriting decisions on a policy-by-policy basis, the company has shifted its focus to underwriting the broker's overall portfolio. Not only has the data entry cost shifted to the broker, but so has a portion of the risk. At the same time the direct access to Phoenix Continental's database has given brokers more autonomy and control over their business.

The company has changed its entire approach to broker and policy management and has achieved a significant competitive advantage as a result. It has assembled a higher-quality portfolio of business resulting in more revenue and improved profitability. Phoenix Continental has also significantly increased the number of brokers (customers) across the country, all of whom are now doing their own data entry for their policy applications.

A New "Image" for the Enterprise

Technology that captures and digitizes images (such as photographs, drawings, tickets, or letters) has traditionally been viewed as isolated technology for stand-alone applications. However, more and more of it is coming into its own, integrated with the rest of an enterprise technology infrastructure.

At United Services Automobile Association (USAA), the company is working to establish a totally paperless environment where all documents are collected and exchanged using image storage and retrieval systems based on laser optics technology. The system enables any of the terminals at corporate headquarters and in its field offices to access a member's file in seconds. The result is faster and more effective customer service.

The airline industry has a very complex and fundamental revenue accounting problem which an enterprise computing strategy using image technology can effectively address. To begin, tickets are purchased from a variety of sources, including the airline, other airlines, and travel agents. As a result, it is difficult to estimate revenue since information is scattered through various databases including those of competitors. The only complete documentation of revenue is the ticket—hundreds of thousands of which pour into airline processing centers every 24 hours. This volume makes it unfeasible to manually add up the revenue from tickets. As a result, airlines have typically taken a sample and then statistically project revenue from that sample. That was the situation before integrated imaging technology arrived.

Northwest Airlines tackled this problem through an image-based ticket accounting system. A ticket sorter with an added digital camera captures ticket images and optically reads their serial numbers for indexing purposes and then physically groups coupons by category. The images are stored on image file servers for 6 months. This enables the cataloging of every ticket issued in Northwest's name and every canceled ticket used on one of its flights.

But the Northwest imaging system is integrated with the rest of its technical infrastructure. A network of mainframes and smaller computers collects information from various other reservation, flight operations, and revenue collection systems and stores all available records associated with the ticket. Each transaction becomes a file that includes information about the ticket plus the location of that ticket on the imaging system. Further, an expert system identifies tickets for which there is a match. Anomalies among the electronic and paper (digitized images) records are flagged and assigned to an auditor. Software that organizes and monitors work flow advises management of backlogs in resolving discrepancies.

The impact has been significant, to say the least. The time to process and account for ticket revenue was cut in half, reducing costs. As well, cash collections were accelerated, response time to customer inquiries improved, and revenue verification simplified (ensuring that correct fares were charged and various agents received correct commissions).[2]

All of this was achievable only through integration combined with associated work process redesign.

Getting at the Information Resource

An important example of enterprise computing is the new trend (and associated technology) to provide an interactive and consolidated picture of the entire operation of an enterprise to support the decision making of senior managers. It is these two factors (interaction and consolidation) that differentiate management support systems from traditional classes of management systems that provided "information." *Management information systems* (MISs) typically provided reams of paper printouts from specific system islands. *Decision support systems* (DSSs) were restricted modeling environments initiated before the days of the spreadsheet.

A step beyond MISs and DSSs is the *executive information system* (EIS)—a system that consolidates information from various sources for senior management. Executive information systems are designed to collect information from a variety of company sources and produce easy-to-understand, on-line, graphical information designed to support better decision making by executive users. The drill-down capability of these systems allows these users to gather more detailed information on specific areas according to their individual needs.

Information accessed through an EIS can cover all operations and divisions of an enterprise and can even extend to externally produced data. Financial statements, cash flow statistics, sales per employee, and on-line information services via electronic mail networks are just a few of the information areas that can be accessed. Many packages also allow the executive to create what-if scenarios to assist them in making future strategic plans.

EISs can give executives immediate information on company and departmental expenditures or any other information in corporate or departmental databases. In addition, specific EIS software can analyze this information in the form of graphic charts to depict a month-by-month analysis of the key performance indicators or update a projection for the year end. Sales analyses, for example, can be done by product category or operating unit.

However, EISs are often kludges rather than part of an architected enterprise computing environment. In extreme cases, armies of data entry personnel (sometimes unbeknownst to the executives involved) reenter output from various relevant systems into a separate EIS.

A broader way of looking at the challenge of management support is the *management support system* (MSS). Behind the idea are the notions that operational responsibility goes beyond executives and that such managers require not just "information" but a complete computing environment to support them in their various communications, information-handling, and decision-making activities. Although managers do not typically constitute a work group as discussed in the previous chapter, they, as members of work groups, have a need to participate in a broader enterprise computing environment. Good EIS implementations have been conducted in this spirit of management support in many companies. For example, at TransAlta Utilities Corp. (based in Calgary, Alberta), executives have access to a wealth of information that includes financial data, energy loads, safety statistics, and other important organizational data. At Noranda Inc., a major North American mining company, EIS technology provides access to metal exchange prices, stock prices, and earnings. Genetech Inc., a biotechnology research and product firm, has made important gains through an EIS that tracks sales programs and markets.

At Dupont Industries, all senior executives have 24-hour access to vital corporate information that includes profiles of the company's largest customers, updates on the company's safety performance, company productivity data, and market trends affecting Dupont. An EIS network at Phillips Petroleum includes information that is updated daily, weekly, and monthly. Information on the network covers areas such as the company's drilling operations, its chemical and plastics production, and the current retail price of gasoline. Information from news sources and other external databases on markets and other developments that may affect the company's operations is also available. All the information that links the company's physical, financial, and human resources is needed to implement enterprise business strategies.

Frito-Lay Inc. provides another example of an innovative use of an EIS. The company uses a system to monitor and analyze inventories and sales transactions on a daily basis, from more than 10,000 route sales representatives who cover 300,000 retail outlets each week. The data are integrated with financial and other corporate databases to provide information on sales patterns, customer responses to both traditional and recently launched products, and market reactions to product promotions.

By changing the access and flow of information, EISs and MSSs are changing the structure of organizations. They are removing layers of management bureaucracy and, like many other current information technology developments, are forcing companies to rethink their hierarchical organizational structures and procedures, and the roles and responsibilities of their middle managers. Executives, who formerly went through layers of management to obtain information on company or divisional operations, can directly access the data they require through this technology. As a result, the middle-management function of gathering information and acting as a liaison between the executive and individual departments of the company is quickly disappearing. With no need to provide information to an executive, many managers either are becoming redundant or are able to apply their expertise and skills to other tasks leading to greater corporate productivity.

The Travelers: Forging a New Business Based on Integration

When the Travelers decided to enter the managed health care business, it was no accident that it turned to Joe Brophy (now president of the Travelers insurance company) to head up the new operation. Over a period of 2 years the Travelers turned from a traditional indemnity insurance business to create a new managed health care business, with considerable results.

The company's transformation is reflective of the massive changes taking place in health care in the United States, as the traditional approach to health care disintegrates. Traditionally customers were insured through a group insurance plan, and they submitted claims to the insurer — who paid them with few questions asked. From the Travelers' point of view the system worked well for years. However,

as health care costs continued to spiral upward, and as evidence of
serious quality problems mounted, it became clear that the
insurance industry needed to take another approach to providing
health care.

The health care industry in the United States has been, and is
largely, an unplanned collection of hospitals, physicians, and other
practitioners. Estimates are that from 15 to 40 percent of health
care costs are unnecessary, and despite quality problems, the
infrastructure in place is underutilized. A key missing element in
this system has been a virtual lack of integration. In all but a few
cases, hospitals, physicians, laboratories, and other providers operate
with a minimal use of advanced information technologies and
virtually without coordination. This has led to a health care system
in which treatment decisions are done in isolation—for example,
based on clinical tests and on a physician's own experience, instead
of on the vast body of clinical experience that exists. Physicians are
influenced by the opportunity to make insurance claims as well as by
practices in their communities, resulting in doctors performing twice
the number of tonsillectomies in one community than in another.

Some people, including those at the U.S. National Institutes of
Health, argue that this situation is due largely to the free enterprise
approach to medicine.[3] On the other hand, companies with an
interest in the private system have had to develop a new approach,
namely, managed care. This is an effort by insurers, employers, and
health providers to deliver health care characterized by both good
quality and managed costs. The trend required insurers to take a
proactive approach to encourage the development and maintenance
of standards of health care quality, as well as to control increases in
health care costs. This has resulted in the creation of *health
maintenance organizations* (HMOs) in which insurers and customer
organizations band with locally based networks of doctors and
hospitals that deliver health care at an agreed-upon fee in return
for a guaranteed number of clients.

Travelers was a latecomer to managed care. As such, it faced
formidable challenges in both developing an effective system and
selling itself to its existing and new customers. It had an important
choice to make: purchase some existing HMOs or build its own.
According to Brophy, it was because of Travelers' confidence in its
information technology capabilities that it decided to build. "The
essence of managed care, as we see it, is information. The more
relevant information that is available to all participants in the health
care delivery system, the more that physicians and hospitals will
provide the right treatment and the right service at the right time
and the care will be of higher quality and less expensive."

The company set out to provide appropriate medical personnel
access to large databases with millions of case histories that could
guide treatment decisions for customers. The goal was to use
information technology to help make the correct diagnosis the first
time without unnecessary tests and to provide the physician or
hospital with the information it needed to select the course of

treatment that had proved most likely to result in a quality outcome for the patient. "It is our view that information technology and access to information will be the diagnostic tool of the third millennium as the microscope was to the second," says Brophy.

Travelers then reengineered its enterprise and all its operations. This included hiring 3500 medical staff and implementing a massive care management network. The CareOptions medical management system can be accessed by any of the 30,000 personal computers in health care offices around the country as well as by more than 1000 corporate customers. Integration is a key theme. For example, the Travelers professional workstation includes a PC with integrated voice mail. Smart "swipe cards" are being used in a growing number of locations to reduce the hassle factor for physicians and improve data capture. The physicians can also use the card to authorize referrals to specialists and precertify hospital admissions. Standard forms and contracts are stored centrally in the system and printed locally on demand, although these are more and more being replaced by on-line customer ordering.

Travelers has concluded that integration is enabling the combination of local medical expertise with the administrative and other resources of a national company. For example, the delivery and management of all aspects of care are conducted at more than 40 local plan sites, while the entire process can be reviewed and audited anywhere on the system. Further, the integration of data, text, and voice has enabled an effective customer service strategy. Agents handle over 35,000 calls a day, which are classified and forwarded to the right person with accompanying customer data displayed on a screen.

As well, databases are being built which provide detailed information on how patients' conditions were diagnosed and treated, what every provider did along the way, and what the outcome was. This is part of a strategy of making available the huge volume of experience so as to make better clinical decisions.

Brophy believes that changes in the business process were key. "The most important thing we have done has been to push authority and accountability to the level of customer contact. Managed care simply doesn't work in an ivory tower, hierarchical environment. That kind of approach would inevitably create tension and animosity between providers, customers and insurers."

Federal Express: Enterprise Technology and the Pursuit of Quality

It is hard to think of a more effective organization or a more spectacular rise to industry dominance than Federal Express. Through pursuing and measuring quality and adopting an enterprise strategy of innovative and integrated systems, the company has become the dominant force in the package delivery business. In all, 420 airplanes, 30,000 trucks, and 96,000 people work in synchronization to deliver over 1.5 million packages a day.

The company strives to deliver its package right 100 percent of the time. If it fails, it may never recover that customer. This makes quality Federal Express's key to service, success, and survival. In 1986 the company changed its mission statement to reflect the importance of information technology in achieving quality. The mission includes the words: "positive control of each package will be maintained by utilizing realtime electronic tracking and tracing systems...."

Essentially, the company had concluded that if you can't measure it, you can't manage it. For years it had measured its service levels dozens of ways. But these measures were all internal, operational measures of success or failure—primarily focusing on the percentage of on-time deliveries. What was needed was a system that actually measured every transaction—hundreds of thousands per day—according to the customer's satisfaction.

Dennis H. Jones is Senior Vice President of Information and Telecommunications and Chief Information Officer at Federal Express. According to Jones, "From the viewpoint of product differentiation we knew that the movement of information was as important as the movement of packages. We also knew that the customer service systems being built could not only provide this product differentiation, but they could more importantly provide us with the ability to measure precisely our service quality."

Federal Express noted at the time that it had a successful on-time delivery rate of 99.5 percent for all packages. Sounds impressive, but for Federal Express that meant 1.5 million failures per year—1.5 million dissatisfied customers!

The company spent about a year developing a mathematical measure of its failure rate, called the service quality index (SQI). This is based on 12 different events that FEDEX knows disappoint and frustrate its customers. Each of these is weighted from a customer perspective on a 10-point scale. For example, if it loses a package, this is rated 10 times more serious than if a package is 5 minutes late. The items and scores are:

Delivery late on right day:
  1 point

Missed pickups: 10 points

Delivery late on wrong day:
  5 points

Lost packages: 10 points

Traces requested: 1 point

Damaged packages:
  10 points

Complaints reopened: 5 points

International delivery:
  1 additional point

Missing proof of delivery
  information: 1 point

Overgoods: 5 points

Invoice adjustments requested
  by customers: 1 point

Calls abandoned by customer:
  1 point

Calculations are performed on every transaction throughout each day. Often the customer isn't even aware that FEDEX has failed. For example, it guarantees Priority One delivery by 10:30 the next morning. If the company delivers a package at 10:31 a.m., the system counts that delivery as a failure, even though the customer may not notice.

Needless to say, all this is based on integrated technology—in this case, integrating the three classes of systems discussed earlier—physical systems that scan or monitor physical events, transaction-oriented systems that use database technology to manage financial information, and end-user systems that directly support users.

Jones describes the system challenge. "Today basically, Federal is a series of networks, and it takes about 17 hours for a package to move from shipper to receiver. During that 17 hours we must do everything possible to guarantee that this shipment does not go astray as it moves from shipper to station, to airport, to one of the sorting hubs, and on to the destination customer. We must have a flawless set of events happen for 17 hours and we must track and measure every critical point along the way."

To understand the role of technology and the engineering of an enterprise around quality goals, it is worthwhile to review what happens to the parcel you send by Federal Express. Every time that parcel changes status, information is recorded through sensors and entered into the COSMOS database. The database contains all the basic customer information—name, account number, address, package pickup location data—and it communicates with a number of other systems and devices to maintain a complete record of every shipment that FEDEX handles, from beginning to end.

When a customer calls in to have a package picked up, that call is taken by a customer service agent at one of the 21 call centers worldwide. The package pickup request is transmitted to the COSMOS system and then relayed to the dispatch center in the city closest to the shipper. Seconds later this pickup request is transmitted to a small computer (called DADS) located on board the FEDEX van, and the dispatch request is displayed on a small screen inside the van.

The courier then drives to the customer's location and picks up the package. It is at this point that service quality measurement begins. The courier uses Supertracker—a small, portable, battery-operated, menu-driven computer having a bar code scanner—to scan the bar code on the package. As well, the courier keys in certain information like the destination ZIP Code. The Supertracker device is very smart. It knows its own ZIP Code, which route it is on, who the courier is, and the time and date.

When the courier leaves the customer and returns to the van, the courier places the Supertracker into a port located on the DADS computer. The package information is automatically transmitted to the dispatch center and to the COSMOS database, making the data available to customer service personnel worldwide.

At that point, less than 5 minutes after the package is picked up, FEDEX has all the information required for the shipper or consignee regarding when the package was picked up, who picked it up, where it was picked up, what type of service is required, where the package is going, and what route it is intended to follow. As the package moves through the system, this information is updated as packages are scanned when they come out of the vans, enter containers at the airport, and so on. Before the airplane leaves the runway, the system knows that the package is on that plane in a specific container. And before the night is over, Federal Express will scan 1.5 million shipments, at least nine times each, as they move through the network.

All during this period of time the company is running massive comparison reports in all systems to determine if the shipments have gone astray. The idea is to be proactive—to spot and correct a problem before there is a failure from the customer's perspective.

When the package arrives at the destination city, it is scanned and sorted for delivery. When it is placed on a courier's van for delivery that morning, a scan is done so that the system knows on which truck each package is going and with which driver. Finally, when the courier arrives at the customer's destination, a proof-of-delivery scan is conducted, including entering the name of the customer who signed for the package. The courier then returns to the van and places Supertracker in the DADS computer, and the final proof of delivery information is transmitted back to the main databases—in less than 4 minutes.

FEDEX now has total information about that package. According to Jones, "What is more important is if that package was delivered 5 minutes late, if there was an exception, if it had been damaged, or misrouted, we have been able to capture all of that information on a realtime basis." By the middle of the afternoon FEDEX will know exactly how many packages have been misdelivered, delivered late, damaged, lost, and so on.

From there many people are advised of problems. The next morning the courier receives a quality feedback report giving details of all transactions that were not 100 percent correct. Other teams are working to understand exactly why an error was made and if there is a dissatisfied customer.

"We believe that information is just as important as the shipment," says Jones. "It provides a tremendous amount of product differentiation and value added to our product."

The business, organization, and business processes and procedures were enabled by an integrated enterprisewide computing environment.

Northern Telecom: Getting the Big Picture

Northern Telecom Limited, the second largest telecommunications manufacturer in North America and one of the largest in the world, is an example of a large enterprise using an EIS to change its operations and improve its effectiveness.

The company operates in a highly competitive global marketplace that requires timely short-term and strategic long-term decision making. Before implementing its EIS, it was difficult for many executives to access information quickly and easily. They had access through different software packages to some corporate data, but the packages had different user interfaces, were not integrated or user-friendly, and were not easily accessible through a communications network. Information was transferred to diskettes, and important data were sometimes not available for up to 30 days.

In many instances, the executive had to rely on information gathered and prepared by others and submitted in an edited report. The lack of immediate and comprehensive information on company operations in a highly volatile and competitive industry was making executive decision making more and more difficult.

Faced with these problems, the company decided to install an EIS. Its purpose was to provide executives with immediate access to the information they needed to run their business operations. All executives at the vice-president level are now using the new system.

The EIS has changed the management style within the company. Before it was introduced, the financial department would review information, draw graphs, and develop reports for senior executives. Between eight and ten people were involved in this weekly exercise. With the EIS, executives are able to determine, immediately, if there is a problem in a particular area or division of the company. The management style, as a result, has become more proactive. Senior executives don't have to wait for information from intermediate levels of the organization. They can do their own analyses of data that come directly from the source.

A user can call up 12,000 screens of information displayed on one screen matrix by progressively selecting options. Executives now have access to revenues and orders according to divisions and product lines within the company. The EIS also offers a 2-second response time, and daily financial data are available 30 minutes after the company books are closed.

Executives can now track all the company's merchandise by customer, product sold, delivery times and costs, and order trends. Before the EIS installation, this information was presented in weekly or monthly reports by each company division. The system also includes expenses, profit and loss statements, and other financial data.

The executive information system has not only enhanced the effectiveness of executives at Northern Telecom, but also improved the productivity of others in the organization. Senior financial executives and managers in the financial group now spend their time analyzing the implications of operational data rather than preparing data and charts. The EIS has eliminated their clerical and administrative duties and enabled them to complete other tasks that will, ultimately, make each person and the corporation more productive.

The EIS implementations at Northern Telecom and other organizations are vivid examples of the innovative use of technology to create an integrated enterprise. Other integrated systems and applications aimed at achieving the same objective are also becoming more prevalent.

Otis Elevator: Building an Integrated Enterprise

All enterprises, whatever their products or services, must serve their customers if they hope to compete and prosper. In increasing numbers of companies, technology is being used to provide better customer service through integrating enterprise operations and making businesses more effective.

One company that has adopted technology to revolutionize the way it operates and responds to its more than 30,000 customers is Otis Elevator, a subsidiary of United Technologies Corporation.

Otis Elevator manufactures, sells, and installs elevators, escalators, and related equipment and offers comprehensive service agreements to cover equipment maintenance. To support these agreements, Otis employs service mechanics who are responsible for both customer callbacks and preventive maintenance.

Like many other organizations in the manufacturing sector, customer service is a large part of Otis's operations. Finding ways to provide better service and reduce service costs was the impetus for automating Otis operations.

The heart of Otis's customer and equipment support service is OTISLINE, a centralized dispatching center that provides an integrated communication network linking Otis's corporate databases, its customers, its service mechanics, and its field offices. OTISLINE, which is staffed by more than 100 OTISLINE customer service representatives, supports the new system and provides 24-hour dispatch service. The center handles half a million inquiries a year. Customers requesting service call an OTISLINE customer service representative, who then pages a local service mechanic. After the mechanic responds via telephone or hand-held terminal, the customer service representative leads the mechanic through a series of questions designed to identify if the elevator needs servicing.

OTISLINE is also linked to Otis's *service management system* (SMS), an integrated database management system that contains information on Otis's customers and their service history. This link enables an OTISLINE customer service representative to access customer information in seconds and to respond immediately to a service request. The representative also enters a closeout report, which is a series of specific questions regarding each callback, into the SMS. The service mechanic provides information to the OTISLINE representative by hand-held computer terminal or by telephone.

Customers access OTISLINE by calling an 800 number, which connects them to the service center. Field offices using PCs can also access the network and track callback activity in their territories. In addition, OTISLINE provides management with valuable data on building history, product performance, and Otis response times.

OTISLINE was implemented to improve Otis's customer relations through offering high-quality and consistent customer service. The company also wanted to operate more effectively and to enable customers to reach Otis employees 24 hours a day. It wanted to be able to respond more quickly to service inquiries, to reduce the paperwork and administrative tasks in both its corporate and field offices, and to establish a more comprehensive and objective customer information base that would provide information on products and service.

Being able to identify problem areas would allow Otis to address these issues and to develop the best solutions through product reengineering or training. The end result would be a reduction in service callbacks, which would not only save millions of dollars in annual service costs but also improve its customer relations.

The investment in OTISLINE has brought Otis the returns it expected. The system has greatly improved the company's response to customer callback requests. The system also produces reports on response time statistics that are available to customers. Having this information has enabled the company to be more proactive regarding its service records and more professional in its customer relations.

OTISLINE also provides Otis's corporate office and field with more information on the quality of service provided to its customers. Before OTISLINE, management became aware of chronic service problems only after a customer complaint. Now, excess callback reports enable the company to identify problem installations and to quickly diagnose equipment problems. Areas of the country where more training and education are required can be targeted more quickly and easily.

OTISLINE has changed Otis Elevator in many ways. It has improved its customer service and engineering operations. By centralizing the response to customer calls, OTISLINE has enabled the company to provide a corporately controlled response to customer service inquiries that is consistent, professional, and measurable.

OTISLINE has also virtually eliminated the paper-based service report filed by its mechanics, manually maintained by the field office, and provided to the corporate office only in the form of summary reports. As a result, the quality, consistency, and timeliness of information available to district, region, and Otis management have dramatically increased.

Several steps are being taken to make the OTISLINE service more effective. In North America, Otis is replacing its paging systems with radio-frequency hand-held computer terminals linked to a private network. The hand-held terminals will eliminate the service mechanic's need to find a public or private telephone to answer paging messages. Otis, as a result, will be able to improve its response times to customer calls and reduce the time a unit is out of service.

The software that supports the closeout procedure for service reports will also be made more flexible. Engineers and management will be able to customize these reports for specific equipment installations. This will make the data gathered on each installation more thorough and comprehensive. Having this customized information will enable senior management and Otis's engineering division to identify which product components should be improved. Otis's ultimate goal is to eliminate all unplanned outages.

Also, OTISLINE is increasingly interfacing directly with installed elevators equipped with remote diagnostic technology. New products may be equipped with remote elevator monitoring (REM) capability. The automated diagnosis will enable Otis to take preventive and proactive approaches to equipment maintenance and service and reduce the number of callbacks and equipment problems. The company, as a result, will be able to significantly reduce its service costs and increase its profitability.

Lithonia Lighting: Managing Enterprise Complexity

Lithonia Lighting, a division of National Service Industries, Inc. (NSI), of Atlanta, Georgia, is the largest manufacturer of lighting equipment in the United States. The company has 13 manufacturing operations in the United States and Canada, with more than 5000 employees. Its lighting products are designed for commercial, residential, industrial, and institutional applications and are sold through a network of sales agents through electronic order entry links with customers.

Lithonia faced the challenge that all market leaders encounter sooner or later. Although the company was number one in the lighting market, its competition was becoming more fierce as mergers and acquisitions began to consolidate what was formerly a highly fragmented industry. The rise of more powerful competitive conglomerates posed a serious threat to its market share. The company had to look for innovative ways to maintain its industry position.

Lithonia decided that it had to help its agents work more effectively with its existing and potential customers. The company determined that providing better customer service was a key strategy in maintaining a competitive advantage. The company was working with more than 80 agents, and the number was growing. However, it was having difficulty handling the increased volume and complexity of its business with just its current staff. It was becoming clear, though, that hiring more people wouldn't be effective in achieving its projected volume and profitability objectives. The answer was to develop systems that would make the operations more effective.

The core of Lithonia's information technology architecture is its Agency Communication Environment+ (ACE+) system which processes all company quotations and orders and serves as the hub of its system architecture. Individual systems that serve the company's distributors, field warehouses, product-line divisions, and customers are directly connected to ACE+. In addition to electronic order entry, ACE+ offers project pricing and order-status capabilities. Other system modules provide computer-aided lighting designs and layouts for use in project quotes, word processing, and business management tools.

Lithonia links this system to its corporate systems and databases and to its product divisions through a communications system called Light*Link. Light*Link also provides the direct electronic links to Lithonia's customers that allow them to access product and inventory data and to place orders electronically.

The company's investment in its enterprisewide systems has produced many benefits and helped to ensure that it will retain its position in the marketplace. Shortly after the systems were implemented, the ratio of outside to inside staff changed from 1:1 to 2:1, which meant that the agents were handling more volume per employee. Sales have also doubled every 5 years.

Light*Link and ACE+ have also enabled Lithonia Lighting to achieve its goal of providing better customer service. The local processing power of the ACE+ system enables agents to generate proposals for lighting applications quickly and easily and to complete projects in one-third the time. With more responsibility and ownership over projects, agents have gained valuable experience and skills. This expertise has added to Lithonia Lighting's competitive advantage and is expected to lead to greater sales volumes and profitability.

The communication of information at Lithonia has changed. Agents at their network nodes can dial in during the day for specific information. At night, Light*Link dials out to each node and conducts a data exchange to update all local files. Each morning, Lithonia's agents have updated information regarding inventory status, orders, and status of lighting calculations from library retrievals. All the available data enable them to generate a complex presentation for a potential customer overnight.

Light*Link has allowed Lithonia to serve its customers directly and has facilitated a whole new way of doing business. Customers can dial up the company's warehouse, determine whether specific products are available, and place orders immediately. Before Light*Link existed, customers had to work through an agent who would call the warehouse and then inform the customer. The problem was that inventory stock would often change in the time it took to return a customer call. Because agents are now only involved in pricing issues, they have more time to service accounts and enhance customer relations. An added benefit of this change has been a lower turnover in the field.

Lithonia is taking steps to further rationalize and improve its efficiency through technology. A new software program will also help Lithonia Lighting provide consistent and competitive pricing. The software will be resident in each agent's computer and enable the company to download updated information on a product without having to poll all network nodes. As a result, communications costs are expected to decrease significantly as the company's need to poll each division and the agent's need to call headquarters for pricing information decline.

Another system planned for the future is a corporate information system that will include information on all of the company's products. The data will include pricing, inventory levels, energy and footcandle considerations, and graphic designs. Information in the system will be passed through the corporate mainframe to the agent's module and in some selected applications to customers. The product departments in each product-line division will feed pricing data to a centralized quotation group. This new group will be able to access the files and screens of the agent and have the authority to authorize new pricing or to cut a better deal in a highly competitive situation.

Lithonia Lighting also plans to operate all of its manufacturing and distribution operations as one unit. A new system called Dynamic Synchronization will determine the capacity of its manufacturing plants through modeling. With the exception of field inventories, the company will eliminate all inventories and establish direct links between its manufacturing facilities and the customer. The result will be a demand-driven system where no product will be created unless it is going directly to a destination. The benefit of this organizational change will result in dramatic savings in inventory and distribution costs.

Supporting all these changes will be the development of new systems platforms that will use computer-aided software engineering and other productivity tools to support current and future system developments. By being able to build better systems and applications more quickly and efficiently, Lithonia hopes to be able to respond to the competitive challenges it foresees over the next decade.

Summary: The Integrated Enterprise—The Shifts

- Technology applications → Organizational restructuring
- Systems islands → Integrated systems
- Three classes of systems
  addressing the three resources → Integrated computing environments
- Single-form systems → Integration of data, text, voice, and image
- Cost reduction → Enterprise effectiveness

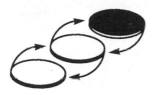

4

The Extended
Enterprise

- A customer in an auto showroom personally configures her car on a screen, selecting options and color. The system calculates the cost and delivery schedule in real time, prepares the order, and upon purchase initiates the order.

- A clothing manufacturer generates purchase orders for its customers.

- A multinational company in the Far East announces the takeover of a major American conglomerate via a globally linked videoconference.

- An automated teller machine in Tokyo gives a business executive immediate access to his cash management account in Seattle, Washington.

- Travel agents worldwide have PC access to the reservation system of a major airline that also allows them to book flights with its competitors as well as to make reservations with a variety of rental car companies and hotel chains.

- A company sends new product information to thousands of on-line customers around the globe.

- A hotel guest reviews her account and checks out using a special software program that she accesses from the television screen in her room.

- A business executive renting a car at an airport enters his destination into a terminal and receives a printout of directions and a map.

- A computer-driven voice response system handles phoned-in requests for market research information and customer reports.

These scenarios are part of another important change in the nature of business. In the last chapter we discussed how the walls *within* organizations are breaking down as enterprise computing enables the integrated enterprise. In this chapter we discuss how the walls *between* organizations are breaking down through interorganizational computing and the rise of the extended enterprise (see Fig. 4-1).

Just as an enterprise can be viewed as a technology-enabled network of business functions acting as clients and servers, so technology is enabling new client/server networks of enterprises. The *value chain* is becoming a *value network* as enterprises reach out through technology to their customers, suppliers, affinity groups, and even competitors.

The discussion of partnerships based on information systems is often cited as the key to competitive use of technology. For example, in a seminal piece Konsynski and McFarlan point out that "information empowers companies to compete, ironically, by allowing them new ways to cooperate. One of the most intriguing is the information partnership, facilitated by the sharing of customer data."[1] And it has become commonplace to discuss strategic alliances in which companies collaborate with an ever-shifting array of partners to achieve mutually held goals. One year before it was announced, the idea of IBM forming a strategic alliance with Apple to jointly develop products for critical markets would have been nearly unthinkable.

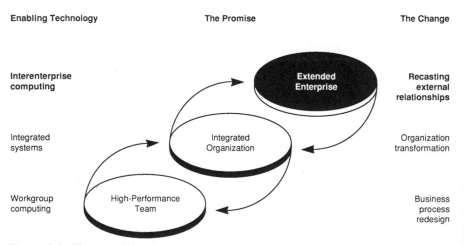

Figure 4-1. The extended enterprise.

However, it seemed that until the early 1990s the examples of such technology-enabled partnerships were few and far between. To paraphrase Mark Twain, about the weather, "Everyone was talking about it but no one appeared to be doing anything about it." But according to Tom Peters, "The fact that the rhetoric of partnership outstrips the reality is really no surprise; not so long ago we didn't even have rhetoric."[2]

One important general driver for partnering is the cost of building systems. According to Max Hopper, senior vice president of information systems at American Airlines, systems that are useful are becoming too big and expensive for any one company to build. This points to the need for a packaged software industry, joint ventures, and other partnerships that distribute the cost and risk.[3] More and more, it makes sense to share a network, share customer data, share the costs of developing a commonly needed application. More and more, companies need to work more closely with various partners, including competitors, to solve commonly held problems and exploit mutual opportunities. And more and more, technology makes such relationships feasible.

While the borderless, seamless enterprise may not have arrived, the shift in technology is marching us inexorably toward it.

Reaching Out to Customers

The initial hype was strongest when it came to systems that lock in the customer to the products and services of the supplier. For example, almost every information management guru on the rubber chicken lecture circuit in the late 1980s rehashed the experiences of two companies that had linked with customers to achieve competitive advantage. In both cases the customer received terminals that facilitated the supplier's ability to close business. The stories of American Airlines SABRE reservations system[4] and the American Hospital Supply's ASAP system[5] have become industry legends.

Clearly, one impediment was the immaturity of organizations in their conceptualization of competitive opportunities. This has changed dramatically with the dispersion of much IS influence into the business units. Line managers and professionals increasingly control the IS agenda, at least with respect to the identification of opportunities. Another impediment has been the far-reaching impact of such innovation on business practices contrasted with the capacity of both providers and customers to absorb such change. (How long did it take you to start using ATMs after the first ones appeared on the market?)

However, the immaturity of the technology itself has also been a factor of considerable importance. Typically such customer systems involved building a proprietary network (often involving proprietary links with customer networks), designing corresponding software applications, and then making a capital investment in terminals to be installed in customer sites. Such systems were expensive, hard to build (typically seven, eight, or even nine figures), difficult to change, and involved an additional massive investment in customer training.

The technology paradigm shift has changed this situation. Systems that link to customers have been made possible by the proliferation of the microprocessor, the rise of standards for interorganizational integration, and the growth of important technologies such as electronic data interchange (EDI), graphic interfaces for software programs, voice response systems, and various point-of-sale (POS) and related devices.

Organizations that add value through technology can win at least temporary competitive advantage. However, it is important to note that the old model of "placing the proprietary terminal of the proprietary system in the customer's office to lock them in" is being bypassed. Given the cost of such systems and the ability of others to replicate them, the trend is to implement customer reach systems based on standards and to cooperate with others in their creation.

Forging customer electronic links has become a basic requirement for competitive parity, let alone competitive advantage, in many industries. For example, for a bank to resist cooperating with others on an ATM network that reaches its customers is tantamount to saying that it doesn't want to do retail banking.

Reaching Out to Suppliers

Steps that can be taken to facilitate the interchange of data, text, voice, and image with suppliers can produce important results in terms of obtaining cost savings, improving turnaround time for goods and services, reducing errors, and even improving quality. Further, the viability, health, competitiveness, and even profitability of suppliers are in a customer's best interest, as having responsive, stable, effective suppliers is an important factor in success. As a result, one reason many companies are implementing systems such as EDI is to strengthen their suppliers and supplier network.

The automobile industry was one of the first to automate supplier links because of the complexity and size of the supply network in that industry. The client is Ford, and the servers are its thousands of suppliers. Ford then becomes a server for its clients—various dealerships, leasing companies, car rental companies—who can communicate with Ford through EDI, electronic messaging, and other vehicles (pun unintended).

Retailers are also forming information partnerships with key suppliers, as the information they hold from POS systems is invaluable to manufacturers. Kmart corporation, for example, has formed a Partners in Merchandise Flow program with over 200 of its largest suppliers. Kmart provides critical warehouse and sales information in return for faster and more frequent deliveries. The goal is, in part, to assist the suppliers to be able to better forecast demand for their products.

Reaching Out to Affinity Organizations

Companies that offer complementary services and/or products may have an affinity that can be strengthened to mutual advantage through information technology. Such affinity enterprises or groups are not primarily suppliers or consumers of your organization (although they can also act in that role). Rather they are first and foremost organizations that share a common interest, that are stakeholders in a common process, and that can benefit from working together.

Given the power of technology and the growth of standards, such affinities may not initially be obvious. Consider the airline company, bank, hotel chain, department store chain, and car rental company which form an agreement to reward customers with frequent flyer/user/guest/buyer/renter points. Points are greater if, for example, the correct airline, hotel, and car rental company are all used on the same trip.

In the management consulting industry, Nixon's law ("Everything is connected to everything else") leads companies from different disciplines to collaborate in marketing and delivery partnerships to conduct large projects. The lead company may specialize in systems integration with affinity companies—specializing in process reengineering, IT architecture, systems development, and change management—all working together on a common technology platform. Such has become the norm in large federal government bids.

Reaching Out to Competitors

The October 1991 *Business Week* cover story announced the "age of consolidation." "Everywhere you look these days archrivals are falling into each other's embrace.... Where acquisitive companies once had to confine their attentions to targets in unrelated industries, or might rarely be allowed to scoop up some much smaller, floundering competitor they can now often embrace their largest rivals."[6]

However, as significant as the consolidation taking place is the new form of technology-based partnership between competitors. Such relationships are less vexing when the domain of competition is limited. Competing airlines exchange frequent flyer points, understanding that they have limited route conflict in the international skies. So fly the friendly skies of Canadian Airlines, Qantas, Lufthansa, Scandinavian Airlines, British Airways, Air France, and Aloha Airlines and you accumulate points on your Canadian card. Ditto when you stay at Canadian Pacific Hotels, Delta Hotels, Doubletree Hotels, Swissotel, or Ramada International Hotels.

However, even more nettlesome is the growing trend for direct competitors to join together in technology-based partnerships to achieve common objectives—rather than simply attempting to acquire each other. Such agreements may make sense when, for example, pooling resources to deliver a capability to the market will benefit all. The agreement among banks to develop the Cirrus, Interac, and other ATM networks is an example.

A striking example is the partnership of 17 hotel chains to deal with the problem of reservations in their industry. Previously these hotels had to build individual network interfaces to the various airline *customer reservation systems* (CRSs) so that travel agents could book hotels through their CRSs. Such proprietary interfaces were costly, cumbersome, and difficult to change. Up to a dozen such CRSs and 17 major chains were faced with the prospect of more than 200 complex systems development projects in the industry. Moreover, each CRS kept a separate database of information about hotel room rates and availability for each hotel, which was infrequently updated.

The hotels decided they could expand the range of rooms available to travel agents, present a unified view to agents, and shift business toward the members of their consortium by working together and avoiding the massive costs of each developing its own interfaces to each CRS. The result was THISCO—*The Hotel Industry Switch Company*.

Initially THISCO enabled each hotel to develop only one interface—to the THISCO switch, which in turn connects to the various CRSs. The reservation made by a travel agent is communicated to the CRS database and arrives electronically at the hotel looking the same as any other reservation. Subsequently a second phase was implemented which provides direct on-line access by the travel agent to the reservation system in each hotel chain. This enables what Gordon Kerr, vice president of MIS for Hyatt Hotels Corp., describes as "last room availability." That is, the last room is available for booking from all distribution outlets, rather than the previous situation in which a travel agent would have to bypass the CRS and telephone the hotel directly to see if rooms were available when they didn't appear in the restricted CRS.

Kerr told us, "I wanted to make the latest possible information available electronically through every possible delivery channel. I also want to be able to provide the best possible rate information through the same channels." THISCO provides additional benefits. The travel agents do more of the bookings, reducing Hyatt reservation costs. And Kerr believes they are providing a much better service to their distribution channels. "We just recognized that it makes sense to band together."

Such consortia and partnerships between competitors are flourishing. The *Insurance Value Added Network Services* (IVANS) links a group of insurance companies with thousands of agents. In the auto parts industry, used parts suppliers cluster around AUTONETWORK to exchange information and make their industry competitive against new parts manufacturers who have united to connect to retailers through MEMA/Transnet—a group initiated by the Motor Equipment Manufacturers Association. Competitors from a wide range of industries have united to agree on critical standards, not just in EDI but more broadly in open systems. These include the User Alliance for Open Systems and the X/Open Xtra process.

The Technology of External Reach

What is the emerging technology that enables external reach? In the last chapter we discussed how the islands of sensor-based, data-processing, and end-user systems are becoming integrated through enterprise architectures based on industry standards. Similarly, standards are enabling external reach.

In the pre-era II enterprise, information in the form of invoices, cash, letters, drawings, reports, designs, and maps is interchanged across the value network in physical form. Such physical documents have been around for centuries. Moving such documents is costly, cumbersome, and time-consuming. Notwithstanding the improvements in land and air travel through the introduction of the automobile and plane, physical documents still move relatively slowly—when compared

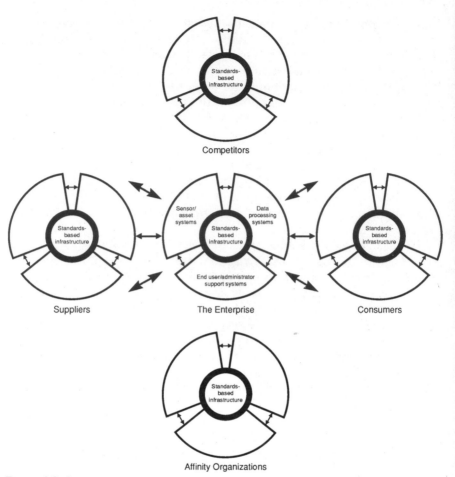

Figure 4-2. Interenterprise computing.

with electronic means. Additionally, traditional face-to-face (since the beginning of recorded time) or telephone communications (for a century) have severe limitations as the sole modes for interactive information exchange.

The extended organization replaces much of this primitive interaction with electronic links. (See Fig. 4-2.) And through technology new relationships with suppliers, consumers, affinity groups, and even competitors are being formed.

This transformation was forecast and described in some detail years ago in a 1986 DMR investigation on the topic of integration. The executive summary reads:

In a number of industries and support areas, the replacement of manual information flow by computer-based exchanges will directly affect the physical nature of the operation. For example:

- Electronic mail and document distribution will reduce mail delivery and courier usage, improving responsiveness and lowering costs.
- Online reference systems and electronic distribution media will affect library functions, extending services, broadening availability and improving access.
- Electronic publishing will transform newspaper and book production and distribution, opening new markets while reducing publishing cycles and strengthening the ability to react to particular demands.
- Various forms of teleconferencing will substitute for business travel and face-to-face meetings, improving time use and providing more timely interaction.
- Office work and associated commuting time will be reduced through more home and mobile use of workstations, reducing the need for office facilities and lowering travel overheads.
- Customer service functions will make more use of online access for routine enquiries and transaction capture, as we have seen in ATMs and airline reservations, reducing or shifting the requirement for physical access.
- Distribution channels will be restructured and distributor links become electronic as new means of providing products and services directly to the consumer are achieved.

The above examples illustrate several different opportunities, each of which affects the three areas of systems by shifting activity from a manual or physical approach to an integrated systems function... and providing a rich selection of relatively untapped opportunities.[7]

But how has the world really evolved since those words were written? Let's take a look at several important *reach technologies* and the impact they are having. Although each of these is a precursor of more sophisticated capabilities to come, each is being implemented today as enterprises electronically extend themselves.

Beyond the Fax Tip of the Iceberg

The explosive use of fax was the tip of the iceberg. Fax is standardized, fast, relatively cheap, and incredibly easy to use. As a result, it has become ubiquitous—used by virtually every business in the United States. (Remember when one would ask the question "Do you have a fax machine?" rather than "What's your fax number?")

However, fax is an extremely limited technology in that it involves media transformation—from computer to paper (you print the letter off your computer), paper to computer (you insert the letter in your fax machine, which digitizes it), computer to paper (the fax is printed at the destination location), and paper to computer (information from the fax is reentered into a computer). Adding insult to injury, it may be photo-copied and distributed within and external to the organization. Each transformation is a source of error, delay, and costs. Also, the fax was initially a fairly limited technology—in that you couldn't electronically forward, edit, file, or annotate faxes.

With the ability to send a fax letter directly from your desktop computer, fax machines are taking on the role of remote printers. You create the document in New York and print it in Seattle. Moreover, with the ability of computers to read fax images, fax machines are taking on the role of scanners for documents (such as a supplier brochure) which are not easily directly accessible through electronic means.

However, as standards for direct computer-to-computer communication mature, the world is evolving beyond fax. Technologies such as EDI, electronic mail, and interorganizational databases reduce the number of media transformations and enable a new realm of external reach opportunities.

Document Interchange
Goes (Fully) Electronic

Chances are your enterprise is, or will soon be, involved with electronic data interchange. Organizations are turning to EDI because of its potential to improve service, increase sales, reduce manufacturing and overhead costs, and improve employee productivity. Overall, EDI is an enabler to new and closer relationships between businesses.

The principle of EDI is straightforward. Rather than have a computer produce a paper document that then has to be manually reentered in another machine at another location, a computer sends required data in electronic form over telecommunication lines directly to the receiver's computer.

The term *EDI* was originally used in a restrictive sense to refer to direct computer-to-computer information exchange of data in a highly structured format—such as an invoice. It has now grown to refer to the computer-to-computer interchange of a broader array of business documents, employing strictly defined industry standards. EDI technologies are being used to transmit not only purchase orders, shipping notices, and invoices but a host of other day-to-day business documents. For increasing numbers of enterprises, EDI is providing the means for establishing integrated electronic communications with their customers, suppliers, and other external entities.

With a growth rate that has accelerated to 70 percent annually, EDI has become a top priority in leading companies around the world. DMR estimates that more than 5000 companies were using the technology in the United States at the beginning of the 1990s. By the end of the 1990s EDI will be used by most business and other organizations for a variety of communications and transactions.

One of the key benefits leading many organizations into EDI is cost savings. The Electronic Data Interchange Association estimates that EDI cuts the cost of sending a bill of lading from $13 to $1.50, for example. It is estimated that as much as 70 percent of the computer-originated information exchanged between businesses is subsequently reentered into another computer. A major European trade group estimates that $15 billion a year could be saved worldwide through EDI by reducing the paperwork required for international trade. A prominent U.S. bank has calculated (we believe conservatively) that the United States could save $6.5 billion annually by generating electronic documents using EDI.

EDI has been found to significantly reduce administration costs. It is estimated that one-quarter of the cost of executing a business transaction is data entry and rekeying. Additional time and costs are also incurred correcting errors made in the original entries and managing related inventory management problems. By removing the need for these steps, EDI enables organizations to achieve impressive savings in the cost of day-to-day administration operations. Several companies have achieved even greater savings by extending the responsibility for the purchase order and invoicing transactions to their suppliers and consumers. When customers enter their own orders, they also gain greater control over order entry transactions.

The greatest benefit that EDI offers, however, is that it enables the integration of interenterprise business operations and eliminates manual business transactions. This results in an improved metabolism between enterprises—for example, shortening turnaround time from weeks or days to seconds. Improved labor productivity and reductions in paper handling and administrative errors are two important hy-products. Companies have also been found to increase sales using EDI technologies by moving orders faster and freeing sales staff from time-consuming paperwork and administrative tasks.

Moreover, the information contained in an EDI message can automatically initiate a whole series of related transactions. For example, inventories can be updated, customers invoiced, shipments initiated, status advisories sent out to appropriate parties, material releases issued against open purchase orders, and suppliers paid, all without human involvement. This has led some people to refer to EDI as intercompany data processing.

As well, EDI is essential to achieve the integrated enterprise discussed in the last chapter. A case in point is the automobile industry in North America which took a serious look at the reasons why it was rapidly losing market share. The industry discovered that it is not possible to compete using the same logistics and manufacturing processes that had been in effect since the assembly line was first introduced. A new means had to be discovered to cut down on the cost of inventories and to provide better flexibility in the changes inherent in this dynamic industry. This led to the adoption of the Japanese *just-in-time* (JIT) concept, where raw materials and component parts are delivered to the assembly line just in time to coincide with the arrival of the partially completed vehicle at the next stage of assembly. EDI was found to be an effective technology backbone to improve JIT manufacturing, and by the beginning of the 1990s it had become a standard for communication with suppliers to the industry.

The major auto manufacturers such as General Motors have created a payment system entirely dependent on electronic transactions. The use of EDI for replacement of invoices, checks, and other financial settlement instruments has become a model for corporate trade payments in a number of industries.

The retail industry faced with shrinking markets and fierce competition in the discount market devised the *quick response system* to replenish stock shelves in synchronization with public buying patterns and seasonal changes in products. Massive reductions in inventory have greatly improved the profit margins in these retailers. One of the earliest examples was agreements made between clients and servers in the clothing industry, ranging from the milling of cloth to the retail outlet. Common interchange standards mean that requirements go across the network, and invoices and funds transfer back electronically rather than through physical documents.

Banks and other financial institutions were among the first organizations to experience the payoff of specialized EDI systems. *Electronic funds transfer* (EFT) applications, which enable these organizations to transmit money across the street or across the globe, and ATM technology, which allows for better customer service, have become a vital part of their day-to-day operations. Providing these capabilities and services is necessary not only to the competitive success of these organizations but also to their survival. They, like most businesses, must operate in an increasingly competitive worldwide marketplace where the need for information is immediate and customer demands are increasing. For many companies in low-margin, competition-intensive marketplaces, EDI is becoming a requirement for survival.

For other organizations that are suppliers to large enterprises such as the automobile industry, EDI is an imperative for another reason. Their customers demand that they use it or else they will be terminated as a supplier. Our experience is that while such demands have met initial resistance, most suppliers comply quickly. For many of these smaller companies that have integrated EDI as part of their operations rather than a simple invoicing tool, we have noted that they soon wonder how they ever did business the old way.

EDI implementation is not restricted to the private sector. The U.S. Department of Defense is developing EDI links for dealing with up to 300,000 suppliers. Public-sector EDI activity in the United States has also focused on payment processing. Vendor Express is an initiative by the U.S. Department of the Treasury to speed payments to government suppliers as an alternative to more time-consuming and costly check processing. The program will eventually affect more than 77 million payments per year.

Customs and excise and port authorities throughout North America are also actively discussing EDI opportunities with shipping and brokerage companies. The St. Lawrence Seaway Development Corporation is implementing a *seaway automated information system* (SAIS) that provides automated facilities and services to ports and stevedores, government agencies, exporters and importers, brokers and forwarders, steamship lines, and other members of the system. Transactions such as delivery orders, cargo on/off status, bookings, bills of lading, invoices, payment orders, and purchase orders are being automated.

In Singapore, such an automated system is already a reality. Funded by the Singapore government, the Tradenet System of Singapore links government agency brokers, freight forwarders, shipping companies, insurance companies, and customs and immigration officials. The system's function is to streamline the vessel clearing process. Since its implementation, the time a vessel takes to clear the port has been reduced from 2 to 4 days to as little as an hour or less. All major international ports are now actively pursuing the introduction or extension of EDI capabilities to better serve the shippers and the broader community of transportation, government, and related service organizations involved in cargo movement. Although there is some necessary and important collaboration, there is also a spirit of competition, as individual ports respond with their own initiatives to the opportunity and threat of EDI.

Overall, EDI is a backbone of the extended enterprise. As EDIA President Jerome L. Dryer puts it: "EDI is a catalyst for change. Internally once EDI is in place, it has a ripple effect throughout the company's whole infrastructure. Externally it radically modifies the company's relationship with its suppliers. The edges between trading partners begin to blur, creating a new interrelated organization that begins to function like a single organism."[8] EDI is also making companies more dependent on each other, and in doing so, is fostering external reach.

Reaching to the Customer at the Point of Sale

You're in a clothing store. You pick up a sweater and try it on. Definitely you! You insert the tag on the garment in the scanner on the side of the rack, put your credit (or debit) card in the slot below, watch the adjacent screen for the amount of your purchase, and validate it by keying in your personal identification number.

While you wait for the message that your purchase is authorized, the screen tantalizes you with discount offers on a matching shirt or pants and news of other items currently on sale. The authorization completed, the scanner deactivates the security tag on your sweater, the screen displays your frequent-shopper credits, and you bag your sweater and leave.

Does the prospect appeal? To some it will; to others not. But it's just another step in the trend of increasing self-service, such as we've already adopted at gas pumps and automated teller machines. The focus is on the convenience and flexibility of self-service, and personal service is provided only where it can provide extra value to the customer.

Or how would you like to do your shopping from home? No, not just the kind of home shopping club we see on television today, but a service where, using your touchtone phone, you can "let your fingers do the walking" through an "electronic mall." You can go to the store you want, browse (in full-motion video) through the items, make your purchase (or not), and move to another store. The goods you buy will be delivered to your home.

Farfetched? Not at all! Just such a home shopping service, offered by J. C. Penney, is now implemented, the initial piloting being in the Chicago area. In Canada, a modified approach, "Alex," is also being piloted by Bell Canada. Alex provides a computer terminal that will enable home shopping, among other things. In France, a similar service called MiniTel is already highly successful. The *electronic mall* in your future will also offer you completely electronic services ranging from travel and theater reservations to banking or insurance transactions.

POS systems are reaching out to customers in a growing number of ways. A striking example is Royal Viking Cruise lines, which has installed point-of-sale systems on all its ships. Terminals are used throughout the ship to capture information needed for managing the inventory, the ship, and the fleet. The system provides detailed reports on which food, bar, and other items are selling. It orders meals from the restaurant electronically and automatically rings up drinks dispensed from computerized bar guns. It provides on-line credit card verification and self-banking that allows customers to pay their bills without a cashier, to name a few features. Customers were found to benefit from "better, faster, service and more accurate billing, which is fortunate because at 500 miles from shore, they don't have much choice."[9]

At a recent conference on future strategies for point of sale, many speakers' definitions of *point of sale* included the words *payment* and *electronic* — an obvious reference to the increasing role credit, and now debit, cards play in the way we shop. Debit cards, which allow your purchase to be directly charged against your bank account, are already used in many countries. Beyond debit cards we are seeing the emergence of the *smart card,* a card with a microchip providing a variety of functions from security information to storage of personal health records to storage of electronic cash. The value-loaded smart card is already in use for phone calls or for other small payments. Hong Kong Transit uses a value-loaded card system for its riders instead of the type of token and transfer system in use in Toronto.

The future value of smart cards at point of sale will be in providing the customer with additional services. For example, the card could keep track of all your purchases and monitor them against a preset budget or provide you with a statement itemized by category of expenditure.

We have presented the customer's view. Let's step to the other side of the counter.

Remember the sweater scenario. As soon as the scanner read the purchase information from the coded item tag, it was only awaiting payment authorization to:

- Deactivate the security chip on the garment tag
- Record the sale by amount, item, color, and size
- Create a record of the discounts offered and whether you had accepted them
- Log that information against your generic customer profile (socioeconomic group, area of residence, etc.)
- Update your personal purchasing history
- Update the inventory position for that item
- Check against reorder levels and, if necessary, issue an order
- Update the store's cash flow position and projections for the month

Any of these transactions could automatically create a further string of electronically generated transactions. For example, the purchase could trigger a robotic manufacturing system to cut or dye new garments to replace the vacant shelf space. The highly successful Benetton Company uses this type of intelligence in two ways: to move a particular item from stores where it is not selling to stores where it will and to dye precut outfits to the colors that customers are buying.

Your reaction to discounts or other sale information might also determine that shelf space can be used more profitably. In other words, the retailer, the distributor, and the manufacturer can all learn much more about you and your wants from the information captured at the point of sale. This can mean better inventory control, better product design, and better use of existing floor or shelf space.

From the consumers' point of view this can lead to a new dimension of convenience in how they shop and potentially a whole new range of services not otherwise available. While these are real benefits, there are some clear issues for the retail industry. Competition, particularly for electronically delivered services, will intensify with the increasing globalization of trade. Home shopping allows manufacturers to become retailers simply by arranging delivery from warehouse to customer. If home shopping and other electronic services start to displace a significant number of our store purchases, there could be a lot of empty real estate. Conversely, the creation of powerful databases regarding customer buying patterns from POS systems has been one factor shifting power from the manufacturers to the retailers. How much will manufacturing come under the control of retail? Further, the growing pervasiveness and completeness of such databases on individuals, their behavior, and demographics has also raised concern regarding invasion of privacy, confidentiality, and the like. There are no simple answers.

It's in the Mail

It was a remarkable achievement, even if it did go largely unnoticed. Last month, a computer at Hughes Aircraft Co. in Los Angeles zapped a short memo to a computer nearly 2,000 miles away at Boeing Co. — and the age of [interenterprise] electronic mail dawned. It wasn't just that the memo took mere seconds to arrive. More impressive was that it crossed previously impenetrable boundaries. With the press of a button, the message left a Hughes IBM computer, was picked up by MCI Mail, transferred to Telemail, then deposited in a Digital Equipment computer at Boeing.[10]

Biologists debate whether two organisms are part of the same species, whether they are different species, or if one is a subset of the other classification. Similar debates occur among information technology aficionados regarding the relationship of EDI to electronic mail or messaging (Email). Without getting religious about the subject, there have historically (if you can apply history in such a nascent industry) been some important differences in the two technologies and their application.

After many months (really!) of deliberation the Electronic Mail Association concludes: "Electronic mail is the generic name for noninteractive communication of text, data, image and voice messages between a sender and designated recipients by systems utilizing telecommunications links."[11] Phew! According to this widely held view, electronic mail is person-to-person communication which, unlike the telephone, is noninteractive. Although the format for addressing the message and determining its characteristics (urgent, certified, copies to, etc.) may be structured, the content of the message is typically unstructured. The content of EDI messages is highly structured—as in the case of an invoice. EDI is also a formal record of a business transaction. It always has a restricted, predefined list of recipients (you know who your supplier is before your supplier invoices you). Conversely, just as you could conceivably telephone anyone on the planet, you may also want broad distribution for sending and receiving Email messages.

Unlike messaging, which is person to person, EDI is organization to organization. EDI makes existing processes electronic; Email creates a new form of communication—store and forward electronic communications which replace modes such as telephone calls or face-to-face meetings, or forms that previously have not existed (for example, across many time zones where telephone communication is impractical). EDI integrates with existing data-processing capabilities, whereas Email has often tended to be a stand-alone capability in a user workstation. However, Email is on a faster track to multimedia. Voice messaging systems are now widespread, with multimedia messaging beginning to take hold.

As a result, EDI often has different security and transmission characteristics and may not be suitable for the same network as Email. Over time, as standards for networking mature, the two communications technologies will tend to share the same networks and converge. Major Email companies have, for example, integrated EDI capability into their systems.

DMR estimates that by mid-1992 there were more than 10 million users of electronic mail systems in the United States. They were using private Email systems purchased from the major hardware vendors, public messaging systems provided by VANS (value-added network suppliers) who enable any company or user to purchase rights to share a network with others, or LAN (local area network) based mail systems primarily for users of PCs.

Given that the business case for Email was typically not based on reducing costs, this is a significant number of users. Whether it is used to
communicate within a work group (where most communications occur),
across an enterprise, or externally with customers, suppliers, affinity
groups, or competitors, Email transforms the nature of human interaction. For those who have used a good Email system, the benefits are
quite apparent, if often difficult to quantify:

- Email saves time for those who use it — through reduction of shadow
  functions (like telephone tag), media transformations (like those of
  fax), interruptions (you communicate with Email when you want to),
  delay (like waiting for something from the mailroom), unproductive
  overhead in face-to-face meetings (next time send me a message), and
  the myriad of unproductive activities associated with paper-based
  communications systems.

- Email improves the quality of communications — through speeding up
  organizational   communication,   creating   permanent   searchable
  records of communications, reducing miscommunications (where the
  communication does not occur) and mistaken communications (where
  a communication was misunderstood), and forcing brevity, clarity,
  and precision. Email, for example, has been found to strengthen relationships with customers, making it easier for them to communicate
  and to resolve problems.

There are many variants of Email. One is the computer conference — a
written meeting that is independent of time and location.[12] Another is
the electronic bulletin board.

However, an important new trend is to integrate Email with business
applications (other software programs). That is, Email can be not only
person to person but both person to application and application to person.

- *Person to application.*   The airline sales agent in the yield management scenario in Chap. 1 sends an Email message to the yield management officer requesting a discount. The message first invokes a
  procedure to interrogate the reservations database and validate the
  information contained in the message.

- *Application to person.*   A software program monitors various stock
  market databases and sends a message to the broker when important
  events have occurred, for example, when a stock has hit a certain
  threshold.

The company Soft·Switch Inc. argues for a third type — application-
to-application — which essentially embraces the notion of EDI as part of

messaging. Soft·Switch was the first to develop the notion of "mail-enabled applications" in which electronic mail is seen as a transport mechanism—"the store and forward transport of electronic objects, across a heterogeneous environment, among people, among people and applications and among applications."[13] While the integration of Email with other applications will be a long process, there are already numerous success stories. Clearly Email is emerging as one of the backbone technologies of the extended enterprise.

Interenterprise Databases, Applications

EDI, Email, and mail-enabled applications are ways of linking the computer systems of enterprises. Another route has been the sharing of access to corporate databases or cross-enterprise distributed computing systems.

Historically this has mainly involved a hub enterprise, giving terminals and database access to key suppliers and/or customers. Agents of Phoenix Insurance have access to various Phoenix databases. Travel agents have access to SABRE, Apollo, and other reservations systems. At Great West Life, corporate customers have direct access to claim submission validation and approval processes through on-line terminals on their premises. The result has been better customer service and a reduction in administration costs. Other organizations such as Federal Express are taking similar steps to provide better customer service by allowing their large accounts direct inquiry access to their parcel tracking system.

Such access has been shown to differentiate products and services—having the effect of strengthening relationships. Often incumbency—being the first one in the door—is a special advantage as the customer invests in learning a specific application, achieves benefit from it, and forms the ties that bond with the supplier.[14]

Electronic links are being established in other sectors such as resources, industrial manufacturing, and financial services. Analysts and traders in Mobil Oil's corporate money market and foreign exchange operations, for example, interact on-line with many external entities such as banks, brokerage houses, information provider services, and securities dealers. Texas Instruments, which operates in 17 countries around the world, has extended its sales and marketing capability by offering its customers direct 24-hour on-line access to information about its entire product line. Customers can order products electronically, which initiates manufacturing activities within the company that will result in just-in-time product delivery.

Major Canadian and American financial institutions have also led the way with everything from direct payroll deposits to shared automated banking machine networks that offer an increasing array of customer services on a 24-hour basis. To deal more effectively with their major corporate customers, many banks, for example, are taking steps to offer value-added alternatives to traditional paper-based check disbursement and collection services. As a result, companies are able to process these transactions electronically and eliminate processing and administration costs. Other financial institutions are offering a wider range of electronic services to their customers that include purchase orders, shipping notices, and acknowledgments.

Innovative public-sector agencies are also linking out to partners through shared databases. The Royal Canadian Mounted Police, Canada's national police force, for example, operates a centralized mug shot and fingerprint identification system for its headquarters and field offices that uses optical disk systems with computerized retrieval and image management capabilities. Other agencies have electronic access (with appropriate security arrangements) to this information.

The system that has enabled this document exchange has resulted in several benefits. Fingerprint matching is now fully automated, with graphically illustrated printouts for court use. Five hundred thousand mug shots on optical disk are updatable and usable to support witness viewing systems. The system will also enable other future applications such as national indexing and access to automatic facial feature matching and photograph aging from any of its field offices or partner locations.

I'd Rather Talk to the Computer, Thank You

It's Saturday. Your paper isn't delivered to your house. You call the customer service hotline and a computer says:

> COMPUTER: "Welcome to the *Toronto Star* service line. To report nondelivery of today's paper, press 1. To register your vacation dates, press 2. To find out how you can become a *Star* card member, press 9. All other callers, press 0."

You press number 1.

> COMPUTER: "Please enter your telephone number."

You type in 783-8123.

> COMPUTER: "If your street address begins with 11, please press *."

You press *.

COMPUTER: "Thank you, Mr. Robertson, your report has been registered. A copy of your paper will be delivered to your door shortly."

Total time 26 seconds. And the paper shows up 14 minutes later because an Email message was sent to the dispatcher in your area requesting an urgent delivery. Now it is true that you didn't get a chance to interact directly with a human, discuss how the day is going, the weather, the ballgame, and so on. But really, you just wanted your paper delivered, and it took 26 seconds to fix the problem. You're a satisfied customer of the *Star*.

This is an example of external reach in which the customer terminal is the telephone. Expect other home appliances to get into the act soon, including your home PC and television set. (We are not predicting the communicating refrigerator or blender in the short term.)

One of the most important external reach applications is telemarketing. In 1992, more than $200 billion of goods were sold over the telephone. Initial implementations of telemarketing systems focused on providing computerized support tools for telemarketing personnel. For example, a salesperson sits at an integrated voice-data workstation that prioritizes calls to be made, automatically identifies numbers, prompts the interaction with a sales script, provides the salesperson with pertinent customer information, and enables the recording of additional information through the call, including updating customer files. Such systems have typically been found to increase sales productivity by 20 to 40 percent. They can also reduce labor costs, enable the collection of comprehensive information about customers, and provide a faster, more personalized service.

The next steps involve computers doing more of the work. Companies such as Dun & Bradstreet are using computer-driven voice response systems to handle product inquiries and capture customer information and orders. Customers call in, and a computer voice response system explains products and guides the customers through the ordering process. The system has enabled Dun & Bradstreet to automate customer phone-in requests for market research information and custom reports. The result has been improved sales of research information, decreased customer service staffing requirements, and improved accessibility and hours of service.

Beyond this there are predictive dialers that call out automatically from a database of prospective customers, and as soon as a call is answered, a salesperson comes on the line. At least that's the theory. Often the prospect is left hanging on the line listening to a message. Better still (or worse, depending on your perspective) are systems that autodial a database and then ask the prospect something like "How would you like to make up to $30 an hour from the convenience of your own home?" Such controversial and usually obtrusive systems have been found to alienate many recipients, but paradoxically have been effective in generating sales. Again, important business strategy questions are posed, not to mention the questions of a social and even ethical nature.

Should You Become an Information Provider?

The marketplace for electronic information has its origins with the various information providers such as Dun & Bradstreet, Reuters, and Dow Jones, which have been selling information since the nineteenth century. The advent of computers and communications brought an important new dimension to this business. Over the last few years we have seen a rich diversity in the kind of information and type of media for providing that information.

You should care about this because probably there is information available electronically which your organization could effectively use. Of greater importance for a growing number of enterprises is the new trend for organizations to become providers of information to their value network, as part of strengthening relationships, improving the capabilities of suppliers, marketing effectively, etc.

The North American electronic information market can be categorized by major information types. These types, along with 1994 revenues estimated by Link Resources Corporation (a New York–based research and consulting company specializing in electronic information services), are:

- *Financial/economic ($3.9 billion).* This includes real-time data on markets such as bonds and foreign exchange. It is used primarily by financial institutions. Information such as public filings by stock exchanges is tending to become automated and interactive as well.

- *Marketing/media ($2.5 billion).* This includes single-source marketing information on individual consumers and markets such as socioeconomic groups and neighborhoods. Interaction with such data enables more selective and effective marketing to individual customers through direct mail, better advertising programs, and so on. There is a great deal of related information about people and their purchasing behavior organized in such a way that it can be integrated with the enterprise's own data about sales and market trends.

- *Credit ($2.2 billion).* This is information about business and consumer credit. A number of on-line services collect data from regional and local credit bureaus. Traditionally this information is used by credit managers. However, given that there is a richer set of information evolving on which to make credit decisions, access to such data is moving beyond traditional risk evaluation. A wide range of business people can now make use of this information to identify and evaluate potential customers and markets.

- *Scientific/technical/medical ($1.1 billion).* These are the bibliographic databases that have been a mainstay of this market. This category includes abstracts of research, chemical structure searching, etc. Currently the information is used primarily by libraries, but more frequently researchers are accessing this information directly. The trend is for data to be moved to the enterprise or departmental computing infrastructure to achieve integration with other corporate data.

- *Legal/regulatory/government/patents ($965 million).* This is information used by public relations departments, investor relations, lobbyists, insurance companies, and lawyers. It can include information on case law, regulations, analysis of what bills are before the legislature, and information on when they're coming up next.

- *Product information/transaction ($534 million).* This is information provided about products by a third party rather than a manufacturer. These providers aggregate, describe, and analyze product information from a variety of sources. They also sometimes provide the ability to order—one-stop shopping through one source. This category also embraces a lot of information that could be provided in support of a product such as electronic customer support databases.

- *Insurance ($460 million).* This includes various kinds of information on businesses that are prospective customers as well as on insurers.

- *News ($444 million).* The problem with news is the amount of it. The more that it can be filtered to corporate users, the more useful it is. Electronic filtering of news, delivered electronically to the desktop workstations of appropriate recipients, helps beat information overload. Examples are new product announcements made by competitors and competitor or customer personnel changes. Filtered electronic news enables users to "read defensively."

- *Real estate ($421 million).* Information includes electronic residential listings, various title search databases, and mortgage databases. On the commercial side, data are available on global markets for real estate.

- *Commercial transport ($320 million).* This includes databases about interstate tariffs that a shipper must pay to get a truckload from one side of the country to the other.

- *Library ($266 million).* More and more, this refers to general reference information. The library is an important node on the corporate network. Its traditional role as a funnel of all information is dying. Remaining funnels are likely to be the specific organizational group with expertise in a given area. For example, the marketing intelligence team funnels marketing information.

- *Travel reservations ($2.7 million).* Corporate travel departments are becoming direct users of the information and services available as enterprises integrate internal and external information about travel.

Should your organization become an information provider? If you are thinking about the great opportunities to cash in on this growing market, you are probably thinking in the wrong direction. While there are certainly such opportunities, the real case lies elsewhere. That is, by becoming a provider you can help achieve external reach. The trend is to take information from a provider, add your own value, synthesize it, and make it available, as appropriate, to your value network of customers, suppliers, affinity groups, and stakeholders. Companies that have done so have found that they can strengthen their network (channel relationships). This helps trading partners be more effective—for example, Kmart working with its suppliers. It strengthens relationships with customers as your channel acquires greater value. It also can provide a vehicle for persuasion—for example, a manufacturer can provide compelling evidence of market trends which would favor aggressive promotion of its products by its retailers.

Rather than competing with information providers, it is more effective to join with information providers to create synergy and a service of considerable custom value.

Unilever, for example, is taking data from Nielsen (an information provider) and combining those data with its own to create a custom database with unique value to its grocery retailers. The on-line information helps the retailers understand how to best spend their cooperative promotion money—directing messages to their customer base more effectively. It also influences the retailers to move Unilever products. This can only be done using data that are collected beyond the regional basis available to the retailers. For example, national trends and product-line analysis data are required. Unilever, the manufacturer, is becoming an information provider by adding value to the Neilson database and then making that database available to its retail base.

Price Waterhouse also takes various kinds of data and textual information from various databases (e.g., legal databases), adds value, and provides the result to its accountants, to its consultants, and directly to its largest customers. In addition to providing added value to accounting and consulting services, Price Waterhouse is strengthening its relationship with customers through an external reach capability.

There is a strong trend in the public sector to becoming an information provider. The typical goals are to reduce the costs of providing information, enable effective response to freedom of information legislation, and make government more open and accessible.

A success story is Montgomery County, Pennsylvania, which provided information initially to employees and then extended this to public access. The county now provides free remote access to civil and criminal case information, miscellaneous and judgment indexes, probate court case files, comprehensive real estate information, records of deed indexes, tax claim files, and attorney-client lists and court schedules. Steps have been taken to protect privacy and ensure against unauthorized access. A solutions center also provides consulting, for a fee, regarding how to access information to solve a problem.

Another public-sector example is BC Online, an agency of the British Columbia government, which has established several electronic information services, including interactive video disks, to provide access to government information. One service, aimed at lawyers, real estate firms, financial institutions, and auto dealers, offers electronic access to three government databases: the Land Title Registry, the Central Registry of Liens, and the Companies Registry.

Using a PC and a modem, searchers can access these databases from their homes or offices. On-line transactions cost at least 15 percent less than manual searches, and so the service saves users both time and money. The geographic breadth of the network also means that most users do not have to pay long-distance charges to access information. The service is also more convenient, as registry information is available 12 hours a day, 6 days a week. The service has been popular, with more than 4000 users making more than 85,000 searches in the first 3 months of operation.

Touch-screen interactive video service provides other types of government information to tourists, students, and other interested users. Both of these services have been established to improve access to government information and provide better services to their customers.

Toys 'R' Us: Extending the Enterprise Is Kids' Stuff

Toys 'R' Us, the world's largest and fastest-growing children's specialty retail chain, has reaped tremendous benefits since it implemented a network to its suppliers in the late 1980s. One of the early innovators with EDI, the company has transformed its relationship with its suppliers.

One immediate result of its work was a streamlined accounts payable process. Toys 'R' Us can now do an immediate electronic line-by-line item match for each of the 500,000 invoices it processes annually. This automated processing has led to significant reduction in labor costs. By eliminating the manual data entry operations, EDI has dramatically accelerated the exchange of purchase orders and invoices and reduced the number of clerical and administrative errors. This increase in efficiency has meant that positions and job responsibilities in the company's accounting departments have become more focused. People are given greater ownership of more directed tasks.

EDI has also streamlined the company's supplier links. Toys 'R' Us uses two EDI network services to link its corporate headquarters to suppliers throughout the United States. Invoices are sent through the network to a Toys 'R' Us electronic mailbox. The company forwards purchase orders to its suppliers using the same procedure. The EDI network replaced a manual system that was time-consuming and inefficient. It was a system where each invoice had to be entered into a corporate database, matched with a purchase order, and matched again with receiving documents.

The EDI network also transmits point-of-sale information to a very select group of vendors who are equipped with sophisticated sales projection modeling systems. Many of these suppliers use the data to determine sales trends and to generate purchase orders on behalf of Toys 'R' Us. In some instances, these suppliers generate their purchase orders and deliver their products directly to Toys 'R' Us stores, an arrangement that saves Toys 'R' Us both administrative and distribution costs.

The company has also added automated distribution centers to the network. These centers are able to receive advance electronic notices of shipments from suppliers. Armed with this information, the distribution centers can prepare the required carton labels and documentation for internal distribution before the shipment arrives. Before the arrival of the supplier network, products had to be manually unloaded, stored in a holding area, and verified. With the data EDI technology provides, Toys 'R' Us can quickly verify the contents of a shipment electronically and distribute products immediately to its stores or its internal warehouse facilities. There is no longer a need for any holding areas. Goods now reach the company's stores and consumers much more quickly.

By extending EDI to its automated distribution centers, Toys 'R' Us has been able to reduce its storage and holding space requirements and, consequently, its operating costs. In highly populated areas of the United States, where land is scarce and expensive, these savings have been substantial.

Toys 'R' Us faced a major challenge when it implemented EDI because it was setting up a technology that was very new to the toy retailing industry. The company chose a small group of third-party networks rather than link directly with its suppliers. Using electronic mailboxes to communicate has enabled the company to rationalize its entire EDI operations and avoid the problems associated with system compatibility and communication protocols.

Toys 'R' Us is continuing to add new EDI applications. One new transaction is remittance advice. This transaction enables suppliers to receive and verify data, which often contain thousands of invoices, and to enter these data into the accounts receivable systems electronically.

The company is also planning to reduce the number of distribution centers by expanding EDI to those centers. The automated centers will have the capacity to handle the company's current and future operational needs. These centers will be able to process significantly greater volume through automation information efficiencies. Toys 'R' Us may also move to implement interactive EDI, which would allow the company to generate a purchase order at any time and be able to further accelerate the order and distribution of products from its suppliers to its stores.

AUTONETWORK: Electronic Mail and the Virtual Warehouse

Automobile dismantling is a $4 billion industry in North America. Auto dismantlers, also known as wrecking yards or junkyards, purchase wrecked vehicles and sell the salvageable parts. Major customer types include auto body shops, insurance companies, auto rebuilders, and the general public.

In North America, there are about 15,000 licensed auto dismantlers. While 10,000 of these companies are tiny, with sales under $150,000 yearly, about 5000 dismantlers have sales that range from $250,000 to $9 million. There are no industry giants. Most dismantler businesses are small corporations that operate from a single facility.

The dismantling industry has two competitors: auto manufacturers that provide spare parts for their vehicles and third-party manufacturers that provide after-market parts. While dismantlers can compete effectively based on the price of their parts, they have one distinct disadvantage: Auto dealers and after-market parts dealers are supplied by central warehouses, while a dismantler's inventory is based upon vehicles that are destroyed in auto accidents. When a potential customer wants a part, there is no central warehouse, as such, that a dismantler can call.

To provide a function that is similar to central warehousing, dismantlers have networked with each other since the 1950s via voice "hotlines," which are telephone party lines. A dismantler who needs a part picks up the hotline telephone and speaks the name of the part needed. That information is heard from speakers at up to 50 to 100 other yards. Anyone who has the part either announces it on the hotline or makes a private call.

In the late 1970s, a small company based in southern California,

Incomnet, brought modern electronic messaging techniques to the
dismantler industry by introducing a computerized hotline. While a
voice hotline gets overcrowded when it has about 100 active
members, there is no limit to the number of messages and users on
a computerized network. Today Incomnet has 400 dismantlers
connected together in the western United States, primarily in
southern California, while another company, AutoInfo, has 1200
yards linked together nationwide. Several other companies operate
in other parts of the country. All told, about 2000 dismantlers are
networked together on computerized hotlines, while 8000 other
dismantlers still use the older, but less expensive, voice hotlines.

With a computerized network, each dismantler has a personal
computer and real-time connection to the network. A dismantler
who needs a part creates a parts request that is broadcast to every
other dismantler on the network or to dismantlers in a specific
region. The network itself is based on leased telecommunication
lines, satellite terminals, or a combination of the two.

To get an idea of the intensity of dismantler networking,
Incomnet's AUTONETWORK broadcasts 5000 parts requests a day
to each of its 400 members. Compare that to a typical electronic
mail user who sends or receives a mere 20 to 25 messages a day.
The dismantling application is 200 times more intensive than a
typical Email application. The reason is that dismantlers use
networking to replace the need for a central warehouse. When voice
and computer hotlines are added together across North America, it
is estimated that of the $4 billion in parts that are sold yearly, at
least $1 billion of those parts are located electronically.

The dismantler industry has its own trend line toward
mail-enabled applications that link messaging systems into databases.
While computer networking continues to spread throughout the
dismantler industry, so too does the use of computerized inventory
systems. Already, several companies in the industry are developing
technologies that will allow inventory systems to read specially
formulated parts requests automatically. This saves the enormous
time required for people to read several thousand requests daily
and to determine if those parts are in stock.

Auto dismantlers have banded together to use electronic
communications to create the equivalent of a virtual warehouse of
used electronic parts. Ranging from simple voice hotlines that
connect five or ten dismantling yards together to computerized
networks of hundreds of dismantlers, the overall industry is living
proof that when a need can be met, even low-tech industries, such
as dismantling, will use electronic networks.

Sears Roebuck and Co.: External Reach, Big Time!

Sears Roebuck and Co. of Chicago is one of the largest
organizations in the United States. The Sears Merchandise Group

(Sears), a wholly owned subsidiary, is implementing an external reach network that involves all of its 5000 primary suppliers throughout the United States. For example, the company processes more than 21 million purchase orders annually. Its suppliers range from companies that do less than $100,000 a year to those that generate tens of millions of dollars in revenue.

Suppliers doing EDI with the company can communicate purchase orders, shipping notices, invoices, remittance and inventory advices, text messaging and changes to purchase order inquiries, and status reports. In addition to communicating with Sears, these suppliers can also link with other networks and retailers.

Sears had several reasons for building an extended network. The company wanted an improvement in the quality of information it exchanged and the speed at which it was able to receive and transmit data to its suppliers. In short, Sears wanted to maintain a competitive advantage by simplifying the exchange of business documents with its trading partners. By eliminating many of its paper-based manual operations through EDI, Sears projected reductions in transaction errors and in processing costs. By freeing its people from the time spent on repetitive administrative tasks, the company also expected greater flexibility to assign its human resources to more productive activities.

The EDI links were also designed to bring improvements in the production of inventory within Sears and its trading partners. As suppliers became an extension of the Sears enterprise (and information was exchanged more quickly and easily), the company would have a greater opportunity to manage its supply chain more cost-effectively and to work more closely with its suppliers to rationalize inventory. Better supply chain management would mean that goods were received at the stores more quickly. This would lead to more sales, better customer service, and more profits for both Sears and its suppliers.

Sears was well aware of the value of electronic exchange of information when it decided to implement its EDI network. For 20 years the company had used a proprietary electronic system to link with suppliers that represented 80 percent of purchases. The company's experience with this proprietary network put Sears ahead of most organizations in making the EDI transition. The company also realized that the EDI applications were really technology-supported business applications. While there were and continue to be technical consultants involved in the network installation and maintenance, the entire staff responsible for the EDI implementation and its current operations within Sears have business backgrounds.

Although the cost of converting 5000 suppliers to EDI totaled over $5 million, the company has quickly experienced a payback in several areas. The benefits to vendors have included a reduction in clerical errors, a reduction in inventory and manufacturing times, a shortening of the order cycle, and improved document processing. The result of all these efficiencies is that goods move more quickly and easily to Sears stores, resulting in greater productivity and profitability for both the company and its suppliers.

Sears will continue to implement EDI with all of its new suppliers. The company is also looking to find new opportunities to use EDI technology to improve its operations. More transactions sets, such as receiving purchase orders from customers, will be created to streamline and automate more business activities.

What will not change in the future is Sears's approach to EDI technology and its role within the organization. EDI is viewed not as an event but as a process that will eventually involve all company operations. EDI is only one part of a continuum of technological change that will continue to alter the way Sears manages all of its business and its relationships with suppliers and customers.

Levi Strauss & Co.: External Reach from Hip Pocket to Bottom Line

Levis Strauss & Co. of San Francisco has reached out to suppliers through a comprehensive network called LeviLink™. The results have been spectacular, contributing considerably to a 34 percent rise in profits.

LeviLink™ is a package of computerized and related business services for retailers that speeds and simplifies the entire process of ordering, stocking, receiving, analyzing sales, invoicing, and making payments for Levi products. It covers every stage of the retailing cycle, including managing and reconciling purchase orders, capturing point-of-sale information, and managing overall market trends. LeviLink™ also allows Levi Strauss & Co.'s trading partners to receive, manage, and pay for Levi product orders electronically. Generating and receiving orders are processes that now take minutes rather than days.

Two of the company's key objectives in establishing LeviLink™ were to increase sales with lower inventory and enhance service to retailers. The company had developed a clear vision of where it wanted to go in the future. It was a future that included a closed-loop business cycle where Levi Strauss & Co. would know, quickly and accurately, what merchandise was selling, what its current product inventory was, what work was in process, and which merchandise was in transit. In short, the company wanted to be able to compare what it was producing to what it was selling and, as a result, take the steps needed to be more productive and profitable.

Meeting these goals meant establishing more efficient partnerships with its suppliers and retailers. The company had to streamline its links with its retailers and offer more business results and other vital information for itself and its trading partners. This has been a key function of LeviLink™.

For Levis Strauss & Co., LeviLink™ has meant a more timely flow of market, sales, inventory, and other important business information.

The company is able to develop better models of what is happening in its business operations. With the information LeviLink® generates, the corporation is in a better position to meet its goal of having the right products in the right market at the right time.

The benefits of LeviLink® to the company's retailers have been equally significant. Users of LeviLink® are generating 25 percent more sales on 25 percent less inventory, while LeviLink® has dramatically improved the retailer's receiving operations. The system sends an electronic packing slip that indicates the sizes, styles, and colors of merchandise being shipped. Bar codes on labels allow retailers to develop their own receiving systems to scan and match merchandise receipts by computer. Scanning the bar-coded cartons also eliminates hand counting, and so merchandise can be sent directly to the selling floor. Stocking inventory more quickly means that goods are available to customers sooner, which in turn has resulted in increased sales.

Enhancing the features and functionality of LeviLink® is one of Levi Strauss & Co.'s key strategies for the future. Another objective is to create a centralized on-line database of sales and manufacturing information for its domestic network users. The company is also involved in an apparel industry effort to draft standards for the electronic exchange of three-dimensional graphics of clothing and fabric designs.

Levis Strauss & Co. also plans to expand its *Levi's advanced business systems* (LABS) and *computer integrated manufacturing* (CIM) operations, both of which are linked to LeviLink®. LABS will be used to generate information on market sales and projections to determine what work orders will be sent to the company's CIM operations. It will use the point-of-sale information generated by LeviLink® to further increase the productivity of the company.

Two other strategies are vitally important to the company's future. One involves the creation of a comprehensive IT architecture that meets the company's strategic business needs. The other addresses the implications of the changes and opportunities that new technology systems, such as EDI, are bringing to the company and its trading partners. The opportunity to exchange semistructured and unstructured information to improve the fortunes of the company and its business partners is already being realized. Because of the EDI links, Levi Strauss & Co. account representatives have more information on what is selling at the retail level and are able to analyze this information and develop strategies that will benefit the customer in the future. With the intracompany administrative activities automated, the company's representatives can spend more time providing valuable consulting advice and meeting the retailer's (and customer's) ongoing and changing needs. They have more time and more information to provide knowledge and expertise and to interact with their customers in a more effective and ultimately more profitable way.

Summary: The Extended Enterprise—The Shifts

- Value chain

  → Value network (suppliers, consumers, and affinity groups, competitors)

- Simple marketplace combat

  → Competition through cooperation, i.e., technology-based relationships

- Manual and physical communications

  → Electronic communication across the value network

- Enterprise technology islands

  → Interorganization computing

- Purchaser of information

  → Information purchaser and vendor

PART 2

The New Technology Paradigm

The next section addresses the three key technology shifts that are enabling the move to the high-performance business team, the integrated organization, and the extended enterprise.

The first of these is network computing, the topic of Chap. 5. The first era saw the rise of host computing and the creation of isolated information system islands. Host computing environments are rapidly being replaced by networks of intelligent computer systems, distributed to best suit the needs of the business.

To achieve effective network computing, it is essential that businesses develop an enterprise architecture to guide the evolution of information technology. This architecture defines the components (software, information, and technology) required at various points in the network. Inevitably, network computing leads to the adoption of industry standards and is part of what we refer to as the *standards-based architecture*.

Under pressure from this shift in the customer world, the computer industry is shifting from the traditional proprietary approaches upon which host computing was based. *Open systems* based on vendor-neutral standards are central to the second era. The role of open systems standards in support of network computing is the topic for Chap. 6.

Another important component of this transition is software development. The costs of software acquisition, construction, and maintenance now far exceed the associated hardware costs and will continue to become a greater proportion of overall systems costs. In the first era, software development was a craft. It is now becoming an engineered, production-style discipline focusing on the use of standardized, interchangeable parts. Productivity of development resources must be dramatically increased through improved use of tools, far greater reusability of software components, and wider use of packages. It is especially important to understand these changes because you, personally, are becoming a developer of software. Chapter 7 examines the transformation of software development and its effects on your organization. These shifts are summarized in Fig. 5-1.

5
Network Computing Comes of Age

- A chief information officer (CIO) establishes a task force to investigate the possibility of "downsizing" applications from mainframes to smaller machines. This is precipitated by a report indicating the growing feasibility of exploiting $300 (per unit of performance) microprocessor technology instead of mainframes which cost $70,000 for a comparable unit of performance.

- A financial executive sees a Super Bowl television ad for a computer company which claims it has "the purest form of client/server computing." On Monday, he asks his IS manager, "What on earth does that mean?"

- A CEO explains to her CIO that the next few years will involve considerable upheaval for the company—reorganizations, mergers, new business launches, and acquisitions and divestments. She needs a computing environment which is easily changeable and in which software applications can be developed very quickly.

- A marketing executive decides to reengineer the work process in his department and wonders about the implications of a team structure on the requirements for technology.

- More than 200 computer companies collaborate on the development of a standardized software package for distributed computing which each decides to integrate into its own products. Customers everywhere investigate what this change will mean for their technology plans.

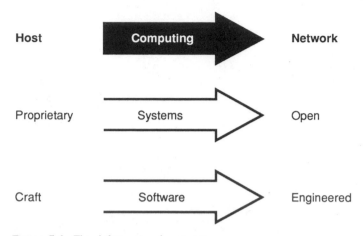

Figure 5-1. The shift to network computing.

These are reflective of a fundamental change occurring in technology itself—the shift from "host" computing environments to network computing in which technology, data, and even software applications are distributed (see Fig. 5-1). Sometimes called *client/server* computing, this shift has far-reaching implications for every organization. It enables the migration to a more cost-effective, powerful, and dynamic computing platform.

Era I Host Computing Environments

For the first three decades of computing, organizations were busy deploying technology to address specific business needs, such as financial management systems, inventory control, process control, and word processing. These era I systems were primarily based on a single, and relatively simple, paradigm—that of host computing (see Fig. 5-2). The host computing model placed the computer at the center and connected all terminals and other devices as slaves. Most of these terminals had limited or no intelligence and were therefore totally dependent on the availability of the host computer to perform their intended functionality. In the 1980s, these hosts were accessed through personal computers that could emulate such terminals.

Host computing environments led to isolated pockets of technology, applications, and information, serving only those users who were connected to the host. Many different applications were placed on these hosts, as application and user needs expanded over time. These users

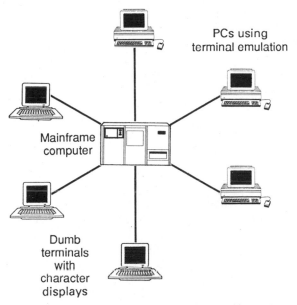

PCs using
terminal emulation

Mainframe
computer

Dumb
terminals
with
character
displays

Figure 5-2. Host computing—centralized master/slave orientation.

were often plagued by poor or inconsistent performance and low availability of service. These environments were complex to manage because of the diversity of applications and supporting system software.

Vendors of these systems competed by using their own proprietary hardware and software products, uniquely designed for each class of computer system. These proprietary systems were largely incompatible, resulting in a customer lock-in to that vendor's technology direction or an expensive conversion. These incompatibilities led to further isolation of individual host networks, making interconnection of different computer systems a major, if not impossible, challenge.

The isolated, independent, and consolidated nature of host computing became very constraining throughout the 1980s. As a result, new business requirements for computing emerged and new types of computing architectures arrived to challenge the bastions of host computing, especially large mainframe operations.

As discussed earlier, the new business reality is creating a pull for a new style of computing—one based on distributed networks rather than hosts.

The business trends of the 1990s have a direct impact on the role of information technology in supporting strategic applications. There is a common theme here—survival in the 1990s is dependent upon effectively linking business units and partners to deliver value to customers.

In other words, there is a need to see business operations not as isolated islands but as highly networked and interdependent functions. Speed, responsiveness, partnering, productivity, and the other key trends are essential to success.

More and more, host computing tends to run counter to this theme. The creation of islands of users, applications, and information combine with the difficulties in integrating across proprietary systems to suggest the need for a new approach to computing.

At the same time that companies are trying to simplify business processes, the scope and nature of operations are becoming more complex. In order to deal with this complexity, it is useful to apply some basic systems theory. That is, the ability to achieve optimum results in any complex set of processes lies in dismantling the systems into a number of standard functions with well-defined behavior and interfaces. These functions can then be organized by defining relationships and associated rules that govern their interaction.

There is a growing need for the integration of previously disparate applications of technology through a distributed networked infrastructure based on standard components and interfaces. This implies that attention must be given to the architecture of the network to support the interworking of the various components. This infrastructure can then be used to further the use of technology in ways that significantly contribute to business operations. It is against this backdrop that a new style of computing—network computing—is emerging.

What Is Network Computing?

A network computing environment provides the means for users to access a wide range of information, applications, and computing resources without worrying about where they are or how they are interconnected.

This is a fundamentally different approach from host computing. Multiple points across the network can deliver computing services, in contrast to the single location of a host computer. The various points of delivery of computer services and applications are referred to as computing platforms. These platforms are typically distributed to a variety of locations to address different degrees of sharing and to provide the most appropriate type of computing or communications capability. Types of platforms include dedicated personal workstations, work-group servers on local area networks, departmental information systems on distributed processors, corporate information systems on enterprise processors, and external service providers on public networks (see Fig. 5-3).

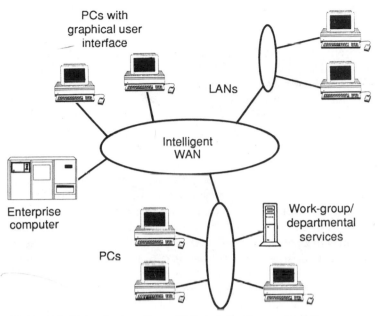

Figure 5-3. Network computing—distributed client/server orientation.

Traditional host computers involved large monolithic software applications running in highly centralized environments. Network computing makes use of a new approach called *cooperative processing*. Cooperative processing involves spreading application components across multiple platforms and using the network to link these components.

For example, the management of user interactions, through displaying information and responding to user inputs, is handled by the intelligent desktop or portable workstation; a communications processor on the LAN handles information transfers with other processors on the wide area network (WAN) to link to applications running on a departmental processor, which in turn accesses data from an enterprise database.

Host computing dictated a master–slave relationship with respect to attached devices such as user terminals. Network computing, however, leads to a client/server approach. The workstation becomes a client platform that requests information and processing services from "servers" connected to local and wide area networks.

The new technology paradigm can best be described by combining the concepts of networked platforms, cooperative processing across these platforms, and client/server capabilities to manage the relationships between the components.

The Client/Server Approach

To achieve a true network computing environment, the IT industry is adopting the client/server model for building and interrelating the various components of the environment. The client/server model has two parts. The client task is essentially responsible for the user interface. It structures the screen including the graphical user interface and responds to user inputs. If a client is not capable of responding directly to a user request, the client passes the task to an appropriate server.

The server actually performs the tasks requested by the user. The tasks may require an enterprise or departmental system, a value-added network, an intelligent switch such as a PBX, or a local area network. It can even be on the same workstation that performed the client task.

Depending on the sophistication of the network design, the server can have any or all of the following characteristics: it can be closely coupled to the client workstation or some other part of the network; it can break its tasks into two or more subtasks; it can activate other applications on different system resources through remote procedure calls; or it can dynamically shift processing to a platform that is best suited to perform the specific task. All these functions are transparent to the user who works with a set of friendly graphical user-interface functions. As far as the user is concerned, the entire process might as well be occurring on the personal workstation.

Another key distinction of the network computing and client/server model is that it is much better suited to handling multiple forms of information, such as text, graphics, images, sound, and video. Over the past decade, there have been many technology breakthroughs in computerized (i.e., digital) techniques. These advances have revolutionized our ability to manage and display information, similar to the effect of advances in audio/video systems.

The workstation is the logical point of integration of these advanced user-interface capabilities. The transition from traditional character-based data-processing terminals to multimedia, multifunction intelligent user workstations incorporating color graphics, moving images, and high-quality sound is the most visible and exciting aspect of the new technology paradigm.

Why Network Computing?

Why is network computing such an attractive alternative to conventional host computing? Is it worth the annoyance and upheaval in architectural and technology direction? Perhaps the most compelling answer to these questions comes from the business thrusts that we explored earlier—our business units and trading partners functioning as an organizational value network. Therefore, enterprise approaches to computer systems should be aligned with the business network.

Operational Alignment

As long as businesses and governments could function and survive as large hierarchical bureaucracies, then large centralized, monolithic host computers were well-matched. However, isolated host systems no longer match the fast-paced, streamlined, and integrated operations of today's well-planned organization. The client/server approach to work organization treats business units as networked clients and servers with well-defined roles, a measurable contribution to the business and equally well-defined relationships with other clients and server units. These units can be both internal and external to the enterprise.

The research shows that network computing is required to implement the networked organization. Modular, dynamic, user-oriented computing platforms have been found to best support and enable new ways for organizing and managing work. The ability to align the various components of information technology architecture with more streamlined and modular approaches for conducting business operations is the main business driver for network computing. Network computing is essential for the successful enterprise of the 1990s.

There are, however, a number of other distinct advantages of network computing over host computing.

Platform Specialization

With many different types of platforms and placement options to choose from, network computing has been found to provide the systems architect with the ability to customize solutions to meet a number of criteria. These criteria typically include function, performance, availability, cost, ease of operation, and ease of management. For example, the personal computer is the ideal platform to perform creative activities, such as writing reports, letters, and memos; developing presentations; and completing forms for data entry. These various tools can be provided as part of the user's "workbench." They can be customized to the personal style of the individual user, providing consistent, high-speed response on dedicated desktop or portable PCs without the associated delays, contention, and costs of being on a network.

An electronic filing cabinet for a group of workers, containing reports and drawings and reference material, is well suited to a document server on a local area network. High-volume, low-cost optical storage technologies can be deployed along with a high-speed local communications link.

Another specialized platform might be a geographical information system for a municipal or regional government, where base mapping and land-use information is stored and maintained for a number of user departments.

The phone system itself, in the form of a digital private branch exchange (PBX), represents another specialized platform that can be integrated in a network computing environment. It is well suited to supporting switching applications between users and networks. It provides a base for delivering voice mail applications and interactive voice response from various messaging and information retrieval services.

And what becomes of the traditional host mainframe or mid-range computer? It too can become a specialized server on the network for selected transaction processing and data inquiry applications, only now it performs like any other server accessible to the user. That is, it no longer is the master or the center of intelligence, but one of many intelligent servers operating as peers on the network.

As these examples illustrate, network computing allows for both selection and placement of appropriate information technology platforms. Perhaps more importantly, it also allows future flexibility to combine, separate, or relocate applications to new servers.

Cost Savings

Mainframes that cost $3 million do have capabilities that an equivalent PC-based system costing $300,000 does not. But the list of advantages is shrinking—creating a compelling cost argument for network systems. It is only a matter of time until all computers will be based on microprocessors (computer on a chip), rather than the traditional semiconductors (in which different specialized chips perform different parts of the logic and operations required for computing) which are found in the mainframe and minicomputers in your enterprise.

Continuing advances in microprocessor technology speed and capacities have upset the basic tenet of the 1960s. Grosch's law stated that the more applications that could be combined on a computer, the cheaper the cost of processing. This "bigger is better" philosophy was followed by a majority of corporate computer departments which experienced a number of multimillion dollar mainframe upgrades over three decades of host computing.

Although it is difficult to agree on appropriate comparative measurements between host computing and network computing, there is absolutely no denying the relative price/performance advantages of powerful microprocessors over their minicomputer and mainframe competitors.

The most powerful desktop workstations in 1986 had a speed of two MIPS (millions of instructions per second). (A comparable minicomputer cost many times more at the time.) Every year since, that number has doubled. In 1987 there was a 4-MIPS desktop machine. In 1988, you could buy an 8-MIPS machine. By 1991 the number had grown to 64. By 1992 there was a 128-MIPS machine, and one with a speed of more than 1000 MIPS is projected by 1995. If the costs of microprocessor-based versus other computers are examined, the data are even more striking. (See Fig. 5-4.) For example a 1992 mainframe costs about $70,000 per MIPS. A 1992 workstation costs well under $300 per MIPS. Now, clearly a mainframe MIPS is not exactly comparable to a workstation MIPS. Further, there are many applications that run on traditional mainframes or minicomputers only. However, the writing is on the wall. The microprocessor will replace traditional semiconductor technology.

Figures 5-5 and 5-6, provided by Dr. Phil Neches, chief scientist of NCR Corporation, give another angle on the issue. Figure 5-5 shows the growth in the number of equivalent transistors that can be located on a single microprocessor chip. Today, a microprocessor-based computer can outperform mainframe and minicomputers by linking a number of microprocessor chips together to work in parallel (called *massively par-*

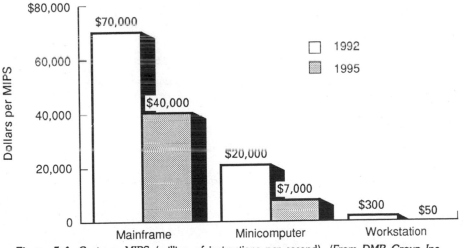

Figure 5-4. Cost per MIPS (million of instructions per second). (*From DMR Group Inc., Emerging Technologies Consulting.*)

Year	Transistors
1979	30 thousand
1983	100 thousand
1986	280 thousand
1990	1 million
1996	10 million
2001	100 million

Figure 5-5. Number of transistors on a micro-processor chip. (*Courtesy of NCR Corporation.*)

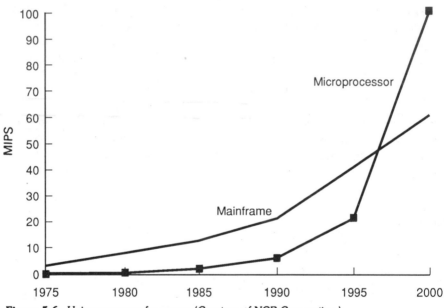

Figure 5-6. Uniprocessor performance. (*Courtesy of NCR Corporation.*)

allel processing). And, as the graph in Fig. 5-6 illustrates, a single micro-processor will substantially outperform a mainframe by the year 2000.

The network computing option is becoming considerably less expensive as enterprises architect software and associated information to make greater use of low-cost platforms and to reduce the requirements for ongoing communication costs.

The countervailing argument is typically based on the added cost of the resources to manage and maintain the decentralized computing resources. These are clearly issues where the technology has been allowed to progress without any coordination. Coordinated planning, management, and maintenance are achievable if network computing standards are employed. Some early adopters of network computing even claim lower costs because of reduced complexity.

The good news is that network computing environments will become increasingly easier to manage and maintain as they incorporate improved facilities for remote access and control of distributed components and platforms. As well, many powerful systems management features (typically found on traditional computers) are appearing in the new technology. These include features such as automatic file backup and recovery at specified intervals, and facilities to synchronize dispersed databases and maintain software components at appropriate and consistent release levels. This can be accomplished using overnight network capacity.

Integration

Network computing environments are, by definition, standardized environments. No vendors can compete in this market unless their technology plugs and plays well with the technologies of other vendors. Furthermore, workstation and server software developed by independent software companies is created for the largest markets — which are based on open standards rather than unique proprietary hardware.

Because network computing can only work with standards, it is part and parcel of the movement toward open systems. As such, network computing is a style of computing that facilitates integration.

Flexibility

In the turbulent times in which businesses now operate, enterprises are requiring more and more flexibility in their operations and the systems that support them. Network computing enables organizations to achieve this needed flexibility by enabling their systems and business operations to be modular. At the same time, they remain linked to corporate entities and have the flexibility to link to external entities. Integrated workgroup and enterprise operations allow the business units of an organization to develop new system applications that meet both the local and corporate goals of the organization more quickly and efficiently.

Corporate reorganizations, mergers, acquisitions, and alliances all have significant implications for information systems. Network computing provides an excellent basis for arranging information management needs around functional, as opposed to organizational, lines. By incorporating personal, work-group, and departmental levels into the architecture in addition to corporate levels, it is much easier to adjust the placement and relationships of the different supporting computer platforms, using the network as the point of integration.

The distribution of intelligence is equally important in linking with external systems. Providing interchange of information with key customers, suppliers, and service providers is a natural and highly strategic extension of network computing.

The flexibility of network computing offers benefits in leveraging existing investments in information technology. Inherent in the network computing concept is the need to evolve the capabilities and to provide an environment that facilitates, rather than restricts, change. Some of the migration options from host to network computing will be explored in the subsequent section.

Once again, it is the modularity that provides the ongoing flexibility of network computing. The ability to pick and choose appropriate platforms and components and to deal with their required network interfaces provides this flexibility. With continual improvement in the use of information technology to increase functionality, exploit the use of multiple forms of information, and extend accessibility and reach, a modular network-based approach becomes essential.

Innovation

A growing number of organizations are adopting network computing as an environment for innovation. For these companies, network computing is providing both the facilities and opportunities for all business units within the enterprise to build upon their existing systems and applications. Because new applications are built upon a network platform, companies are able to integrate these applications into the corporate infrastructure. They are no longer supporting an outdated organizational structure or producing brilliant applications isolated to one PC or work group.

Enterprisewide access to new systems and applications is enabling other business units to build additional system innovations on an ongoing basis. In short, network computing is allowing organizations to share new system innovations and to encourage faster and more efficient development of new applications in other business operations.

Whither the Host?

The flexibility inherent in network computing also provides benefits when it comes to determining migration approaches from host computing environments. Most organizations have experienced a proliferation of personal computers over the 1980s. This led to many adopting one or more LANs as a means of providing shared services to work-group users, such as laser printers, file servers, and communication servers.

The first issue is to choose standard platforms and software components at the work-group level and then to choose the appropriate workstation, LAN, and server standards. Next is to enable the exchange of messages, documents, and files through electronic mail. Then come considerations for application and data access on the departmental and corporate host computers.

Turning hosts into servers requires a strategy. The most simple, but least desirable, option is to link the PCs to the host by emulating host terminals. This requires extensive user knowledge of the associated host log-on and access procedures for each host to be accessed. As well, it reduces the powerful PC, with its graphical user-interface capability, to a character-based display using only rows and columns of alphabetic and numerical data. With terminal emulation, interactions are controlled by the host and based on the application programmer's screen design. Thus the complexities of the host environment and limitations and inconsistencies of user interfaces are all very visible to the PC user.

A much preferable migration option involves camouflaging the complexities or idiosyncrasies of the host by using the intelligence of the PC to provide a graphical user interface. This allows host application user interfaces to be converted on the desktop to present a similar look and feel to that of PC applications. It also means that the PC can look after host log-on and security procedures as part of its normal start-up. With this method, the host still thinks it's in control while the user views the host application as just another open "window" on the desktop.

Ultimately, a purer form of network computing is desirable to gain full and ongoing advantages. In this case, software is cooperatively processed simultaneously on the various platforms, implying adoption of a standard set of distributed environments and interfaces. With full network computing in place, the goals of transparency (independence of location on the network), portability (movement of software between types of platforms), and scalability (adjusting the size and capacity of the platform to meet user requirements) are achievable.

Network computing requires the adoption of a set of enterprisewide standards. Conversely, it is this lack of a common infrastructure that has complicated and frustrated many systems initiatives of the past. This leads us to the next topic—open systems.

6

Open Systems for an Open World

- Software developed internally by a consumer products company runs on the computers of more than 50 of its subsidiaries, even though there are dozens of different hardware platforms.

- A large retail company reports that it saved tens of millions of dollars in a recent hardware purchase by choosing an open systems platform.

- The European Community (EC) adopts a set of information technology standards that shape systems procurement in all EC countries from the federal to the municipal level.

- Hundreds of computer vendors — many of which are direct competitors — join together in consortia to create standard platforms and products for the future marketplace.

- A very large government department determines that it can save billions of dollars in software development and maintenance costs through the reuse of standardized so-called Lego software modules which it is storing in its softwarehouse.

- An international consumer products company adopts something it calls "open systems" as part of its business plan — deeming open systems to be critical to its survival as a global enterprise. The company then mandates this policy for more than 200 subsidiaries around the world and launches a program to convince its trading partners to do likewise.

- Every major computer vendor announces that its main strategy for the 1990s is open systems.

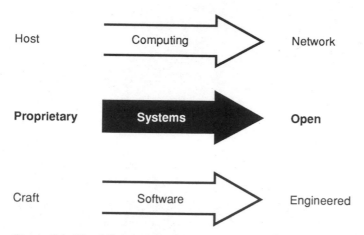

Figure 6-1. The shift to open systems.

All these events are reflective of one of the most profound aspects of the new era—the shift from vendor-proprietary systems to open systems based on industry standards (see Fig. 6-1).

In the 1990s, the topic of open systems—heretical as recently as the mid-1980s, has moved to the center of the information technology industry. Along with the epochal restructuring of the global economy, markets, and geopolitical environment, IT has entered its own *glasnost*. Open systems are creating a *perestroika* of the IT industry and opening a new era of opportunity and peril for both vendors and enterprises alike. If your organization has not adopted an open systems policy, it should as soon as possible. The growth of such adoption is shown in Fig. 6-2.

What Are Open Systems Anyway?

The question—posed to computer pundits—elicits answers reminiscent of the religious debates of the thirteenth century regarding how many angels can dance on the head of a pin. However, when posed to planners of companies who are adopting open systems, clear themes emerge.

A widely accepted view is presented by the X/Open consortium, which defines open systems as "systems and software environments based on standards which are vendor independent and commonly available."[1] That is, computing has matured to the point where stan-

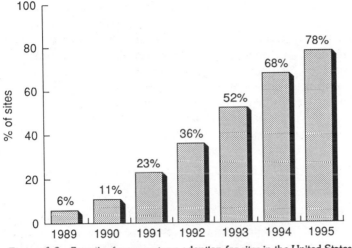

Figure 6-2. Growth of open systems adoption for sites in the United States and Canada with more than 50 people.

dards that are outside the control of any one supplier are becoming widely adopted. This profound change opens up a new world of possibilities, and challenges, for customers.

Two main buzzwords describe the characteristics of open systems:

- *Portability.* Software applications and information can be relatively easily moved to various computers of various sizes or brands. This enables the skills of people to be portable as well—that is, to be applicable to different computing environments.

- *Interoperability.* Computers of different sizes and brands can communicate together—sharing resources, information, and even software applications.

Initially, companies that adopted open systems in the late 1980s and early 1990s tended to seek two main categories of benefits. Open systems have been found to reduce IT costs in the areas of hardware, software, information management, and the human costs of managing change. Second, open systems also provide value-added benefits such as reduced risk of vendor dependence, architectural flexibility, better software integration, easier migration to new innovative technologies, and better choice of packaged software.

However, the DMR research noted a shift in the early 1990s.[2] More and more companies are concluding that the issue is not just one of benefits of open systems. Rather, open systems are becoming an imperative for companies to function effectively in the new competitive environment. They are part of the rise of computing architectures, which, through standards and a modular network orientation, are dynamic and cost-effective and can enable linking with external organizations, the reuse of software, the embracing of technological innovations from unpredictable vendor sources, and overall the effective building of work-group, enterprise, and external reach computing.

Before we examine this change in emphasis, it is important to step back and review how open systems came about.

The Origins of Open Systems

During the first few decades of the computer industry, vendors, as a rule, engineered and marketed nonstandard, proprietary products. Each claimed to have the best processors, operating systems, networks, computer languages, and application software. When a vendor had been chosen, the customer was locked into that manufacturer's architecture and products, because the cost of rewriting all the software or porting it to a different architecture was prohibitive. This was euphemistically referred to by vendor marketing personnel as account control. The vendor controlled the customer account and, as with the Hotel California, "You can check out any time you like, but you can never leave."

All aspects of the customer relationship, from the proprietary nature of the technology to the use of leasing programs, tended to foster dependence on the vendor. Naturally, standards were of less interest to manufacturers who had a large market share. Standards were anathema to many suppliers, as product differentiation and market share were based on the competitive advantages of proprietary technologies.

However, proprietary technologies did not flow from nefarious motives of the manufacturers. The computer industry was in its infancy, and proprietary technologies supported the need to experiment and innovate. Moreover, the industry had not matured to the point where clear standards could be supported by vendors or even demanded by customers. The account relationship model advanced the interests of all parties.

In the early days of the computer industry, the American National Standards Institute (ANSI) led efforts in the area of creating de jure standards, but compliance was voluntary and limited. The U.S. government, which was the largest-volume purchaser, was able to bring considerable pressure to bear on the industry for standards. Today, it is generally accepted that most early standards exist as a result of that pressure. The U.S. National Bureau of Standards was established in 1901 as part of the Department of Commerce and Labor. In 1965, it was given responsibility for standards development for U.S. government computer users. In 1969, the standard ASCII format for coding and using alphanumeric characters was adopted for government computing. IBM, which used its competing EBCDIC format, succeeded in watering down enforcement of the standard. EBCDIC, in turn, was widely accepted as a de facto standard in the commercial world.

This situation changed dramatically with the introduction of the microcomputer. More than any other technology, it has thrust organizations into the second era. By the early 1980s, standard microprocessors became the dominant force on the desktop. Microcomputer peripherals became standardized around a small number of bus architectures and peripheral interfaces. Standard operating systems at the micro level began to appear. Most important, we witnessed the rise of a software industry that was independent from hardware vendors. Whereas traditional software companies created programs that were tied to a specific vendor's products, these companies created shrink-wrapped software packages that would work on any vendor's personal computers, without modification. That is, they were binary-compatible across different hardware platforms. The software programs written by developers did not have to be modified and recompiled into the "object code" (ones and zeros) which can be understood by a computer, that is, translated into transistors being either on or off.

With the emergence of the PC and the standards-based environment in which it operated, users in departments and divisions throughout organizations suddenly learned the power of standards in enabling information technology to solve their business problems and make them more productive. These were people who had little or no access to corporate mainframe or minicomputer systems. They reveled in their newfound power and independence as, for the first time, a wide range of applications could be purchased off the shelf. These shrink-wrapped packages would run on virtually any microcomputer, regardless of manufacturer.

The success of these standard programs showed people that there were ways to use technology other than through proprietary systems that were under the control of the data-processing department. Users also became aware of the advantages of being able to choose from a variety of packages from a multitude of vendors. It was becoming clear to software developers that, with the market awakening to the power of standards, proprietary systems would no longer be able to retain their power and position in corporate computing. One by one the software developers abandoned the proprietary market and shifted to creating products for the rapidly growing open environment. By the turn of the decade, the trickle had turned into a flood.

But the success of the microcomputer begged the question: What about other levels of technology? Might it be possible to have standards so that software would work on the products—from the desktop to the largest mainframe—of any computer vendor? Might it be possible to have standards that would enable interoperability among the products of many vendors? The answer to these questions has become open systems.

During this period a move was afoot inside the largest manufacturer—IBM—not only to adopt open systems, but to attempt to standardize within IBM proprietary environments as well. A far-reaching set of standards called *systems application architecture* (SAA) was adopted. IBM announced that it would have, for the next historic period, "two strategic architectures"—SAA (based primarily on IBM standards) and systems based on the Unix operating system (open systems). Moreover, it said, the two worlds would work together well. In late 1991, IBM extended this view, announcing that SAA would become open as part of IBM's single *open enterprise* strategy. This was a major shift for IBM, which throughout its history has had various incompatible, and to some degree, competing product lines. As a rule, the software that worked on one family did not work on another, and, especially in the early days, products from various families did not communicate well. In fairness to IBM, however, the company was one of the early innovators in the area of software portability. Before the introduction of its 360 family of computers in 1964, software from any hardware manufacturer was tied to its own computer. When a customer needed a larger computer, a conversion (that is, a rewrite of the software) was required. The 360 family introduced a radical notion—that software would work on a family of products from one manufacturer.

With open systems, the computer industry moves for the first time to industrywide standards. While this may be new to the computer industry, it has many historical parallels.

Standards: Not a New Thing

Throughout the history of the world, adoption of standards has led to growth, industrial development, progress, and prosperity. The adoption of standards has also produced casualties—typically, suppliers who lost in the standards battle or who were unable to modify their proprietary approach. In the long run, however, standards have benefited both suppliers (as a group) and consumers.

A standard is a recognized unit of comparison by which the correctness of others can be determined. The world's first standards of length, volume, weight, and money were established in ancient Greece, Egypt, Babylonia, and India. Standard measures were kept in religious temples or places of commerce. Formal standards have been developed to achieve consistency and compatibility and to protect personal safety or society as a whole. Most standards have been developed by government or parapublic agencies in association with industry and other interest groups. Below are a number of historical analogies.[3]

In 1689, Boston was destroyed by fire. The city fathers recognized that standardization would facilitate the rapid and economical reconstruction of the city. They passed a by-law making it a civic crime for brickmakers to make bricks other than 9 in. by 4 in. by 4 in. Subsequently, the industry gravitated toward uniform dimensioning (standards) for other building materials such as lumber, blocks, wallboard, and piping.

Initially, standards meant smaller inventories and speedier service for dealers. Standards permitted architects to spend less time drafting and more time improving design. The contractor benefited from easier estimating, more efficient methods on the job, and less construction time. Although the need was not initially understood, a world without such standards is unthinkable today.

One of the most important standards ever developed in North America was the railroad's standard track gage. Early railroads each had unique gages, resulting in a small industry of freight consultants who made their living carrying goods between incompatible lines. These people naturally opposed standards, but lost out when, after negotiations with the railroads, the U.S. Congress passed a law making the 4 foot 8.5 in. track gage universal.

This gage, subsequently adopted in Canada, enabled expansion of the west and was an essential prerequisite for the development of trade, mining, industry, and commerce.

Few businesses have standardized as fully as the electric lamp industry. Through consolidation of numerous companies into General Electric decades ago and cooperative efforts among electrical manufacturers, power companies, insurance companies, and others, electrical standards codes encompass virtually every phase of electricity transmission and use. For example, there is complete mechanical interchangeability between the electrical components in both incandescent and fluorescent lamps. There are also codes that help ensure the safe installation, maintenance, and operation of electric lines and equipment.

These standards have created a huge market by enabling mass production, distribution, and use of electric lamps and appliances. This has resulted in the growth of the industry and, for consumers, better convenience, greater safety, and cheaper prices.

In the early 1900s, the movie industry used nonstandardized motion picture machinery, irregular perforation spacing in films, and nonstandardized methods of handling film and equipment. These nonstandardized practices led to stoppages in theaters and imperfection in films and, overall, inhibited the development of the industry and the international market for films. In 1916, the Society of Motion Picture Engineers cited such stoppages as a main cause for the lack of popularity of motion pictures. Standards eliminated such difficulties. For example, in the 1930s, the location of the sound track on 16-mm film was adopted internationally. Today, a motion picture film can be projected on standard equipment in any country in the world. And the winners are both the industry and the consumers.

Do Standards Inhibit Innovation?

Overall, standards have played key roles in the advance of many industries. Construction standards have allowed the industry and its suppliers to manufacture products and build houses, offices, and other structures more productively. Doors fit into wall brackets because a standard measurement is used. A light bulb fits a socket because socket manufacturers and light manufacturers agree on a standard size. Transportation standards have enabled industries to use roads, railways, and waterways to transport goods quickly and efficiently. In such areas as bridge construction and aircraft design, they have created levels of safety that benefit other users of these facilities. Knowing that the maximum load level is based on established standards rather than a decision by one individual or company is reassuring to anyone who is driving beside a large tractor trailer on a busy highway.

Standards have also enabled people to take advantage of technologies that would otherwise be either unwieldy or impossible to use. Communication standards, for example, have enabled consumers to view television programs that originate in countries around the world, view the latest video on their videocassette recorders, or listen to their favorite music on their compact discs. Without such standards, consumers would be faced with a myriad of technologies from which to choose. (Remember the VHS versus Beta battle?) Broadcasting and recording industry producers would have to decide what format would be most profitable. The result would be a world of technologically fragmented and very costly products.

Arguably, some standards have inhibited innovation and the introduction of more advanced products to the market. For example, the VHS video format has won the lion's share of the home video market and prevented the introduction of smaller-cartridge formats and higher-quality video technologies. But what consumers have lost in innovation they have gained in widespread access to prerecorded films and low-cost technologies.

On balance, standards have enabled innovation. The standard voltage system didn't inhibit the innovation of consumer appliances; it enabled such innovation.

Information Technology Grows Up

Likewise, standardization around the IBM PC was the single largest factor in creating the explosive growth of the personal computer marketplace and the development of an innovative third-party software industry.

Now emerging from its relative infancy, the computer industry has matured to the point of consolidating around standards. Events far beyond the industry itself are accelerating this recognition. The business environment demands powerful, flexible, network-based architectures that can only be achieved through standards. The ability to compete and trade worldwide is becoming critical for the health of companies and national economies around the globe. The proliferation of computing combined with instant global communications is transforming all industries from banking to manufacturing. The free flow of information is changing the structure of the world economy and the relationships between and within nations. There is a growing need to deliver information technology anywhere in the world, and no one vendor can provide all the technologies and associated support that global enterprises require.

In response to these worldwide developments, the second era of information technology is bringing standards-based architectures (where technology is built from interchangeable parts and common reusable components) from a variety of suppliers. Computing in this era will consist of peer-to-peer networks, distributed intelligence, and vendor-independent standards. Like voice communication technology that allows people to use their telephones to connect to other people anywhere in the world, the computer industry is moving to offer users equally transparent connectivity.

Achieving Open Systems: Six Critical Areas of Standards

While the possibility of creating open systems environments seemed remote only a decade ago, several recent developments have occurred to change this prognosis. Customer demands, political events such as the establishment of a new European Community in 1992, the influence of government purchasing practices, the rise of standards bodies, and the foresight of leading vendors have combined to make the goal of truly open systems a feasible concept.

Achieving an open systems world is no simple challenge. Software portability and interoperability of systems are required across the entire spectrum of information technology. This includes common operating environments, cross-systems communications, shared and distributed databases, common user interfaces, and cross-system development environments. DMR has developed Strategies for Open Systems, the model to describe the areas for which standards are required. This model is called an *open systems environment* (see Fig. 6-3).

1. Operating System

The operating system is the layer of software that sits between a computer and an application program such as an accounting system or

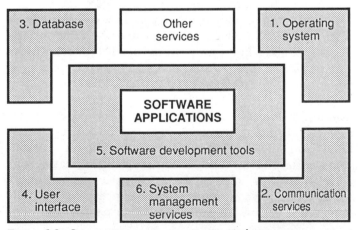

Figure 6-3. Open systems environment—six critical areas.

Email. Operating system standards are essential to permit applications to be transportable to any hardware and to take advantage of the services and capabilities they offer.

Although open systems are much more than the Unix operating system, Unix was significant in the creation of operating system standards, and more broadly standards-based architectures. Unix was developed in the early 1970s in AT&T's Bell Laboratories. By 1990 it had been adopted by virtually all manufacturers as the operating platform for their open systems strategy.

Ironically, it was the MS-DOS personal computer (a quasi-proprietary computing platform) which heightened the interest in Unix. The success of MS-DOS showed that there were other ways to succeed than through a proprietary strategy. Moreover, it became clear that with the market awakening to the power of standards, many proprietary architectures would fall by the wayside. Unix, which had been developed for minicomputers, had the scope and capabilities needed to quickly exploit 32-bit microprocessors. Unix also began to be viewed as a standard operating environment for larger systems. Some emergent and second-tier minicomputer vendors identified Unix as the main candidate for the open systems market and developed Unix products and strategies. Chip designers began to design new-generation chips with Unix in mind. Microprocessor-based supermicros appeared on the market as competitors for proprietary minis. Unix was ported to mainframes. Supercomputer manufacturers looked to Unix as the only standard multiuser operating environment.

Unix was also important in the drive to create formal, or de jure, standards. In particular, ANSI's Institute of Electrical and Electronic Engineers set up a group of standards committees dubbed POSIX. The POSIX standard has been adopted by every major vendor along with the largest customer of information technology—the U.S. government. POSIX carries massive weight in the move to open systems.

Other standards-based operating environments followed Unix, in particular the IBM product OS/2. OS/2 is the workstation operating platform for IBM's SAA, and, as such, it plays a central and historic role in the shift to standards. While OS/2 was initially proprietary in that it was (and is) controlled by its progenitors, it has become a de facto standard. Moreover, it is an operating platform that will be POSIX-compliant, meaning it will correspond to the POSIX specification of what an operating system should be. This will bring it into the open, or at least quasi-open, world.

Throughout the 1990s we will continue to see other important operating platforms based on multivendor standards. Important initiatives include Microsoft's attempt to replace MS-DOS and the results of IBM's agreement with Apple to create an "object-oriented" operating platform (see Chap. 7).

2. Communication Services

The information highways of the next century will offer new opportunities for information technology users to develop and utilize many creative and innovative applications. Communication highways will open up new and existing markets in areas of the world that were previously unreachable. They will enable companies to use better techniques to reach their existing customer base or dramatically improve corporate productivity through an expansion of technology applications such as EDI. These highways will be possible, however, only through standards. Only when an open systems environment (one that is based on well-established standards) truly exists will technology be able to offer organizations effortless and transparent communication around the corner or around the globe.

Standards to interconnect various computer and communications systems fall into two categories. Arguably, the most important are those created by the International Standards Organization (ISO), which has adopted a seven-layer *open systems interconnect* (OSI) model. This important and widely known (in the computer industry) model was introduced in 1978. The model includes standards at various layers of communications ranging from the actual physical transmission of electrons at the bottom layer up to protocols for software such as electronic mail at the top layer. Each layer in the model utilizes services of the layers below and provides services to the layers above. The arrival of high-level (called *application*) standards has delivered some sophisticated era II capabilities. For example, high-level standards (called the X.400 message transfer and X.500 directory management standards) are required to create electronic mail that works like the telephone. You can call anyone in the world using the telephone system of any computer vendor simply by knowing his or her telephone "address."

These developments, however, are merely a taste of what is to come. Communications standards will enable all forms of communication. Both the user and application will be isolated from differences in various network environments. Users will be able to connect computers from different vendors into a distributed processing system or network. In particular, software applications will be based on client/server standards that enable software applications to be divided, parceled, and processed on the network, rather than on a host computer. The underlying technologies that will enable such communication will be transparent.

In an open systems environment, transparent connectivity will occur at all levels. Basic network services of file access and transfer, electronic mail, and virtual terminal will evolve into a very rich set of enhanced services that will include network management, directory, and document exchange. Multimedia document exchange services might include text in various fonts, images and graphics, animated graphics, equations, voice, voice mail, and voice-annotated mail. Specialized business forms such as purchase orders, invoices, and letters of credit could also be part of these services. All these and other OSI-based applications will come about after specific industrywide standards are established for each layer.

A second, competing, yet in some ways converging, set of standards for communications are those contained in IBM's SAA. These protocols are based on IBM's proprietary *systems network architecture* (SNA)—a set of protocols and services that were designed for IBM computers. However, given IBM's importance in the computer industry, SNA became a de facto standard, with many companies creating SNA-compatible offerings.

3. Database

The way information is stored, managed, and accessed will be another important issue in establishing open systems standards. Initial approaches stored records in a long list or hierarchy. When information was requested, the computer would search through the file until it found the required record. Depending on the size of the information bank, this procedure was often slow since it could take time for the computer to find the appropriate record(s). It also caused problems for programmers, as software applications were dependent on the structure of the information. Further, if the information was restructured for any reason, any application that used that information needed to be modified.

The first important development to change this situation was the relational database and corresponding fourth-generation language. Relational databases have a tabular or matrix structure. The data are grouped into tables with rows and columns that have a relationship to each other. In a simple example, all the employees in a given department can be found by searching through the department number in each employee record. Because relational approaches have been found to provide better performance, flexibility, integrity, and security, they have proliferated. The arrival of relational database systems and fourth-generation inquiry languages has escalated the need for such standards. A step in this direction is *structured query language* (SQL). SQL was designed by IBM and has achieved acceptance as a standard by software vendors and users. SQL has formed the basis for cross-system compatibility of database systems for numerous environments.

The next trend in the organization of data and the construction of systems is called *object-oriented* systems (discussed in Chap. 7). These systems break information into chunks which contain data and also some programming which enables the data to do things. Standards are even more critical for this approach, as objects need to be able to work with and communicate with other objects. As a result, many standards efforts are under way to define structures and rules of objects.

4. User Interface

The typical user interface of the first era was a terse, cryptic, difficult-to-learn set of unnatural commands that used only alphanumeric characters. Such character interfaces were euphemistically dubbed as "user-unfriendly," although some more appropriately could be called "user-vicious." Computer messages such as "system dead," "illegal entry," "execute," "kill," "abort," and "fatal input error" were all legacies of an era when computers were used primarily by systems personnel or specialized operators.

As we make the transition to the new paradigm, everyone is starting to be directly supported by a workstation of some kind. Second-era interfaces that integrate data, text, graphics, and voice are appearing on the scene. In 1974, the first "wysiwyg" (*what you see is what you get*) interface for word processing appeared. Unlike its predecessors, it allowed direct manipulation of text (versus going through a text compiler) and a consistent appearance in the document whether it was on paper or on the display—hence the saying "What you see is what you get." The arrival of this interface heralded a new era in computing because the user could more easily concentrate on the task at hand rather than on the irrelevant complexities of operating the machine.

In the 1980s, a graphical user interface popularized by the Apple Macintosh became a historic innovation. The Mac allowed the user to operate the machine through the manipulation of icons using a pointing device, or *mouse*. Each application or document was represented in a "window" on the display screen. Multiple windows could be opened at one time, allowing the operator to work on several documents or applications. Other graphical interfaces proved to be quite Mac-like, and although there is not one standard, all are similar. Dubbed the *WIMP* (*w*indows, *i*cons, *m*ouse, *p*ull-down menus), graphic interfaces began to provide a relatively consistent look for both users and software developers.

Such evolving GUI standards are a central requirement for open systems. The GUI represents the users' view of the computing environment. Having a standard graphic user interface is necessary to achieving three key benefits of open systems: providing productivity gains, extending the reach of information technology to more people, and

providing a standard platform to allow software developers to write
consistent and portable applications. Industry studies have found that a
GUI can double and triple productivity compared with a character-
based environment. A standard user interface also means that the time
and effort users spend learning additional applications is dramatically
reduced. A consistent interface eases both user training and support.

As various GUI products on the market converge, the "look and feel"
also transforms the job of the software developer. The *look* involves the
appearance of each application (i.e., the windows and dialogue boxes
should look the same). The *feel* refers to what happens when the user
interacts with the application. A standard GUI benefits developers who
write up to 80 percent of their code to support a specific user interface.
Rewriting applications for a different interface can, therefore, be a massive task. The solution lies in the development of consistent *application
programming interfaces* (APIs) which enable programmers to develop
an application for different (yet similar) GUIs. APIs also help programmers build consistent applications that integrate well with each other.

5. Software Development Tools

There have been many different versions of popular programming languages. By having standardized languages, it is easier for programmers
to develop software that is portable. For example, ANSI has adopted a
standard compiler (the software that turns programming into electric
impulses that computer hardware understands) for the popular "C"
programming language. This is a positive move toward language standardization.

Open systems will also extend to the tools and techniques used to define, create, test, and maintain applications. The increasing use of
CASE tools, for example, is emphasizing the advantages of using computer tools to develop software. The arrival of *repositories* further extends this support. Repositories enable software developers to share
data definitions and reusable modules of software. They also provide a
tracing mechanism from cradle to grave for the software development
process.

The open systems world offers programmers and software engineers
a variety of "portability tools" that will allow applications to be moved or
ported from one system environment to another. Utilities include:

- General utilities that enable directory comparisons, page-by-page file
  display, printable string location, and data compression

- Software development utilities such as cross-reference file creation
  and symbol tables for object files

- System management utilities such as batch programming process status reports

Beyond the user interface, other APIs define the interface between the application and the environment — for example, the operating system and communications environment. The APIs surround and insulate the application from the environment components. The developer pays attention to the APIs and what they do, and not to the underlying mechanics of the operating system. The result is that the underlying technology and programming become transparent. (See Chap. 7 for a more complete discussion.)

6. Systems Management Services

As computer systems and networks get more complicated, they need to be "managed." This includes the ability to instantly learn about problems on the network (for example, when a server in Tulsa fails), and then to be able to diagnose the problem and fix it from a remote location. Networks need to be reconfigured and altered, for example, when new user groups are introduced. Networks need to be monitored for response time and much more. Traditional system management approaches tend to apply to single computers, or at best to linked host computers — typically from only one vendor. With the rise of client/server computing, the computer becomes a network of different computers of different sizes and brands. This requires the adoption of systems management standards.

Standards in Other Areas

Standards are also evolving in various areas ranging from systems security, on-line transaction processing, real-time computing, and document architectures. Tracking such standards has now become an important requirement for any organization serious about making a transition to the new era.

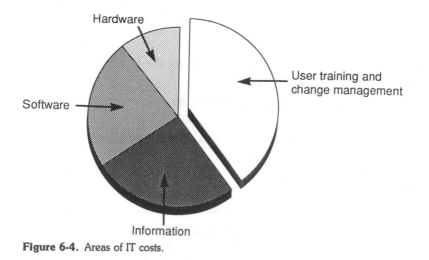

Figure 6-4. Areas of IT costs.

of an innovation into an organization. This is depicted in Fig. 6-4. This model presents a conservative view, as it could be argued that software, information, and human costs are successive orders of magnitude greater than hardware costs. The cost of all levels of the technology investment model would be dramatically affected if software applications were portable and technology were interoperable across a heterogeneous hardware platform.

Reduced Hardware Costs

The savings can be substantial if hardware becomes a commodity and it is purchased from the vendor that provides the best price/performance. Lacking account control, vendors compete more aggressively, and they accept lower margins. The customer benefits.

This is similar to other commodity markets such as wheat or oats. Since competing products have essentially the same characteristics, purchasers simply choose a supplier that has the best price for a given standard measure of the commodity. Similarly when software runs on the hardware of any supplier, the customer is free to select hardware from the supplier with the best price for a standard measure of computing performance.

In fact, the Strategies for Open Systems research showed that many customers conduct "benchmarks"—testing different equipment with the same software programs to see which performs the fastest.

Open systems also go hand in hand with microprocessor technology that has inherently better price/performance than the traditional semi-conductors found in today's mainframes and minicomputers.

In a sense, we now have a free market for computers.

Competition around a common set of standards has brought the research and development capability of the entire industry to focus on a single set of problems. Spectacular gains in hardware price/performance are the result. For example, symmetric multiprocessors based on commodity microprocessor chips can offer 10 times improvement in price/performance over mainframes when performing some tasks.

Hardware cost savings also result from scalable systems. Various parts of the organization may run common applications, yet require different-sized processors. With software that works on, or can be easily ported to, machines with various performance characteristics, the customer can select the optimal system for a given situation.

Some vendors have scalable systems within their proprietary product line. Scalability in a multivendor environment, however, provides much more scope across the entire range of processor alternatives. Scalability provides the flexibility to acquire and install systems of appropriate size and power for each branch, office, or organizational unit.

A good example is the replicated-site application, in which an organization has remote business sites performing similar business functions. Typically there is a need for computing capability on each site and networking between them—for example, between branches of a bank or stores in a retail chain. With an open strategy, where customers can make any given hardware purchase from any supplier, the cost savings tend to be spectacular. Kmart Corporation, for example, has saved tens of millions of dollars on a single purchase for its stores. Whether it is retail outlets for a budget chain, bases of a military organization, or processing plants of a paper box company, open systems is becoming the dominant strategy—justified on hardware savings alone.

Customers do not necessarily choose to be "promiscuous" with suppliers. In fact, they typically maintain one or a small number of key relationships. They still enjoy significant savings on hardware, however, because the relationship is based on the customer's free choice rather than software lock-in.

Reduced Software Costs

One of the biggest savings identified was from the reusability of software. According to Paul Strassmann, chief information officer of the U.S. Department of Defense (DoD), the biggest saving is realized from the reuse of standard software components and the consequent reduction in software maintenance expenses. The Defense Advanced Research Projects Agency conducted an in-depth economic analysis of open systems and concluded that the DoD can save tens of billions of dollars before the end of the decade through its Software Components Reuse Repository.

Software building blocks (or as Strassmann calls them, "Lego modules") are being "warehoused" as part of an open systems strategy. The warehouse already has over $50 million in software components manufactured to DoD standards, and they are reusable across different hardware platforms. Pilot programs in software reusability are achieving better than 60 percent savings in coding and in program maintenance through the recycling of quality-assured software modules across a wide range of applications.

A key question for the DoD is how quickly it can stock this softwarehouse and make its inventory easily accessible. Strassmann says $100 million is being invested to quickly "move software development from a craft cottage industry to a manufacturing environment."

Standards enable a software strategy based on the purchase of software packages rather than on costly custom software development. Note the mass packaged software market created by the MS-DOS standard. Scalability also eliminates the need to maintain multiple implementations of the same application across multiple technology architectures.

Moreover, because applications are not tied to a specific processor, there is no need to rewrite them when converting to a different machine. Application portability allows software to be moved from a smaller machine to a larger machine with minimal conversion—for example, from a microcomputer to a mainframe.

In the second era of information technology, software is often created in a business unit rather than in the central systems function. With application portability, such software can be made available to other parts of the organization.

Conversely, software portability can also encourage and enable the coordination and even centralization of software development and maintenance, again reducing costs. For example, these activities can be accomplished on a centralized machine and distributed to many different target machines. A unified development environment can produce substantial cost savings.

Efficiencies can also be gained by reducing the programming support required across incompatible systems. System modifications, updates, fixes, and the like can be done once and a new release easily installed across a heterogeneous hardware environment.

Reduced Information Management Costs

Often the costs of managing information are a substantial part of the overall technology investment. These include the costs of designing databases, entering and capturing data, establishing and maintaining data dictionaries, and managing information. Changes to the structure of this information resource, which result from such things as improvements in proprietary hardware, can pose significant costs and risk. Open systems tend to reduce these costs.

Information can be thought of in terms of two components—the medium and the message. Costs associated with the medium include the costs for hardware, software, and other inputs. Costs associated with the message may include organizing, formatting, arranging, structuring, and presenting information in a manner that is useful to users with particular problems in particular environments; adding value at points in the information life cycle by adding, deleting, and updating information content; and using or not using information. Costs associated with information management (the medium and the message) can be reduced. Many factors can affect the magnitude of these costs. Much of the expense incurred in these areas, however, arises during a system conversion. Because applications in an open systems environment are not tied to a specific processor, there is no need to rewrite them or fundamentally reorganize the data when converting to a different machine. Application portability allows software and information to be moved from a microcomputer to a mainframe with minimal conversion. In most instances the cost of porting applications from one system to another pales in comparison to the cost of converting the information.

Costs of Change Management and User Training

The most overlooked and, ironically, the largest components of system costs are the human costs of change. These are so poorly understood that they often do not appear at all on the cost side of a systems cost-benefit analysis. Overlooking these costs is a significant oversight by any organization trying to become profitable in a highly competitive market.

The main function of information technology is to transform human work and make employees and the organization more productive. IT can dramatically alter the design of jobs, work processes, organizational structures, corporate cultures, and individual skills. Systems require new human work procedures, working relations, work flow, job content, job descriptions, and organizational structure.

Open systems are also making computing easier for users. In an open systems world the user interface will become increasingly graphical and standardized. The look and feel of every application and tool will be similar no matter where it is in the environment. Applications that work in similar ways require less training and support. Open systems applications will also be able to interoperate with each other and provide a broad range of functions to the user.

A massive amount of work is required for both users and implementers every time a new system is introduced. Human "conversions" across disparate systems involve learning a new user interface, reorganizing personal work files, learning new applications and new work processes, changing management procedures, etc. In short, system changes mean that a tremendous amount of time and resources must be devoted to change management.

Experience has shown that the costs can be substantially reduced with a common platform, portable applications across heterogeneous hardware, and a common user interface.

Value-Added Benefits of Open Systems

In addition to cost reduction, the DMR research found that many organizations were adopting open systems to achieve "value-added" benefits.

Reduced Risk of Vendor Dependence

For example, the evidence is strong that an open systems strategy is less risky than a proprietary strategy. In turbulent times such as these, a vendor may no longer meet the criteria for which it was originally selected. A supplier can go out of business. It can be acquired by a larger company that discontinues product lines and architectures. Products can go off on a tangent that no longer corresponds to a customer's requirements. They can lose their technological edge or be leapfrogged by another vendor's hardware. Such changes can be extremely risky to a customer who is locked into a proprietary architecture. These risks are minimized when applications are portable.

The difference in environments is comparable to a market situation where a company depends on one major customer for its sales, while the other has a varied customer base. The auto parts manufacturer that depends on automakers may suddenly find its revenues and profits down with any slump in auto sales. The more diversified company is less vulnerable.

Easier Migration to New Technology

It is easier to migrate seamlessly to new technology with an open systems strategy. An enterprise is less tied to its installed base when a significant hardware innovation appears on the market. If the installed base is proprietary and the upgrade requires a significant change to the applications, the natural tendency is to be reluctant to change. The danger is that the enterprise will fall behind and not take advantage of new technologies. With open systems, the enterprise is in a position to always select the best technology.

Architectural Flexibility and Scalability

Another advantage of open systems is that users can incorporate organizational changes more easily. Changes that result from mergers or acquisitions or expansion of a company's operations, for example, may require that software be migrated from a mainframe to minicomputer environment or vice versa. An organization that was highly centralized may decide to adopt a decentralized business strategy that involves moving business units to new locations or linking divisions or new affiliates through local or wide area networks.

Often, organizational changes or growth may require the migration of software developed for a small machine to a larger machine; software developed centrally, or in a business unit, for other part(s) of the organization; or software developed in a parent organization for a new affiliate. Many of the organization studies found that open systems provide the flexibility to do this more easily than proprietary systems.

Software Integration

Standard operating systems, user interfaces, networking, database tools, and programming languages make it easier to integrate applications across a heterogeneous environment. Improvements in integration have been shown to enable business benefits. In the first era of proprietary computing, these corporate changes would be costly to the enterprise and a logistical nightmare for the poor MIS manager responsible for coordinating the transition.

Better Choice of Packaged Software

Independent software vendors (ISVs), in the face of dwindling markets for proprietary software, are shifting to open systems. Software for an open systems environment can be easily and cheaply ported to many different hardware platforms. This vastly increases the market potential for a new software product. For users, this means a wider range of packaged software to choose from. Organizations that don't take advantage of this software risk being bypassed by competitors.

Four Seasons Hotels: Open for Business

Four Seasons Hotels has approximately two dozen luxury hotels in major cities in North America and in London, England. New properties are being developed in other areas such as Mexico City, Paris, Singapore, and Tokyo. The company manages hotel properties on behalf of other ownership groups such as insurance or real estate companies. It has more than 7250 guest rooms and employs more than 10,000 people. The company has established a prominent position in its marketplace by operating medium-sized hotels in the high end of the market. The corporation's goal is to operate the finest hotel or resort in each of its locations. Although each property is distinctive, all have the same facility standards and quality of service. Each hotel, however, functions as a relatively autonomous business.

A key business objective for Four Seasons is to offer the highest guest service possible. The company's information systems are targeted to achieving this goal. Technology, for example, is used to perform accounting, reservations, property management, and other functions, freeing management personnel from the back office. The result is that management can be closer to the guests and offer personalized service. This attention should help maintain customer loyalty.

Information technology is also instrumental in ensuring repeat business by capturing information about guests and their unique requirements. This information is then made available across all company hotels.

As part of its strategy to bring information and technology tools closer to its operating units, Four Seasons Hotels is converting its corporate and hotel data processing to a decentralized open systems environment. Each hotel will have a minicomputer running the Unix operating system and a number of PCs all tied into a corporate network. By making this change the company hopes to achieve a greater competitive advantage and maximize its customer service.

The decision to implement new technology in an open systems environment was made for several reasons. The hotels and marketing departments were placing heavy demands for improved functionality to achieve corporate objectives and compete more effectively. At the same time, the existing technology base, which had become outmoded, could not accommodate or integrate with PCs that had proliferated across the chain. Furthermore, the company's computer vendor had fallen behind in technology, and given that the company's software would only work on that vendor's hardware, this posed a serious problem. Four Seasons management concluded that being locked into this particular vendor—or for that matter, any vendor in the future—presented a considerable business risk.

It was clear that a conversion—the rewriting of the company's software environment—was going to be required. Management concluded that this conversion should be the last. It decided to adopt an open strategy in which its investment in software could be ported to almost any vendor's hardware in the future.

The company needed to link applications and share common information across various remote sites, each of which perform identical functions. Rather than build custom interfaces for data transfer between heterogeneous proprietary systems as had been the policy in the past, it also made sense to create a common software environment across all systems. Such an environment would be the most effective way to provide the foundation for future system growth and meet the rapidly evolving requirements of hotel operations and marketing.

The strategy worked. The new open systems technology has given Four Seasons Hotels tremendous flexibility to quickly and easily expand its communication network and information technology resources to new locations. Because the connectivity and other technology barriers inherent in incompatible proprietary systems have been eliminated, the company has been able to simplify and thereby improve the effectiveness of its corporate communications.

All hardware was provided by one vendor, which was chosen from responses to an RFP. In its selection of a vendor, Four Seasons Hotels looked for a high-performance hardware commodity and a vendor who provided value-added service and support. Moreover, the Four Seasons relationship with the vendor is conditional on the evolution of the vendor's technology and directions being consistent with portable open systems software applications. If the current vendor doesn't keep up, Four

Seasons can easily switch to another vendor as its software is built on industry standards, not proprietary vendor equipment.

The technology base varies according to the size of the hotel. In small hotels the company installed a 386/486-based microcomputer with four attached terminals, six additional PC connections, and several printers. The hardware in the larger properties consists of a larger minicomputer, approximately 24 terminals, 10 PC connections, and 12 printers. Installation has occurred on a staged basis.

New corporate applications that were not possible in the previous proprietary environment include creating hotel guest histories, setting up group business and corporate travel agency databases, and doing financial planning.

Within a few years, all company systems including reservations will be running under an open systems environment. In addition, every hotel will have a minicomputer, PCs connected to the mini in a client/server architecture, and on-line dedicated or dial-up access between locations. While the future requirements of marketing and operations and other personnel are unknown, Four Seasons Hotels believes it is building a foundation on which systems can be quickly implemented and adapted to meet all its future needs.

The Changing Case
for Open Systems

The Four Seasons entry into open systems is typical of early adopters of open systems. The company chose an open strategy to achieve cost savings in hardware and software and also to harvest certain value-added benefits. Through experience, however, the company and others like it came to a broader understanding of the benefits of the new paradigm.

As expected, the data from the Strategies for Open Systems program showed that organizations are adopting open systems to reduce the costs of hardware, software, and support; reduce the risk of vendor lock-in; achieve a more rational procurement process in the public sector; and the like. The evidence is strong that substantial benefits are actually being achieved in these areas.

The emerging drivers for open systems go far beyond the traditional view of benefits. The DMR project team found massive evidence that the shift to open systems is part of the broader technology paradigm shift—driven by a business need for more flexible, powerful, integrated architectures that can meet a new set of business requirements.

The investigation identified a growing group of organizations that seek to use information technology to improve the effectiveness of products and services, link with customers and suppliers, and improve the effectiveness of managers and professionals. These organizations are most likely to be adopting open systems and, more broadly, the new paradigm. The old—as one participant described it, "Ceaucescu"—model of computing based on proprietary, host-based, rigid, top-down, unintegrated, vendor-controlled architectures is proving unable to meet the needs of a new global, volatile, competitive business world.

Essentially, many of today's enterprises are locked into the technology of the past—costly, inflexible, limited islands of technology. These system islands make it harder and harder to get the information necessary to run a complex business. They prohibit the integrated computer applications required for today's enterprise to transform itself for competitiveness. Moreover, these system islands are self-perpetuating as applications continue to grow, often at rates approaching 25 percent per year.

Rather than upgrading their current platform, leading organizations are setting out on a course of migrating to the new platform based on linked, interchangeable parts. The research shows that enterprises that are retooling invariably conclude that a new, dynamic, network-centered platform can only be achieved through the adoption of standards.

The challenge is one of planning for and implementing something new—an enterprisewide architecture that exploits the new technology paradigm.

A case in point is Procter & Gamble. According to Chief Information Officer Frank Caccamo, open systems enable the company to pursue key business strategies, for example, globalization; truly global management work is possible only through a global computer and communications infrastructure that ties the corporation together worldwide. This requires open standards. Caccamo says that streamlining business procedures is feasible only through "linking systems and databases to serve the business in a way that 'closed' systems were never designed to do."

Open systems also enable P&G to develop software applications "sooner and cheaper," he says. It also allows P&G to link up with customers and suppliers. "Most important...is the broad acceptance of open systems in the industry group in which we compete. That means our trade customers...suppliers who produce bottles and cartons for us...and across the 51 countries in which we do business." Overall, he concludes, "Open systems is right for Procter & Gamble's business. It is the way we operate. In fact it is part of our business strategy."

The Standards-Based Architecture

Many enterprises are attempting to define an enterprisewide architecture for computing. Just as today's office tower complex is designed according to an architecture, enterprise computer systems require a similar discipline and approach.

This was not much of an issue until recently. If used, the term *architecture* typically had limited meaning. An example would be the design of a single data-processing system, or a given vendor's product strategy or configuration — in hindsight perhaps better called a *product architecture*.

For most enterprises there was no architecture — that is, the disciplined organization of information technology implemented to realize a business vision. Rather, their architecture could be better described as the historical sum of various systems implemented over the years to address the business requirements of the day.

For the first time it is now feasible to plan for, and achieve, a coherent, evolutionary, enterprisewide architecture based on a vision of the needs and future of the enterprise. Information technology, standards, and the IT industry have matured to the point where it is possible to define an architecture, owned by the enterprise, and independent of the products of computer vendors. The goal of such an architecture is to provide a means of cost-effectively supporting enterprise-level requirements while at the same time providing a platform for user-driven innovation in the business application of technology across the organization.

This has led to a new view of enterprise architecture. *Architecture* is the underlying framework which defines and describes the technology platform required by a business to attain its objectives and achieve a business vision. It is the structure given to information, applications, organizational, and technological means and to the groupings of components, their interrelationships, and the principles and guidelines governing their design and evolution over time. Because such architectures must be based on standards, the Strategies for Open Systems team coined the term *standards-based architectures* to highlight the issue.

Open Standards and Standards That Are Opening

The research showed that there is widespread confusion among both users and vendors regarding standards. This is understandable given the complexity of the issue and the embryonic stage of IT standards diffusion. It is therefore generally realistic and appropriate to take a broad view of standards. The "standards" in a standards-based architecture can be:

- Open (vendor-neutral) or proprietary (controlled by a vendor or small group of vendors)
- De jure (specifications resulting from formal standards organizations) or de facto (specifications resulting from widespread acceptance in the marketplace)
- Documents (specifications of a standard) or products (actual implemented technology)

Such a broad definition of standards is necessary. While the research shows that the addition of vendor neutrality to standards provides considerable additional benefit, the adoption of proprietary standards (such as those in IBM's *systems application architecture,* or SAA) can, in many situations, facilitate the migration to a standards-based architecture.

This is necessary given the massive installed base of proprietary systems, the long-term challenge of coexistence and migration, and the fact that the dominant proprietary approach—SAA—is becoming more open. Consequently, a comprehensive standards-based architecture may include standards that are both open and opening. Further, the approach embraces product standards, not just specifications. Given the fact that standards-based products tend to lag the standards themselves, standards are a *necessary* but not *sufficient* condition to link architecture with actual implementation.

Open Systems Don't Simply Provide Benefits

Through standard components and interfaces, organizations can create a dynamic technology platform that can address constant change and unpredictable requirements. Standards enable architectures to be modular, vendor-independent, and loosely coupled with interchangeable parts.

Yet at the same time standards can enable the construction and evolution of a coherent, integrated technology environment as an enterprise backbone. Standards can also act as a basis for computer interaction with the external value chain of suppliers, consumers, stakeholders, and business partners.

Arguably, it is superficial to discuss the benefits of open systems. For example, in hindsight, it was superficial to discuss the benefits of a previous paradigm shift—viewing the world as flat to viewing the world as round. The case presented then was something like: "If we invest in the round world view and can exploit this new view we can reduce the costs of spices." The savings on spices of the paradigm shift turned out to be relatively minor, as will computer cost savings through open systems. The truly significant case lies elsewhere in most instances.

Standards in general, and open systems in particular, do not simply provide benefits. They are becoming an imperative for business success and survival in the 1990s and beyond.

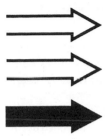

7

The Industrial Revolution in Software

- A customer service manager requests a small but important change be made in an order-processing system. The central IS group informs her that the change will take 8 months and cost $300,000. Everyone wonders if there isn't a better way.

- A CEO discovers that well over three-quarters of his entire IS expenditures goes to software development, and of that, half goes to maintain and update old programs rather than to create new ones. He gets depressed thinking about it.

- A major business magazine has a cover story about something called "object-oriented programming" which, the magazine proclaims, is finally making software simple to develop and use. CIOs around the country are called into their bosses' offices to discuss how to exploit this new technology.

- A huge software development project costing millions of dollars is late—90 percent complete for over 2 years—with a big budget overrun. The user awaiting the project is convinced it will never be completed.

- A group of end users develops a software application on networked workstations to support the business process in their work group. The system, which appears to work well, was done with 5 percent of the effort estimated by the internal information systems department to do the same thing on the central mainframe.

- An aerospace manufacturer sets forth on a course to reorient and re-educate thousands of programmer analysts and engineers in a completely new approach to software involving new methods, languages, tools, and procedures.

These examples are reflective of a third fundamental aspect of the technology paradigm shift—the transformation of software from a craft to manufacturing (see Fig. 7-1).

You should care a lot about the way software is developed in your organization, especially since software is a major portion of overall IT costs (typically from 60 to 90 percent). As hardware continues on its road to becoming a commodity, the software proportion will continue to grow. Moreover, as information technology plays a greater role in organization effectiveness, software costs will grow as a portion of overall business costs. Software, not hardware, is where business value is added.[1]

But, more important, it is software that enables computers to deliver value. It is becoming the backbone of business. It is the differentiator for competitive advantage. The usability, usefulness, and speed with which applications can be developed and changed are critical factors determining the effectiveness of the organization. As a result of this, the demand for software has outgrown the ability to deliver it. As the gap between demand and supply grows, a crisis in software has developed.

This affects every business user. Just as "war is too important an issue

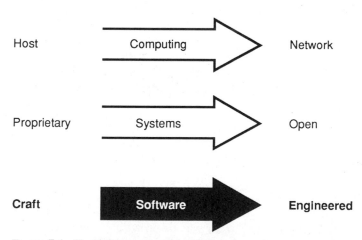

Figure 7-1. The shift to engineered software.

to be left to the generals," the issue of how your organization develops this precious asset should be important for every stakeholder.

Software as Art or Craft

Most of the people creating software in the era I enterprise were artisans, not unlike the craftspersons of preindustrial times. In the first era, a typical software program was a long list of instructions written line by line in an arcane computer language. Each piece of software was custom-designed and produced to meet the specific needs of users. Developers lacked access to software manufacturing tools and know-how (and up until the early 1980s, there wasn't much help out there!).

As the president of a software engineering firm observed in a recent article, the traditional software culture was project-based and tailored to one specific set of requirements. The "organizational unit impacted is usually the department directly affected by the project. The time frame is as short as it will take to produce the required solution. The goal is a program, or a few programs. The bricks of which this program is made are program elements: modules built for the occasion."[2]

The programming languages were low level, requiring many instructions to get the computer to do something relatively small—like displaying a set of data when requested. In an era when hardware was expensive, this made some sense because high-level languages are faster for programmers but require the computer to do more work. With powerful commodity hardware, continuing the practice is false economy.

Era I programs have many characteristics of art. Programs are complex and often big, or huge (involving thousands or even millions of lines of code). We estimate, for example, that somewhere upward of 150 billion lines of code are written in an era I language called COBOL. Like a musical score for a symphony, a single mistake (one note in the second cello part) could mess up the entire program. Finding the mistake and fixing it is typically a major challenge, and (unlike a symphony) by changing the cello part you're likely to have a ripple effect that messes up the tuba.

Moreover, the size of these intricate programs means that they take a long time to create. Like a symphony, the era I software composer could labor for years creating the work of art. Unfortunately, many software works are never completed—leaving many latter-day Schuberts with at least one unfinished symphony to their credit.

Adding something to the program is often a major problem due to the ripple effect. Each *part* of the software symphony is typically created from scratch, as is each *new* software symphony. The software you create to alphabetize cash receivables can't be reused to alphabetize electronic mail messages.

Ironically, today's musical composer who has adopted current information technology has it easy by comparison. Modern-day, era II musicians have musical workbenches that aid immeasurably in the creation, review, and testing of scores. Music as an art has developed standards for instrumentation, for notation, for sound, for harmony, and so forth. When the score is completed, the trumpet part can be played on trumpets of different brands.

Era I software composers had primitive tools. The era I software composer used a variety of different programming languages with different "dialects" and nonstandard compilers (which turn instructions into machine-readable code). Portability to different hardware platforms was lacking, and there was also no standard look and feel to the user. For example, errors in the accounts receivable application looked different from similar errors in the general ledger.

But software is not music. Business users want good, consistent, integrated functionality that helps solve business problems. They want it delivered to them fast and at a low cost. And they want to have the flexibility to make changes quickly and inexpensively. Sure they want esthetics. But they would like to avoid learning a new art form every time they use a new application.

Seven Problems with Software as Art

Seven important problems arise from the era I approach.

1. *There is limited reusability of software.* It is almost as unthinkable to reuse a piece of era I software as it is to reuse a section of a painting. The result is that software costs a fortune and takes a long time to build. In the new business environment, this is unacceptable. Users need applications in days, not years. Moreover, because every new application consists of new software, there are typically extensive quality problems.

2. *Software maintenance is a 4000-pound gorilla.* In the analogy presented by Kathleen Melymuka,[3] the majority of funds spent on information systems are allocated to feeding or subduing the gorilla—just keeping things working—that is, fixing and changing software after it

has been implemented. IBM (it ought to know) estimates that 80 percent of the working hours of IS professionals is spent on maintenance of software. The problem is that era I software is not based on interchangeable parts that can easily be replaced, fixed, or updated. Because of its complexity and lack of modularity, it often has serious quality problems. The consequence is that most investments in systems maintain the past rather than build for the future. In the United States these investments translate into tens of billions of dollars annually. As Melymuka's excellent article says, "the gorilla won't go away, it can't be subdued, and it certainly cannot be ignored." This has left organizations looking for ways to make it technically feasible to shrink and recondition the gorilla into an ape of a lighter kind.

3. *Systems are islands of technology.* Symphonies don't talk to each other. They are stand-alone works of art. Linking two era I systems is a massive undertaking. Linking era I systems across an entire enterprise is typically not feasible. Linking era I systems with external enterprises is unthinkable because of the complexities involved. This situation is not acceptable given the needs for enterprise integration and external reach discussed earlier.

4. *Users must make a huge personal investment in learning different, inconsistent, and poorly designed systems.* Each piece of art has different esthetics—a different look and feel—typically determined by the software developer, as opposed to experts in person–machine interaction. A user accessing six applications often learns six ways to display information or print a document. This represents one of the huge hidden costs of era I software: a massive investment of human time.

5. *Hardware is expensive due to platform dependence.* Era I applications typically work on a mainframe *or* a minicomputer *or* a workstation. They are not portable across platforms or across vendor brands. Customers therefore pay the high cost of traditional semiconductor technology for mainframe and minicomputer applications. Customers also pay the high margins of proprietary systems, rather than purchasing the commodity hardware available through open systems standards.

6. *Only programmers can create programs.* Because of the highly specialized nature of era I software development, such activity is restricted to highly skilled professionals. A different approach, however, is possible. For example, business people use spreadsheets to develop budgets and various computer models that would have been considered data-processing applications in era I. Such applications, which were designed and developed by programmers in era I, were costly and time-

consuming. What took months yesterday now takes minutes using a spreadsheet. The spreadsheet was the tip of the iceberg. Today, new tools and approaches enable end users to quickly link together elements of a system which are prepackaged—either internally or as products from software companies.

7. *Software focuses on process.* Era I applications looked at automating existing or projected business processes or functions. (Remember those flowcharts!) A better way to design an application is to examine the business decisions and cluster the data (or information) to support this decision making. Sadly, we have learned that process-oriented (rather than data-oriented) systems are more costly to maintain. The gorilla is gaining weight!

These seven problems create a significant obstacle to success for the new enterprise. The new business reality makes this situation unacceptable in terms of cost, time to develop applications, quality, integration, and usability. Moreover, it places impossible demands on software developers themselves.

The Shift: From Craft to Manufacturing

Fred Brooks, author of the seminal work on the issue of software called *The Mythical Man-Month: An Essay on Software Engineering*,[4] argued some years ago that there is no silver bullet that will kill the software werewolf:

> Of all the monsters that fill our folklore, none terrify more than werewolves, because they transform unexpectedly from familiar into horrors. For these, one seeks bullets of silver which can magically lay them to rest. The familiar software project, at least as seen by the non-technical manager, has something of this character; it is usually innocent and straightforward, but is capable of becoming a monster of missed schedules, blown budgets and flawed products. So we hear desperate cries for a silver bullet—something to make software costs drop as rapidly as computer hardware costs do."[5]

There may be no *one* silver bullet, but there is a fundamental shift that promises to ameliorate the software crisis. An alternative to software as craft or art is emerging. The transformation is roughly equivalent to the changes of the early industrial age in manufacturing. Software is going through its own industrial revolution.

In the 1850s, rifles were built by hand from parts made by highly skilled craftsmen. The craftsmen created each rifle from scratch. Each rifle was slightly different. If it broke, a part had to be manufactured by a gunsmith to fit it. In 1860, Winchester Rifle started using standard-sized parts to assemble its rifles. Manufacturing production increased tenfold, and Winchester rapidly became the "standard" rifle of the wild west days. Workers began to specialize in designing the parts, manufacturing them, and assembling the rifles. The major thrust of this significant change was that the worker was not manufacturing a custom part, but rather manufacturing for inventory.

Henry Ford took the interchangeable parts idea the next step with the creation of the assembly line. Each worker added a part or component to the Model T chassis as it moved down the assembly line. His production costs were reduced enough so he could sell the Model T profitably for a few hundred dollars. Importantly, by improving the quality of the subassembly, Ford improved the quality of the automobile.

The same kinds of productivity and quality improvements are possible by moving to a standard production model of software. Using standards, well-machined tools, new disciplines and methods, production environments, interchangeable parts stored in the organization's *softwarehouse,* and additional parts purchased off-the-shelf from software vendors, it is now possible to manufacture software.

The manufacturing analogy, however, is imperfect. Software production is manufacturing with a difference. The software production worker still requires a high degree of creativity to fabricate both individual parts and broader systems. Similarly, the business professional's creativity in combining various software modules into an application that delivers business value is critical. Nevertheless, the writing is on the wall for the do-it-from-scratch software programs of the first era.

The goal is not to *replace* human creativity by discipline, methods, and tools, but rather to *extend* the creativity, ingenuity, and capacity of programmers and eventually all knowledge workers through the approaches and technology of the new paradigm. As Peter Drucker prophetically indicated back in 1964,

> Any first attempt at converting folklore into knowledge, and a guessing game into a discipline, is liable to be misread as a downgrading of individual ability and its replacement by a rule book. Any such attempt would be nonsense, of course. No book will ever make a wise man out of a donkey or a genius out of an incompetent. The foundation in a

discipline, however, gives to today's competent physician a capacity to perform well beyond that of the ablest doctor of a century ago, and enables the outstanding physician of today to do what that medical genius of yesterday could hardly have dreamt of. No discipline can lengthen a man's arm. But it can lengthen his reach by hoisting him on the shoulders of his predecessors. Knowledge organized in a discipline does a good deal for the merely competent; it endows him with some effectiveness. It does infinitely more for the truly able; it endows him with excellence.[6]

There are six main themes to the new approach.

Theme One: The Rise of "Lego" Software

A fundamentally different approach—called *object-oriented software*—is now a reality. In the first era, as explicit in the term *data processing*, software applications processed separate "data" in various data files or databases. Object-oriented systems combine data and programs into chunks that are like objects in the real world. That is, object-oriented systems represent information in units called *objects* which consist of data and a set of operations to manipulate them. An object can be an invoice, a filing cabinet, a type of employee, or a computerized representation of a part in a jet engine. Each includes data and logic enabling it to do certain things. For example, the engine object includes data about the characteristics of the engine and software that determine the kinds of things that the engine can do, such as rotate in a certain direction.

The outcome of an object orientation to software is reusable software elements that can be used for large numbers of applications:

> The unit is beyond an individual project, a department, a company and sometimes an entire industry. The time frame is long-term. More than a program, the goal is to build systems. The bricks are software components, which distinguish themselves from mere program elements by having a value of their own, independently of the context for which they were initially designed.[7]

You will now hear people talking about *object-oriented programming* (OOP), object-oriented languages, object-oriented databases, and object-oriented user interfaces. Because object-oriented systems group data and the operations performed on them into objects, they dramatically reduce the amount of code a programmer must create. Each object has the ability to receive messages from other objects, store this information, and perform a limited number of operations based on the data. As such, they are intelligent (they contain logic as well as data), enabling them to link with other objects. For example, a banking system could have an object called *customer* that includes the data as well as the programming needed for a wide range of operations, such as calculating balances, evaluating credit level, and sending promotion material. This object could then be used to build capabilities related to handling various accounts: mortgages, life insurance, credit cards, cash management accounts, and ATM cards—all of which are also objects. A change in the customer's address would apply across the board, as would an event in one account that could affect credit risk in the others.[8]

The appeal of an object-oriented approach is that information in each object can be reused repeatedly in a variety of applications. Classes of objects are arranged in a hierarchy and based on principles of inheritance. Each object inherits the general characteristics of the one above it, leaving only the differences that apply to a specific application to be coded.

A standard word-processing program allows lawyers, accountants, and marketing managers to use and modify stock paragraphs from a variety of databases to compose, or build, specific client letters. In an object-oriented environment, the programmer can save time and effort by choosing and, if necessary, modifying one or a combination of objects to build a new software application. By merging two or more existing objects, a developer inherits all the functions and data of the objects; these can then be used to build the new application. Importantly, the developer inherits all the expertise of those who used and improved the object in the past. We now start to retain accumulated experiences and improve the quality of the resulting new application.

This object-oriented approach is, in effect, a form of standardization. The software developer, like a house builder, can choose from a wide selection of doors, instead of designing one for each new house. The time previously spent in this often redundant and unproductive phase of application development is now being spent on new development requirements and better design approaches.

One of the primary benefits of this approach is to significantly reduce the number of design and programming errors by reducing the complexity and programming operations required to develop an application. Using objects to develop software programs also has the potential of increasing the productivity of the developers of software by reducing development life-cycle costs and increasing software portability. The speed at which new programs can be created is accelerated. This is a benefit that is especially valuable to developers of large and complex systems and applications. In addition, when something breaks down, it is possible to get a new part, rather than having to undertake the cumbersome maintenance and repair work of the massive, intertwined era I program. All these advantages will translate into less expensive and more timely application programs.

Recognizing these potential benefits, the major database management system vendors are now supporting object-oriented programming. In these systems, objects that represent complex and highly structured data are stored within a database. These data, which were extremely difficult to store in a conventional database, can be easily accessed and manipulated in the object-oriented environment.

Theme Two: Software Goes Gooey

In daily life, humans take actions on objects to accomplish tasks. We turn off the alarm clock, turn on the shower, pull on our underwear, load up the coffee machine, open the car door, turn on the ignition. Such directness and simplicity are now accomplished with computer systems through the *graphic user interface* (GUI). Interestingly, object concepts appeared at the level of the interface between user and machine (GUI) before they had matured in the world of the programmer (OOP).

For example, rather than entering the electronic mail application, a user with a graphic interface can take action on objects: send the letter, spreadsheet, voice message, auto part, filing cabinet, or whatever. The send command works the same way for all objects. The print, file, delete, calculate, and myriad other commands also work the same way for all objects. This significantly reduces the requirement for the user to learn the unique ways of accomplishing these activities in various applications. Software is not only friendlier; it is inviting. The rise of the GUI also profoundly changes the way in which software is developed. It is also at the heart of the transformation of the software industry and a key area of standards in the shift to open systems. As explained earlier, in the first era each software development team developed its own home-grown user interface for each application it developed.

The development of the first GUI occurred two decades ago. In 1974, researchers at Xerox's *Palo Alto Research Center* (PARC) developed the first wysiwyg ("*what you see is what you get*") interface for word processing. Dubbed "Bravo," the word processor was the first to allow direct manipulation of text instead of going through a text compiler. It provided a consistent appearance to the document, whether it was on paper or on the display.

The creation of this interface heralded a new era in computing. The user could concentrate on the task at hand instead of having to deal with the irrelevant complexities of operating the machine. The GUI allowed users to operate the machine through the manipulation of icons using a pointing device such as a mouse. Each application or document was represented in a window on the display screen. Multiple windows could be opened at any time, allowing the operator to work on several documents and/or applications.

From the perspective of the software developer, the GUI has several important components. An *application programming interface* provides the system calls that an application uses to manipulate the windows, actually write something on the screen, or react to a user's mouse click. An *imaging model* describes how graphics and text will be displayed on the screen within each window. This model is where character fonts and basic graphic objects are defined. A *desktop manager* is essentially a metaphor for the physical world and includes various objects and procedures for actions such as opening, copying, and naming files. The ultimate goal of the GUI is consistency, simplicity, and reusability for both users and developers. We should note that complete user interface consistency across applications may not be appropriate because some interfaces may be better fitted for some applications than others.

A growing range of input devices is extending the GUI concept. For example, in pen-based systems, which don't use a keyboard, a digitizing pad recognizes handwriting and interprets handwritten data. Our research indicates an explosion in the use of these newly arrived devices due to the need for data capture in situations where keyboards are awkward.[9] Another input device that is growing rapidly is voice annotation and recognition technology. Although it has lagged behind the integration of data, text, and image, voice input is becoming a central component of the new computing environment that must be addressed by software developers.

Theme Three: Software Can Be Engineered

A more disciplined approach to software development, one that incorporates engineering principles used in other industries, is emerging as part of the solution. *Software engineering* has become a cost-effective way to enhance existing software and fulfill the demand for new programs to meet continually changing enterprise needs.

Establishing engineering principles has involved building better tools for automating and redefining the development process, creating more building blocks to assist in the creation of future programs, and setting up more efficient management and control policies. The move to software engineering is establishing a software delivery framework that replaces traditional ad hoc software development. It brings to the industry a discipline that previously didn't exist. Although the notion of software engineering has been around for some time, it had limited impact when applied to the construction of era I software. A much broader change—the shift from craft to manufacturing—is required.

In the mid-1980s, several software companies started work in establishing a new software delivery framework. Some focused on techniques (How do I model this object?), some on the tool (What diagraming notation do I use?), and some on understanding the software process. For example, DMR Group created a software process (called DMR Productivity Plus) that set the cornerstone for software engineering. Digital Equipment Corporation saw the long-term value of this approach and adopted this process (as did MIT, Boeing, and others) within its organization.

In the late 1980s, IBM introduced its AD/Cycle environment as part of its 1990s architecture SAA. This was instrumental in popularizing the notion of engineering and manufacturing software. IBM argued that similar to flexible manufacturing, in which modules or components are premanufactured and assembled to meet specific needs, new software development environments would transform the process of creating and maintaining software. Soon after IBM's announcement, Digital went public with a comparable offering called COHESION.

Combined with the other key themes in the shift from art to manufacturing, software engineering provides the discipline required to realize the shift. A software engineering approach defines the development sequence, the order of required deliverables, and the quality controls. It provides a framework within which a project can be assessed on an ongoing basis and changes made in a more cost-effective way. In the end, it provides a foundation for building and maintaining better software.

Software engineering involves three important elements:

- *Methods.* These provide the basic framework and design instructions for developing software. Methods can include project planning, system and software requirements analyses, data structure design, program architectures, and program testing activities.

- *Tools.* These are the system tools used to develop the software. For example, to achieve the design of a data structure, a series of well-defined techniques can be executed. A tool supports these techniques. In more sophisticated environments many of these tools are fully automated.

- *Procedures.* These allow the enterprise to control the process of software development. Procedures may include specific monitoring activities or development project milestones.

The functions and role of these three elements in a software development project depend on the application technology. For example, the software engineering process differs for an *on-line transaction processing* (OLTP) system and a decision support system. Then within technology type, what is the application type? Does the project require reengineering the workplace? Does it mean making minor changes to the workplace but renovating the technology? Within this application type, the user can now focus on the application approach. For example, development projects may take a systematic sequential approach that proceeds from analysis and design to testing and maintenance. Standards and guidelines are established to define the major development components. These standards can then be customized to meet specific project requirements. Another approach involves prototyping or creating a model of the proposed software. The model can be in a conceptual form or can be a working prototype. Alternatively, a software package could be acquired. Frequently, the software approach for larger projects is a mixture of approaches.

Companies are also implementing fourth- or "four-and-a-half-" generation techniques and procedures for software development. This approach makes the development process more visible to the software engineer. The intermediate software components can now be tested by software teams before they are stored in the softwarehouse (quality becomes more explicit in the process). In some cases, the software process has embedded automated tools that translate the desired results into source code to produce those results. These approaches involve software tools that automatically generate source code based on the developer's specifications, bypassing traditional programming. All these innovative methods represent a variety of software engineering approaches designed to improve the quality of the software that is created and to reduce the price of developing new programs.

Software engineering disciplines hold one of the keys to the migration from craft to effective manufacturing environments. As put by Stan Rolland of DMR:

> I think that one of the fundamental differences between craftsmanship and manufacturing is the intuitive approach to quality that is applied by the craftsman and which is possibly compensated by life-long learning through experience and his close relationship to his client. To get consistent and predictable quality results in a manufacturing environment, modern statistical process control must be applied. We will not

be able to get consistent results in software development and evolution until we can apply to these processes the scientific quality control principles currently applied in other industries.[10]

Theme Four: Computers Can Help Develop Computer Systems

The idea of computer-aided software engineering (CASE) has also been around for some time, but it was—as Mark Twain said about the weather—something everyone is talking about but no one is doing anything about. With the maturing of the other elements of the shift however, CASE is becoming feasible. There is a growing case for CASE.

Whereas software engineering focuses on discipline and structure required to obtain economical and reliable software, the objective of CASE is to support the consistent use of software engineering principles through the use of a variety of automated computer aids. CASE is not just a technology. It involves a fundamental change in the process of creating software.

The appeal of CASE is that it enables software developers, through the use of coordinated computer aids, to apply software engineering principles, methods, techniques, and concepts such as parallel processing, object orientation, and reusable code more easily. All these developments take advantage of or are based on a variety of automated tools that support software life-cycle processes such as software specification, design, configuration control and testing, and in some cases code generation and maintenance.

CASE supports users involved in all essential software development life-cycle functions. CASE users can communicate with each other as well as with various technology platforms. CASE also provides support tools that assist analysts, designers, programmers, and those responsible for system testing and maintenance. It offers enterprises the capability to develop and store all documents and code for a particular application or for an entire system.

A CASE approach to software development means that software needs, analysis, design, development, and implementation are coordinated using a computer-based life-cycle framework. Comprehensive management tools control and support the entire environment. The major benefit of this approach to software engineering is that it can optimize reusable code and concurrent processing. It also fosters controlled rather than ad hoc software development environment. This allows developers to create and maintain both small and large software systems from a variety of reusable components. Through the use of an integrated set of computer aids, CASE provides the factory approach to software engineering and development.

Benefits from CASE include increased productivity for software analysts, designers, and programmers and higher-quality software. These result in reduced maintenance costs and improved system performance for users. CASE technology offers developers a wide selection of innovative software tools that can be used as automated components of an engineering process. The end result is more efficient and cost-effective software development.

Theme Five: Rise of the Software Parts Industry

The independent software industry enabled by the PC (and later, open systems) is taking a turn as well. The software industry is becoming a *parts manufacturing industry:* building key parts which any user, work group, enterprise, or interenterprise partnership may acquire to build its customized computing environment. Correspondingly, the software market is becoming a standard-parts marketplace where customers with high-level problems to solve look for low-level, pluggable software components to assemble into higher-level solutions.[11]

The so-called horizontal applications (usable across various industries such as banking, manufacturing, or government) of the 1980s, for example, word processing and spreadsheets, were an early sign of this trend. Rather than creating financial models or budgets from scratch, customers used a spreadsheet to leapfrog them 98 percent of the way. The trend continued with the creation of software — such as databases — that could be *used to create software* customized for a given organization. Now with object orientation, the forced consistency of the GUI, the fabrication discipline of software engineering, and the machinery of CASE, the preconditions are there for the software industry to move further along the path. Customers will care about how the parts are manufactured as much as tradesmen care how bricks are manufactured — very little. What counts is the interface specifications — how the software, or bricks, can interact with other software, or bricks.

Theme Six: You Are Becoming a Programmer

A fundamental change is occurring in *who* will develop software. A division of labor is occurring in the software industry. Independent software companies build tools and interchangeable parts. Internal IS groups (centrally located or dispersed) manage the internal softwarehouse—ensure standards, procedures for use, and the like. They also do the software engineering to integrate parts into large, complete business solutions.

Increasingly, however, software development will be in the hands of business users who, through linking icons together on the screen, or simply talking to their computer, will create business solutions to their problems. For example, a work group needs a new application to support its newly designed business process. The application consists of a number of objects that correspond to objects in their real world linked together. This is the real challenge of the object designer: to provide the user with powerful, but simple, generic, but context-sensitive, operations on objects in a fashion similar to that of the print or send operations.

It is not possible to meet the growing demand with business as usual. The powerful economic forces for business value through information technology are pushing for a new view of software. This is having the effect of tapping the genius of millions to create the kind of applications that can add a new world of value to information technology. It also has important implications for today's programmers.

As Al Sutherland, an IS manager at the Weyerhaeuser company told us: "I've told my programmers that they are pony express riders. In the future the best of them will be those who can help and coach users in developing software rather than doing it themselves."

However, in the short term, programmers should not fear elimination of their profession. This is a transformation that will continue well into the twenty-first century. Further, the job of programmers will evolve as technical expertise and knowledge grow and change. Today's artisans are tomorrow's engineers.

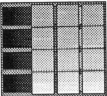

PART 3

The Transition

> *"We, at American Airlines, are in the process of making the shift to era II. Conceptually we are there. If you understand conceptually that the new paradigm is the goal, the big issue is how to get there."* MAX HOPPER,
> SENIOR VICE PRESIDENT
> FOR INFORMATION SYSTEMS,
> AMERICAN AIRLINES

The DMR research identified a growing desire to make the transition to the new paradigm. However, when asked what were the major barriers, clients repeatedly raised the question "How do we get from here to there?"

Part 3 tackles this issue. Given the major shifts in application of information technology as discussed in Part 1 and the enabling shifts in technology as presented in Part 2, it is not surprising to find corresponding shifts in the way we approach planning and organization in the new era and leadership for it. This section explores five primary themes:

1. The challenge of achieving a new vision of the business enabled by the new technology paradigm

2. The new issue of reengineering the business

3. The role of architecture as a means to retool information technology to embrace the new paradigm

4. The functional realignment of the information systems organization required by the new era

5. The challenge of leadership in making the transition

Part 3 has been organized into five chapters corresponding to each of these themes.

Chapter 8 explores the integration of IT planning with the strategic directions of the business. Effective use of IT requires a common vision of where the business is going and an understanding of the supportive role that technology will play. The days are numbered for the old "IT strategic plan" which was developed separately from the overall business strategy process and which focused on budgetary planning for IT expenditures. New approaches must integrate IT investments with strategic business initiatives.

Chapter 9 explains why the new technology paradigm is required to create the new enterprise. It also presents principles and guidelines for reengineering the business. This occurs at three levels—redesigning business processes, restructuring organizations and the enterprise, and recasting our relationships with external organizations. Traditional system implementations often resulted in automating the current ways of conducting business—otherwise known as "paving the cowpath." Traditional business process redesign did not appreciate the role of the new paradigm in redesigning work systems—otherwise known as "building new cowpaths." The new reengineering creates new IT-enabled processes in support of team structures that significantly impact performance. This chapter discusses a new approach that can move beyond the traditional as well as presents the story of an organization that succeeded in doing so.

Chapter 10 looks at establishing an IT architecture as the basis for driving systems development and deployment of technology. In many ways, this is an entirely new approach to systems planning, which takes a holistic view of identifying requirements and opportunities. It discards the project orientation of earlier methods in favor of modeling the many relationships and connections that exist across application areas. Architecture planning addresses the opportunities for leveraging commonality, making use of shareable and reusable components. These components include information, applications, and technology.

Chapter 11 tackles the issue of realigning the information systems function with the business. The IS department grew out of the needs of the first era. Many organizations are concluding that it is poorly equipped to meet the needs of the second. There are new strains on IS, new principles that must be determined to realign IS, and new approaches for allocating functional responsibilities across IS and user organizations. This sets the stage for the final discussion.

Chapter 12 confronts the issue of leadership. Our research has shown that lack of effective leadership is the largest single impediment to making the transition. Different kinds of leadership are required to make the transition, and a deficit in any area can be lethal, having toxic repercussions for the enterprise. Moreover, leadership can, and should, come from throughout the organization—in a hierarchy that is in transformation, from top to bottom. A controversial role—the chief information officer—has been established by many companies to help achieve leadership. But does this make sense? The chapter also investigates the issues of achieving awareness and commitment, the broader changes occurring in the computer industry, and the even broader issues raised by the paradigm shift for nations and governments.

8

Achieving
a Shared,
New Vision

- An international survey of CEOs finds that many question the value of their considerable investments in information technology.

- A disgruntled general manager wonders why the prioritized list of systems projects developed by the department managers bears no resemblance to her view of business priorities.

- Members of a strategic planning study team for a telecommunications company discover that programs to automate and reengineer their network facilities over the past decade have significantly lowered the direct costs of communication services. The costs of supporting and servicing the customers (as well as other overheads) have become the dominant cost factor. The team members focus their efforts on finding ways to drastically improve productivity in these service areas.

- The marketing department complains that this is the third time in 2 months that it has been asked to participate in a study. Why are the quality improvement committee, new organizational design task force, and strategic systems planning team all asking similar questions?

These scenarios reflect the enormity, complexity, and sensitivity of the transition to the second era which is under way. Achieving a vision for business initiatives and strategies enabled by the new technology paradigm will certainly prove challenging.

As the information age accelerates into its second era, organizations do not have the luxury of making a gradual progression over two centuries of progress as the industrialists have done. Paradoxically, the very technologies the organizations are trying to master have greatly compressed the time frame for innovation. They have also raised the stakes for success or failure.

Through our research and consulting to organizations in transition, we have come to a number of conclusions regarding the challenge of making the transition. These have been packaged into a framework to define the key *thrusts* and *plateaus* in planning and managing the transition.

The Era II Transitioning Framework

There are three transformation thrusts which every enterprise must undertake to move to the new era.

The first of these thrusts is to *reengineer the business*. This occurs at all levels of the organization from work group and business process, to enterprise, to relationships with external organizations. Organizations must be prepared to drastically change and streamline operations to change the cost base, if appropriate, and improve effectiveness. This requires a critical reassessment of what is being done and why. As advocate Michael Hammer proclaims, "Don't automate, obliterate."[1] New and evolving means of producing, distributing, and servicing products must be investigated. Programs to move to a team structure and the open networked organization must be undertaken. Customers and suppliers and distribution channels must be viewed as partners in a value network upon which all depend.

The second key thrust is to *retool the information technology infrastructure* within the organization or enterprise. We must determine how best to deploy the enabling effects of the new technology paradigm so as to provide an infrastructure that allows for continual improvement of knowledge and service worker productivity. The architecture and design of information technologies are as critical to success in the information age as the placement and design of factories were in the industrial age. The available information resources are equivalent to the raw materials of production. The communication networks linking computers and information bases to their users are analogous to the vital transportation infrastructure supporting industry and trade. The importance of developing the skills and motivation of the industrial workers to deliver quality cost-effective goods now has a parallel in developing the skills and motivation of knowledge and service workers to deliver quality business results.

This leads to the third key thrust in making the transition, to *realign the*

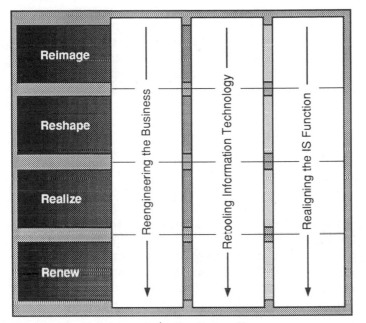

Fig. 8-1. The four plateaus for making the transition.

IS function with the business. It is no longer advisable or even possible to keep all of the IS specialists under tight central guard. As the technology, applications, and information become dispersed throughout the organization, approaches to deploying the human resources required to plan, design, build, and operate must be rethought. Just as industry has learned (although it took a long time) to involve the front line workers in quality circles and in planning for improvements in production, the new user of information technology and the user organization have a key role to play in conceiving, implementing, operating, and evolving the new.

These three thrusts are not independent. In fact, they are tightly linked. The importance of aligning these thrusts is illustrated in the transition framework shown in Fig. 8-1. The three thrusts are the subjects of Chaps. 9–11.

To make the transition — to move from conception to reality — each of these thrusts must move through the four plateaus shown in Fig. 8-1. During each plateau, the thrusts are aligned or synchronized to support a common business result.

1. Achieve Vision (Reimage)

The first plateau is to *achieve a common vision of the desired nature of the business.*[2] This plateau requires the creation of a strategy that positions the organization in its future business context, sets the direction for reengineering the business, identifies the opportunity and role of IT in fulfilling this vision, and identifies the need to restructure the IS function. As important as the creation of a vision is its communication. Visionaries must involve key players to gain organizationwide commitment to the new vision.

2. Structure the Solution (Reshape)

The next plateau for making the transition is to *structure the solution.* This is the role for the architects, who have a broad base of knowledge and experience and who can translate the vision into a workable set of blueprints to enable construction to begin. As with their counterparts in the building profession, the architects of business, information technology, and organizations create models to achieve the desired results. They must define the appropriate components, understand their interrelationships, and make decisions on how to structure and place these components to create the best solution. The architects must be skilled at relating to the many and diverse interests involved in (and impacted by) the changes they are planning.

3. Develop and Deploy (Realize)

The third plateau is to *develop and deploy the planned changes* throughout the affected areas of the organization. This is the role of the construction crew with its many specialized building and implementation capabilities. As with any major engineering project, there are many parallel and interdependent subprojects and activities that require the overall coordination of the prime contractor or senior project director. Typically, the architects identify migration stages that define different delivery capabilities based on the organization's ability to absorb change and to finance and provide resources for the various delivery projects. Each of these stages typically involves work-systems redesign, user training, development of new applications, building of related information bases, deployment of necessary technology, and establishment of the required operational support capabilities.

4. Continuously Improve (Renew)

The final plateau for making the transition involves *the ongoing measurement and operation of the reengineered business processes, and supporting IT infrastructure, with a focus on their continuing evolution and improvement*. As with quality circles in manufacturing, this requires the active participation of the users of the new work systems to identify areas for improvement. The goal is to establish a continuous learning organization in which the support functions perform a coaching role to the empowered user. The result is a partnership, where knowledge and service workers, in addition to production workers, collaborate to achieve the common goals. This requires the ongoing measurement of key performance indicators to define quantity and quality targets and results. These desired improvements and benefits are the glue that connects the four plateaus of transition planning and provides the basis for evolving the work systems and related information technology and support infrastructure.

How can you begin to lead and execute the transition—to reach the first plateau? The remainder of this chapter looks more closely at plateau 1—achieving a common vision. This is the domain of direction setting and strategy. But first it's important to discard some more era I baggage.

The Demise of the IT Strategic Plan

You've probably heard of it. No doubt you were interviewed for one—to determine *your* information requirements. If you saw one, it was likely a thick document. It is unlikely that you read one. Most were read by a select group of technologists. Often the document was read only by the authors—members of the IS department or consultants on contract to the IS department. The document was the result of a planning event—that is, the creation of the document was a project with a beginning and an end. The document focused on internal IT issues, not the market or customer. Systems issues tended to be grouped like an organization chart. The document addressed data-processing or management information needs and opportunities, and included a cost-benefit analysis or investment plan showing the payback for the IT investment. The time between creating the document and harvesting the benefits from implemented systems was typically long. It was called the *IT strategic plan*.

While such documents served a useful purpose in the past, they are being obviated by the new business environment, changes in our enterprises, and the new technology paradigm. As a result, there are a number of shifts occurring in how to go about achieving a vision for IT-enabled business transformation. These are illustrated in Fig. 8-2 and discussed below.

	Era I: The IT Strategic Plan	Era II: Continuous Learning Action
1. Relationship to business strategy	Separate or tenuously linked ⟶	Part of business strategy
2. Ownership	The IT function ⟶	The business function
3. Process	Planning event ⟶	Continuous learning
4. Domain	Internal ⟶	Integrated internal and external
5. Structure	Reflects the organization chart ⟶	Based on client/service model
6. Information class	Data processing ⟶	Multimedia information processing
7. Time frame to results	Long cycle ⟶	Quick hits

Fig. 8-2. The demise of the era I IT strategic plan.

How can your organization achieve a shared vision that repositions IT in a strategic business context? There are seven guidelines that correspond to the seven shifts in planning shown in Fig. 8-2.

1. Achieve Strategic Synergy

IT considerations are becoming part of business strategies. The strategic use of IT has been a popular theme in many business and technical publications over the past few years; yet most organizations are still struggling with linking technology plans with business plans. One fundamental problem lies in traditional approaches that separate responsibilities and processes for strategic business planning from those for IT strategic planning.

IT is no longer an afterthought, an area of planning reserved for technology specialists. The discussions of the high-performance business team, the integrated organization, and the extended enterprise in Part I show the key role that technology can play in supporting the kind of strategic business initiatives required to succeed in the new business world. The individuals and teams involved in developing business strategies must therefore be cognizant of the enabling effects of IT and the corresponding impacts on business opportunities.[3]

In fact, the DMR and Cognitech research on aligning IS with business found an inverse relationship between formal, separate IS plans and the degree of IS contribution to the business. That contribution could be best increased, the project concluded, by ongoing contact between business and IS professionals and managers, rather than through highly structured, formal plans as has been the case in the past:

The ultimate goal for IS planning is integration with the business planning process. The business planning process in the Performing Organization embraces IS as an equal partner. As new business plans are formulated, the IS component is as important as the marketing, distribution or manufacturing and operations parts of the plan. The IS justification becomes part of the business justification, not an afterthought.[4]

Many organizations have embarked on "total quality improvement programs" or similar quality initiatives. Again, it is difficult to separate these programs from the related opportunities for IT. They are simply another way of determining business requirements and opportunities for improvement. Implicit in these programs is the need to establish quality standards, to measure performance against these standards, to develop controls and tests to improve compliance, and to determine the results of these programs. All of these are highly information-intensive activities where information management and communication applications offer strategic solutions in combination with other improvements.

Even an acquisition strategy should include an assessment of both the IT capability of the organization to be acquired and the way IT can be used to support its integration into the new organization. In other words, it no longer makes sense to create IT strategies separate from business strategies—they are too intertwined.

This is not to say that IT professionals should not do planning or develop *technology* plans and strategies. The need is greater than ever for carefully developed plans to support the retooling and development of the IT infrastructure. However, the orientation, process, and culture of IT strategic planning—the development of a strategy for the application of technology in business—will disappear as such activities become part of business planning.

2. Put the Onus on Owners

Because of the tight linkage of systems strategies with business, it follows that the leadership and sponsorship role of systems initiatives is shifting away from the IS department and into the user community. Senior business management must take responsibility for positioning the use of IT as an enabling force in shaping business plans and initiatives. This implies the need for executives and managers and other users to become more aware of the opportunities and the associated competitive threats presented by information technology. They must provide strategic direction to the IT architects.

This shift represents a further nail in the coffin for separate IT strategies. More often than not, IT is a component of a strategic business thrust. The responsible architects, developers, and implementers work as a team in managing the opportunity from its initial vision through to the realization of the business benefits. This implies the evaluation and coordination of many changes, including redesigned business processes, shifts in roles and responsibilities, skill development, development of new systems, deployment of technology, and changes in the IT support organization.

Although business managers can rely upon the advice and support of many specialists, including various IT disciplines, the ultimate responsibility for directing and coordinating these related changes is theirs! After all, they "own" the results.

3. Leverage Learning

Traditional approaches to IT strategy development were top down. Senior management conducted or commissioned a plan — a project or planning event. Input was sought from the users. The strategy was developed and adopted. The challenge was then to get "buy in," to sell the plan to the users. The plan could then be implemented. Often such events coincided with budgeting cycles.

What's wrong with this picture? Basically everything. The new paradigm makes virtually everything in this picture inappropriate. The process inevitably results, at best, in plans that cannot be implemented. And often it results in counterproductive plans.

The orientation was old paradigm — command and control, rather than commitment. Among other things, it assumed that people could buy in to a transformation of their working lives by reading reports or hearing presentations.

Because of the historic significance of the transformation under way, the challenge is generative, rather than adaptive. We are creating the new rather than adapting or fixing the old. This is essentially a learning challenge.[5]

To develop a shared vision, individuals need to learn together, in teams, what new possibilities exist. Equally important they need to learn how to translate these into action. More and more "it's not what you know, but how you apply what you know."[6] Making the transition to the new paradigm will require conscious action on a continuous basis by everyone in an organization.

Rather than creating a planning event, the shift will be toward establishing a working-learning environment where IT thinking becomes part of the life of every person and the activity of every organizational unit. Buy-in is not achieved after the fact, but occurs as part of a team learning process.[7]

In the seminal work on the learning organization, Peter Senge writes:

> Where there is a genuine vision (as opposed to the all-too-familiar "vision statement") people excel and learn, not because they are told to, but because they want to.... The practice of shared vision involves the skills of unearthing shared "pictures of the future" that foster genuine commitment and enrollment rather than compliance.[8]

Many implications flow from this shift in orientation. If you view planning as continuous learning, you will find yourself behaving differently. For example, one of the themes of the new enterprise is empowerment to act. Ironically, individuals need to be empowered *to create* that enterprise. It is necessary to foster informal contact between business people and IS professionals or outside experts and change agents, to involve people in a process to reimage their world, commit to the new, and translate the shared vision and energy created into further action. Planning must be thought of as action—the involvement of people in a process of transformation. And you need to make your most recent IT strategic plan your last one.

4. Extend Externally

The focus for opportunity assessment is shifting away from inward thinking to include the external business relationships of the organization. More and more, it is the boundary transactions where major gains in productivity and business effectiveness are possible.

For example, in looking at strategies for improving customer service, consider the seven kinds of information flows that affect the level of service:

- Assessing business needs of customers and prospects
- Providing information on products and/or services relevant to those needs
- Capturing specific order, delivery, and service request information
- Providing current status information on order, shipment, or service status
- Acknowledging receipt of goods or services and reporting any problems
- Disseminating and collecting invoices and payments
- Collecting feedback on customer satisfaction

Depending on the nature of the goods or services involved, there are many possible scenarios for how IT can improve the communication and management of these various types of customer interchanges. The ability to deal with requests or inquiries in real time and the ability to streamline administrative procedures are key service and productivity improvement areas. Determining where and how these apply to your products, customers, and competitive environment is central to establishing strategic business initiatives.

A corresponding list of information exchanges exists on the supplier side. By extending this information-flow modeling technique to include all major external sources or requesters of information, an information view of the business context results. The business is seen as a hub for an information exchange network that represents its role in an external value network.

5. Chuck the Chart

One of the greatest hindrances to effective systems planning is the organization chart. Traditional planning approaches have encouraged each department to develop a long-range information plan or an information resource plan. These plans, not surprisingly, reflected a very inward view of requirements and reinforced the differences, real and perceived, which existed across departments. They also typically resulted in a prioritized list of systems projects, which then competed for limited resources, both financial and professional.

These projects were developed and implemented as independent systems for each organizational unit, creating a "stovepipe effect." The overlaps and inconsistencies became obvious, but the pride of ownership and the feeling of control within the department discouraged interdepartmental initiatives. The resulting diversity of solutions because of lack of standards, or difficulties in their enforcement, created further barriers for integration or sharing. As a result, the evolution of systems began to reflect the organization chart. With the business pressures of the new era often resulting in downsizing and restructuring, these systems now present a barrier to organizational development.

An entire provincial government in Canada set out to determine the opportunities for cooperating on systems initiatives that crossed the many departmental boundaries typical of provincial or state administrations. With the support of the Management Board of Cabinet and a steering committee of deputy ministers, a number of working groups of departmental managers and staff tackled various aspects of government use (current and potential) of IT. To their surprise, given the wide-ranging jurisdictions of the various departments, they discovered they had much more in common than previously thought.

For example, there were many instances of common business processes, since many departments were involved in functions such as licensing, certifying, inspecting, counseling, granting funds, and collecting revenues. Instead of each department designing and developing independent systems to support these common functions, they would all benefit from sharing reusable components if they were willing to agree on a set of architectural standards.

Rather than viewing the business through its organization chart, it makes sense to define *logical service units,* or LSUs. LSUs are basic functional components of a business which describe *what* a business does rather than *how* it does it. LSUs exhibit the following characteristics:

- They constitute a necessary and sufficient set of functional components of the business.
- Each LSU represents distinct responsibilities for which there are measurable results, benefits, and costs.
- They are dependent on other LSUs and external players in order to deliver results. (These relationships form the basis for the client/server organizational model.)
- Their definition is independent of organization structure.
- Their definition is independent of where the work is performed.
- Their definition is independent of the human resources that perform the work activities.
- Their definition is independent of the degree of automation of these activities.
- They may change if there are fundamental changes in the nature of the business (mission).

LSUs can typically be classified into the following five groups: business planning functions, promotion and selling functions, production and delivery functions, collection functions, and internal support functions. They are fundamental components for developing business models, work reengineering models, and IT architectures. Because of the above independences, they provide a stable base for evaluating and tracking changes to functional capabilities, interrelationships, contribution, and costs. Because they are logical, not physical, they also provide a valuable basis for work reengineering. After modeling their businesses using LSUs, a number of clients have remarked, "This is so basic, why aren't we organized this way?"

6. Indulge in Information

"Information is a strategic resource" is a somewhat tired rallying cry of the information engineers of the 1980s, popularized by James Martin.[9] Although many organizations have invested a great deal of effort (and in some cases millions of dollars) in information engineering, there is not a lot to show for it. We believe this is primarily due to the limitations of first-era information technology. The concepts of organizing information across the organization, developing standard and consistent definitions for software developers, and providing secure access to authorized users are all fundamental to the technology paradigm shift.

What is different now, however, is the recognized need and the corresponding technological capability (although still emerging) to manage information in all its forms — that is, data, text, sound, and image (graphical, pictorial, and moving). Era I was primarily concerned with organizing and managing data. However, *data* represents the smallest portion of information used in most business transactions. It is the other forms, particularly sound (voice) and image, and multimedia combinations of the four forms that provide the most information-rich exchanges.

With the advent of optical storage techniques (similar to those used in digital recording CDs), high-bandwidth communications, and high-speed processors for conversion and manipulation of information, we are now capable of working with even high-quality video images and associated information bases.

In studying the information management requirements across the various departments, our example government organization identified many common uses for certain types of information. This was particularly true in the area of land-use information. The growing interest in *geographical information systems* (GIS), which was occurring in many departments, provided an excellent opportunity for cross-departmental collaboration.

By sharing a common base map produced in one area, each department could overlay its land-use topographical information, such as roads, forests, water courses, environmentally sensitive areas, and agriculture. Each department would benefit by seeing a more complete picture of current and planned land-use activities — provided, of course, that it was willing to comply with a standard GIS environment and to share information! By extending this opportunity for sharing to other levels of government (particularly municipal), to power and communication utilities, to transportation services, to developers, and to many other interested parties in land-use information, incredible opportunities for productivity remain to be exploited.

By identifying the major types of information involved in operating the business and their relationships with the various LSUs, many opportunities are uncovered for turning corporate information resources into valuable business services or businesses in their own right.

7. Make a Beeline for Benefits

Another guideline concerns the approach to justifying IT expenditures. The project-oriented approach of era I was built upon cost-benefit analyses in an environment of controlled expenditures through the yearly budgeting process. IT project costs were estimated and benefits predicted. Very often only the visible IT expenditures were costed while the benefits were dependent on ensuring changes in the impacted areas of the business. The so-called best business cases presented by a convincing sponsor would gain budgetary approval. Very often, no one was asked to account for the promised benefits.

Consistent with the above shifts, it now makes sense to view IT expenditures as part of larger business initiatives. IT will be one of several types of investments requiring capital and operating expenditures involved in the initiative. The approach to benefits involves looking at the strategic impact of the initiative. Opportunities should be evaluated and measured based on business performance objectives, not IT measures.[10]

One of the key business performance impacts is time to results. Given the pace of change in era II, we cannot afford to wait years or even months to see results. We must look for quick hits to establish the merits of second-era approaches and exploit short-term opportunities for benefits. Rather than large projects with fixed deliverables and long schedules, it is necessary to create learning environments that will encourage ongoing evolution and improvement of IT contribution to the business.

The empowered and motivated user and associated work groups, with the support of enlightened management and user-oriented IS support functions, will ultimately drive the process. But first the era II infrastructures for reengineered work processes, IT services, and support must be established.

Five Guidelines for Achieving Vision

As Peter Senge explains in *The Fifth Discipline: The Art and Practice of the Learning Organization*:

> Many leaders have personal visions that never get translated into
> shared visions that galvanize an organization.... What has been lacking
> is a discipline for translating individual vision into shared vision — not a
> "cook book" but a set of principles and guiding practices.[11]

It is not our intention here to present a new approach to strategic
business planning that embraces the considerations of the new technology paradigm. However, from working with transitioning clients, we
have developed a set of five guidelines or steps to achieving vision that
can be integrated into your organization's business planning process. It
should be noted that we do not seek to create a new top-down strategic
planning discipline, but rather the opposite. These five steps can be undertaken and completed in a short time frame, in just days, or in a
longer time frame as part of a broader plan. They can also be applied to
an enterprise, to a division or separate line of business, to a major organizational function, or to a group of enterprises (such as a supply network or an interrelated industry such as health care or justice). They
work equally well for private-sector businesses, private or public institutions, and governments at all levels.

1. Initiate a Learning Process

*How do you ensure that the best ideas are brought to bear on the problem,
gain a shared vision and commitment, and ensure that plans lead to actions and results?*

Unfortunately, it is often easier to create a vision than it is to gain the
necessary organizational commitment to that vision. The steps below
are not intended to lead to the creation of a prizewinning strategic planning document, which gets blessed and then gathers dust on the shelf
while the organization continues on its merry way.

The necessary commitment comes through involvement, communication, and follow-through. Earlier, we placed the onus on the owners to
sponsor and drive the formulation of the new vision. We also encouraged you to leverage learning and view planning as a learning process.
Having key business managers and influential professionals involved in
the process is critical to gaining commitment. It is important to balance
the time and cost factors of involving a good cross section of the organization in this process with the critical need to expedite the process.

For the first round of setting a new vision, it is probably more important to gain organizationwide commitment than it is to have the best
possible vision. Spend no more than a few weeks, not months, in moving through the steps below; then determine the plan of action for re-

solving architecture requirements and getting on with some short-term strategic opportunities. Make a beeline for the benefits that will show results and build momentum in support of the vision; then refine it.

Transfer the responsibility for these actions into the affected parts of the organization, with clear accountabilities and performance measurements established. Develop a formal communications program to clearly indicate the new directions and the seriousness of the organization to these changes, and then follow through. Invite reaction and participation and be very open in discussing and tracking progress through the next plateaus.

2. Reimage Your World

What are the main shifts in your organization's external context, and what is your corresponding business architecture?

Start by reviewing the business environment of the organization under study from the perspective of the four new paradigms—world, business, enterprise, and technology. Typically, there is some form of deliverable from the strategic planning forays of the 1980s that identifies the mission, strategic goals, and critical success factors (or key result areas). There may also be a set of company values that characterize the culture of the organization. These should be gathered, summarized, and updated (quickly) if necessary.

The forces for change that determine the business environment of the organization should also be identified. The following are examples of forces of change that act upon our organizations:

- *Stakeholder interests.* Financial expectations, organization's contribution to the community, integrity of operations
- *Economic.* Shifting investment climate, recessions, inflation, exchange rates, interest rates
- *Market.* Globalization (new markets), industry trends, substitute products/services, quality considerations, product requirements
- *Competitive.* Current competitive activity, new entrants, competitive innovations
- *Regulatory.* Trade barriers (up and down), taxes, various regulatory agencies, union contracts, regional incentives
- *Environment.* Pollution control programs, waste management, energy conservation
- *Labor supply.* Available skills, cost of labor, mobility, work ethics

- *Social/political.* Political stability, various lobby groups, social programs
- *Technology.* Production and process technology, information technology, materials technology

Notice that each of the forces of change represents a necessary flow of strategic information for the effective management of the organization. How well is the organization able to cope with these forces? Where are the risky areas where specific strategies are required to overcome weaknesses or exposures?

Do you have a document that describes the *business* of the organization? To our continual surprise, this does not typically exist—certainly not in a concise, coherent, and current form. In its absence, we suggest defining the *architecture of the business* from an external perspective as a basis for establishing current and future context. Figure 8-3 shows a representation of the components of a business architecture and their key relationships.

The products and/or services that an organization produces or offers are the fundamental component for defining any type of business or organization. The ability of a business to deliver these products to its customers in selected markets is based on the ability to differentiate these offerings from those of the competition (through better price,

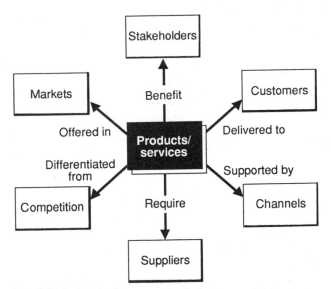

Fig. 8-3. Architectural components of a business and their primary relationships.

quality, service, etc.) and to do so at a cost that produces acceptable results to the stakeholders to which the business is accountable. An organization accomplishes this by being aware of the requirements of customers and of the competitive activities in its markets and adjusting products and services accordingly, by making the best use of available sales, service, and distribution channels, and by selecting the most effective suppliers.

Where there is considerable movement of goods involved, it is useful to describe this business context as a physical transformation and transportation network. In any case, it is important to define the relationships between these fundamental business components. For example, what types of customers in which markets use which products or services delivered through which channels?

Develop both a current and future picture, choosing an appropriate strategic time period (sooner rather than later!). This becomes the first deliverable to define the vision of the future state of the organization. It provides a framework for presenting desired or predicted shifts in product mix, market penetrations, new or shifting distribution channels, and changes in stakeholder interests, all related to the mission and goals of the organization. These same business components can be used to quantify business performance objectives.

The next extension of this context model is to view the business, not in terms of physical flows of goods, but in terms of primary flows of information which govern the interactions between the organization and its external business partners. Not only does each physical exchange of goods result in a corresponding information exchange, but many relationships are primarily information-related.

3. Identify Strategic Drivers

What are the critical thrusts for your organization to achieve the desired new position?

This step involves identifying the key strategic drivers for the organization from a new paradigm perspective. Drivers are determined by evaluating the forces for change that operate on an organization, by assessing their impact on assisting or restricting the achievement of business objectives, and by developing the resulting strategic responses. Drivers provide focus to the follow-on planning activities and day-to-day management of the organization. There are typically one to five drivers, depending upon the complexity and context of the organization.

By assessing these forces and the organization's capability to respond (both offensively and defensively), the strategic drivers can be identified and pursued. The productivity of service and knowledge workers in addition to production workers is a key driver for most organizations, whether private or public sector.

Consider some recent examples of strategic drivers for which many organizations were not properly prepared. The rapid implementation of the U.S.-Canada Free Trade Agreement (FTA) has caught many Canadian manufacturers and retailers flat-footed (and without any government remedies). Those manufacturers whose plants did not meet North American production efficiencies, or lacked adequate scale of production to achieve these efficiencies, lost their customers or simply disappeared as their parent companies consolidated branch plant operations in more favorable business environments. The retailers in Canadian border towns watched hopelessly as their customers headed to the neighboring state to fill their cars with cheaper goods (and gasoline), avoid a new consumer tax, and enjoy the privilege of Sunday shopping.

As a consequence, companies that have been in business for decades are being forced to fold their tents or declare bankruptcy. These results were clearly predictable! Those companies that foresaw these changes developed strategies to upgrade production facilities, diversified their markets and possible production into the United States (and elsewhere), or simply cut their losses.

A common strategic driver in government circles these days is to balance the budget—or in some cases to go further and actually reduce the public debt! The need to cut costs and increase revenues while improving services without increasing taxation sounds impossible. However, progressive government departments and agencies are discovering the opportunity to increase service and knowledge worker productivity through work reengineering and information technology. One regional government we worked with declared that "information technology may well be the underlying mechanism for transformational change within government."

4. Reimage Your Organization in a Business Model

How can you best describe the way in which you would like to operate in this new business environment?

By far the best mechanism for creating and communicating a new vision is to develop a model to represent the desired result. Just as architectural scale models are used to evaluate concepts for building or subdivision development, a model of how the business will function in the future can be used to assess the impact of the proposed changes.

The business model originates from the information view of the business context and proceeds to decompose the functions of the business into internal components of the value network. As we emphasized earlier, do not resort to using the organization chart as the basis for this decomposition—it represents a management control view of the business and rarely corresponds to how the organization actually functions. Also, do not restrict your modeling to only internal activities; external linkages are becoming key to business transformation and success.

To encourage planning approaches that reflect business requirements that are independent of how you are organizationally structured, you must understand the underlying architecture of the business and how to structure your systems to address basic functional and information management requirements in a modular and flexible way. An architecture also provides the basis for identifying commonalities and opportunities to share or reuse components, rather than allowing organizational units to hide behind their differences.

To conduct business modeling, proceed to identify the logical service units using the guidelines presented earlier. LSUs should have generic descriptive labels that retain their independence from organization (e.g., *order processing* rather than *order department*) and from location (e.g., *sales management* rather than *sales office*). Also, avoid using technology-related descriptions such as *data entry* or *word processing*. LSUs can be further defined by listing the distinct subfunctions or major responsibilities assigned to each.

The model is developed by diagraming the relationships between LSUs and with external players (from the context model) using information flows to represent the relationships. It is useful to view these relationships as *client/server* interactions. For example, a request for product availability from a prospective customer would be serviced by a customer service LSU, which would then become a client of a warehouse management LSU to determine the in-stock status, which, if not in stock, becomes a client to the production management LSU to request an expedited production allocation. Each of these client/server interactions proceeds (it is hoped, in real time) using the established request-for-service format with expected responses and time frames preestablished.

By modeling the business in this manner, the opportunities for using era II client/server technologies to parallel the LSU structure become obvious. Each LSU can develop applications to support its business functions and use standard communications over the network to other LSUs. In fact, the above illustration could be accomplished using EDI between the customer site and all the LSUs to totally automate and service the customer request for product availability (and subsequent ordering).

A further way to develop the business model is to classify the LSUs according to the three levels of impact — work group, enterprisewide, or interenterprise. This classification not only will help qualify the opportunity for IT but will identify the parties that must participate in the development of the opportunity. For example, production management will typically have a work-group orientation and will therefore be a good candidate for distributed and localized IT applications, with appropriate communication links to other client and server LSUs. Human resource services, including payroll, employee benefits, and travel services, will usually be a corporate support function with a more centralized orientation but requiring an enterprisewide access network. Various financial services, such as payment processing, cash management, and foreign exchange, are generally interenterprise functions that can take advantage of external financial service networks and processing facilities, accessed through the enterprise network.

By viewing the business as a network of interconnected functions (LSUs), each with a defined and necessary role and associated costs and contributions, the areas of the business that are most involved in affecting the strategic drivers can be identified. Use the drivers to identify and evaluate the opportunities to streamline these areas and to support both the internal activities of the LSU and the electronic interchange of information between LSUs.

5. Establish Business Principles for Work Reengineering, Information Technology, and the IS Function

What direction and guidance can you give to the planners and architects to help them shape the new vision into projects and programs for implementation?

With the context established, the drivers identified, and the vision of future operations embodied in a business model, the next step is to give some further direction to the architects who will be involved in the next plateau. A useful technique is to develop a set of business principles pertaining to architecture.

Principles are simple direct statements that describe what is determined to be good practice. They are typically accompanied by one or more points of rationale and by a list of implications. Principles are extremely valuable because they eliminate recurring arguments and alternative evaluations regarding key planning decisions. For example, in an organization where similar functions and services are performed at multiple sites, it is very useful to establish business principles regarding whether or not business processes, IT applications, structure of information, and use of support functions are going to be standardized across all locations. Clearly, where consistency of service delivery and productivity are identified as business drivers, one would adopt a principle in favor of standardization—it has certainly worked for McDonald's. On the other hand, where a high degree of product or service customization is required and there are many contextual differences across sites, a principle of nonstandardization is more appropriate. Either way, it is valuable to have this principle established on a sound business rationale before proceeding with planning structures. For example, architecture and supporting standards thrive on exploiting opportunities for commonality.

Another typical example of a business principle involves the era II technology direction regarding the transition from proprietary to open systems. By establishing a business principle that favors open versus proprietary standards, organizations can cut through the resistance to change, and provide their architects with the direction, and clout, to promote more open solutions.

Principles can be used to signal the types of changes that are expected with the new vision. After establishing principles, it is very common to find that the current situation is in violation of many, if not most, of them. They are the flag bearers of the paradigm shift. If you can establish a sound business rationale, tied to the strategic drivers of the organization, in support of these principles and gain their acceptance, you have reached the first plateau in making the transition. The commitment to change in light of the new vision signals a cultural shift that must be communicated to the entire organization and then acted upon.

In the previous government example, there was a strong cross-departmental interest in sharing common IT infrastructure services. Shared communication facilities linking all geographical areas with hubs in major cities would allow many departments to make more extensive use of networked applications. It would also make advanced applications, such as videoconferencing, affordable, where they could not otherwise be justified. The common infrastructure would provide a number of network services, such as access to core financial and human resource applications, electronic mail, EDI services for internal and external transmissions, and electronic funds transfer services for financial transactions. These network services would require the adoption of common communication and network standards across the various departments.

The response to these findings was so encouraging that the government received strong departmental support for establishing the required architectural standards and is now making solid progress in implementing them. Departments with noncompliant technology environments are finding creative ways of working with their vendors to become early adopters of the new governmentwide principles and enabling standards.

Example principles for work reengineering, information technology, and the IS function are presented in the following three chapters, respectively.

9

Reengineering the Business

The process of creating the new enterprise is one of generative learning. Rather than fixing the old, we are setting out on a course to create the new. This involves considerable change in virtually everything we have come to know in our work lives.

Most of the cases we have presented involve a fundamental transformation in the business—the way it operates, its structure, its business processes, its people, and to various degrees its organizational culture. Each has made progress in making the transition to the second-era enterprise. Each has made significant progress in *reengineering the business, retooling the technology* environment to embrace the paradigm shift, and *realigning the internal IS function* to reflect the new realities.

What has been learned about how to achieve the reengineered second-era enterprise? What are the driving principles enabling us to create the new enterprise? By what process is reengineering possible?

Reengineering the business requires the achievement of a vision, the creation of new structures, the development and implementation of the new, and the institutionalizing of feedback and continuous improvement systems. This is depicted in Fig. 9-1. Reengineering must occur at all levels of the enterprise, from the individual (each person's job) to the work group, subenterprise, and enterprise levels. Reengineering should also encompass a recasting of relationships with external organizations.

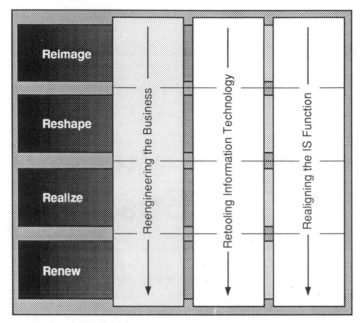

Figure 9-1. Reengineering the business.

New Technology—New Enterprise: Ten Corresponding Themes

Until very recently, the major difficulty in creating the new enterprise was that the technology preconditions to eliminate traditional hierarchies were simply not there. The technology paradigm shift, however, enables us to begin actually reinventing the corporation. Paralleling the main characteristics of technology, achievable organizational goals are emerging.

Technology theme

Open systems. There is *portability* of software and information across hardware platforms and *interoperability* of technology extending out to the external value network (of suppliers, consumers, affinity groups, and competitors). The shift is from proprietary systems in which each computing platform acted in a unique, self-interested manner.

Interconnection. There is a shift from era I islands of technology to enterprise networks that enable communication and sharing of information and technology resources.

Distributed computing. There is a shift from host-based hierarchical networks where all the intelligence was in the "host" (typically a mainframe or minicomputer) to network computing where computer intelligence is distributed close to the user. Host-based systems worked well with centralized command and control organizations.

Organizational theme

Openness. The enterprise is a network of business functions that interoperate. The organization is also viewed as the extended organization or interorganization. Walls between enterprises blur, and strategy is developed in a broader, open, outside-in, rather than inside-out, context. Organizations become more in touch with their customers. In the open organization people act not only out of their own proprietary self-interest, but out of a shared vision and commitment.[1] The work force is also portable—achieved both through outsourcing and through undertaking varied assignments (in which, for example, everyone spends some time in customer contact).

Integration. The new technology now enables integration of modular, independent organizational components—an integrated network of businesses. Functional overlaps and unclear or conflicting definitions of responsibilities in processes that cross functional boundaries can be eliminated. The concepts of seamlessness and transparency are as applicable to organizations as they are to computing architectures.

Empowerment. Individual employees and work groups are empowered to act and to create value. *Intelligence*—the thinking, planning, human processing of information, application of knowledge to business problems, decision making, action—is distributed. Lacking empowerment, many of the real or potential capabilities of individuals in the era I enterprise were not utilized.

Technology theme	Organizational theme

Real time. The technology is applied to capture information on-line and update information banks in real time — giving an accurate picture or enabling the management of a production process second by second.

Immediacy. The new enterprise is in fact a *real-time enterprise* — continuously and immediately adjusting to changing business conditions. This is achieved through information immediacy. Goods are received from suppliers and products shipped to customers just in time. This reduces or eliminates the warehousing function and allows enterprises to shift from mass production to custom on-line production. Customer orders arrive electronically and are instantly processed. Corresponding invoices are sent electronically, and databases updated.[2] Enterprises seek to *compete in time* effectively.[3]

Cooperative processing. Applications are processed on client and server devices, as appropriate, effectively using microprocessor technology. The processing capability that exists throughout or beyond an organization is exploited.

Cooperation. According to Joe Arbuckle, the new organization is a *cooperative infrastructure*.[4] Individuals and groups act as clients and servers, cooperating not out of some moral principles, but out of mutual self-interest. The notion of cooperation is extended beyond labor-management relations to become the *modus operandi* of the business.[5] Reward systems are designed to achieve desired behavior. Interdependencies across the enterprise are defined and built into the new infrastructure.

Peer-to-peer network protocols. Network rules shift from centrally controlled hierarchies to protocols that treat various devices on the network as peers. Peers communicate with other peers under carefully defined rules. For example, on some networks an information token circulates on the network, ensuring that any device that is committed to follow the rules can use the token to send information to another destination.

Commitment. The new enterprise is based on commitment rather than control. It focuses on accomplishment rather than accountability. Organizational clients and servers are motivated through interpersonal and intergroup commitment rather than the authoritarian command and control structures of the traditional hierarchy. As with the technology, centralized command mechanisms are replaced with new horizontal and diagonal communications patterns and protocols allowing for cooperative functioning. Commitment models have been found necessary to enable structures for shared expertise and goals.

Technology theme

Architectural modularity. Rather than being a giant monolith, computing architectures consist of standardized, independent parts that can be grouped together as required to meet business requirements. These can include standard computing platforms (discussed in Chap. 5), operating software (discussed in Chap. 6), or interchangeable application software components (discussed in Chap. 7). The goal is to create a dynamic, flexible computing environment.

Platform specialization. Computing hardware in a second-era architecture is specialized—meeting the customized requirements of the individual, work group, or other organizational unit. Unique computing capabilities, not only those in the area of processing, but input devices (such as scanners) display technologies (such as touch-sensitive screens), and output technologies (such as color laser printers), are applied as appropriate to meet specialized requirements. Various specialized servers are placed on the network, for example, file servers, application servers, communication servers, and database servers.

Organizational theme

Organizational independence. The organizational counterpart to the technology module is the business team. Networking enables the seemingly contradictory achievement of integration yet independence of organizational components, businesses, or modules. Modules or *clusters*[6] are grouped together as required to achieve business objectives.

Skill specialization/competency building. The new enterprise focuses on the knowledge worker—more and more the professional, not the manager. Knowledge, by definition, requires specialization.[7] Rather than discouraging or killing the development of professional competency by promoting professionals to become managers, the new enterprise provides professional career paths and programs in which a professional can be as, or more, "senior" than managers (excepting usually the CEO).[8] As with technology that is specialized to meet unique requirements, specialized competencies are encouraged and developed in individuals and teams. Individual contributors are rewarded based on competency and accomplishment rather than span of control.

Technology theme	Organizational theme
User friendliness. Systems are designed to be easy to learn and use. This is achieved through graphical user interfaces, application consistency and simplicity, effective training programs, and the integration of data, text, voice, and image into multimedia systems.	**Accessibility.** According to Davis and Davidson, a principle of the new enterprise is user friendliness.[9] The "organization man" of the 1950s, who identified with the corporation and stuck with it for life, is dead. He has become the independent, multicareer professional of the 1990s. The networked enterprise must seek to be an accessible, learning organization, uniting members around a shared vision. This is not a command and control vision imposed on the organization, but rather a vision to which people are truly committed "because it reflects their own personal vision."[10] Employees have access to decision making and share in corporate ownership (equity).
Global networking. The corporate network becomes the backbone of the enterprise and the key delivery system for supporting business operations. It is based on standards, and it enables both real-time communications and store and forward communications. This is required when people are not able to reach each other directly. It also enables access to the collective information resource, as appropriate, from any location.	**Time and space independence.** The new enterprise redefines time and space for its employees and stakeholders. In the open networked enterprise any individual or team can communicate and, as appropriate, share information with any other individual or team. Work can be performed from a variety of locations, including employees' homes. The office becomes a system rather than a place. The network becomes a repository for the time-independent communications of people who access the communications of others when they are able. The enterprise becomes an infrastructure rather than an organization. Networks of business teams cooperate globally to achieve business objectives.

The Travelers: Nonmanagers Are People Too!

As part of a program to create a new IT-enabled enterprise, the Travelers set out to address the problem of its "individual contributors"—those who had an important professional competency and could make important contributions to the organization outside the realm of management.

Among the principles adopted are the following:

- Individual contributors have no less value to the company than do managers.

- The value of an employee is based on individual contribution to the corporate mission rather than the number of employees managed.

- There must be clarity of organization for there to be clarity for individual roles and responsibilities.

- Measurement standards for individuals and organizations must be clear and achievable. You don't have to own it to control it.

- The span of control of a manager should be such that the manager spends a majority of his or her time in management activities.

- An individual work activity should be structured in such a way that the individual spends the majority of his or her time in activity that is primary to that individual's responsibility.

Thirty Principles of IT-Enabled Work Reengineering

Reengineering must occur at all levels—at the level of individual jobs, work-group processes, broader processes, and structures (even at the enterprise level). It must also extend beyond the organization to include the recasting of relationships with external entities. A good starting point is at the basic levels of the individual and business process. A number of guidelines or principles of work reengineering have been found useful by our clients. Below is a selection, which can act as a basis of discussion for your organization. It is noteworthy that such principles could typically not be implemented in the first era of information technology. It is only through the enabling effect of the new paradigm that organizations are able to achieve the spectacular benefits of these new approaches to work.

- *Work systems will have a customer focus; internal tasks that do not contribute to meeting customer needs will be minimized.* Personnel will be aligned to customer requirements rather than to tasks. This involves establishing local and corporate goals around customer needs, and not the organization, so that all internal processes serve the customer. It also involves, as much as possible, electronic communication with customers and technology-supported customer service.

- *In work reengineering programs, the focus will be on improving and changing the business, not just the organization.* The issue of being more competitive will be continually reviewed. How can customers be better served? How can productivity be improved? What steps can be taken to improve quality in this process? How can the time it takes from beginning to end be cut? Every task performed must have added value to business objectives.

- *Work activities and processes will be performed in parallel.* Using shared databases, communications tools, and process management applications, it is now possible to take activities that were previously done in sequential steps and conduct them in a parallel fashion. However, care will be taken to ensure that players in various aspects of the process have visibility over other aspects, receiving inputs at appropriate points, eliminating redundancy of information collection, etc.

- *"Whole" jobs with attendant responsibilities and commitments will be created.* The piecework of the past will be eliminated to ensure that individuals understand the entire process, to enable buy-in to the vision, and to reduce friction and alienation. People will be empowered to deal with customer problems.

- *The role of management is to support those who are dealing directly with customers—the front line.* Management works for those at the counters and in the airplanes who are giving customer service. An upside-down view of the organization chart will be used, where customers are at the top, those who work with customers are next, and those who work for those who provide service to customers are at the bottom.

- *Individual contributors will be able to play more than one role.* In selected processes this will involve the rotation of jobs to bring fresh ideas into all aspects of the process, to strengthen and refine team commitments, to eliminate bottlenecks and reliance on specific individuals, and to improve quality of work life through variety and change. All employees will, even if on a rotation basis, have responsibilities involving direct service to customers.

- *All management support information will be captured as a by-product of doing work and not as an additional set of activities.* This involves eliminating many of the traditional data entry functions to capture information and to create and transmit memos and other enterprise correspondence. It also means that team performance data will be generated automatically by the system.

- *"Virtual functions" will be created independent of location.* The starting point will be to ignore geographical distances, assuming that through technology single work process can be performed from a number of different locations. Various business teams will have overlapping members. One person may participate in multiple teams remotely.[11]

- *Information will be available to answer customer inquiries at all times.* Technology will be established to streamline the internal processing of information and information retrieval systems for workers who deal directly with customers.

- *Processes will be designed for flexibility.* Processes and work will be controlled proactively. Rather than always reacting to external events, work processes will anticipate new developments and have the flexibility to embrace them. Design will focus on continuous improvement, in full appreciation of the fact that the reengineering of your work processes will continue past the turn of the century.

- *Where possible, work activities will be broadened to include all tasks that involve meeting a local or enterprise goal.* Internal supply functions, such as purchasing, will be redirected toward higher-value activity such as negotiating supplier discounts.

- *Hierarchical bureaucracy will be eliminated.* As many layers of management as is feasible will be eliminated. The ultimate objective is to have self directed teams throughout the plant with *no* layers of management. For example, quality control methods will be redefined, identifying potential applications of technologies. An example would be executive information systems that allow the enterprise to perform more efficiently with minimum management.

- *Redundant activities will be searched and destroyed.* The reasons for redundancies (i.e., people do not know that the activity is being done elsewhere, or there is a lack of trust in another worker's information or performance capabilities) will be removed. Unnecessary "traditional" activities will be eliminated. This involves assessing the "we've always done it this way" activities and, if necessary, removing inefficient organizational sacred cows.

- *Saved time will be reinvested and tasks delegated.* Time savings have no value unless saved time is reinvested in desirable new activities or divested in actual reductions in personnel costs. Rather than doing old things in new ways, new things will be done in new ways. Some of the greatest time savings can be achieved through eliminating lower-level clerical activities and then delegating high-level activities to the individual involved.

- *Shadow functions will be minimized.*   Shadow functions are unproductive activities such as playing telephone tag, waiting for meetings to begin, looking for things, revising inappropriately, and waiting for the input from another process.

- *Shadow records will be minimized.*   Shadow records include duplicate information transcripts and media records. Making copies of information before the information is finalized will be avoided. In general, making physical copies of anything will be avoided.

- *Miscommunications will be minimized.*   Miscommunications occur when information is inappropriately or inaccurately exchanged, resulting in an incomplete, misleading, or false impression. Miscommunications can be reduced through provision of shared database access and electronic communications rather than by telephone or face-to-face. They can also be reduced through better structuring of the communications process.

- *Media transformations will be minimized.*   Media transformation is the conversion of information from one form of conveyance to another. For example, the head office sends a telex to all the regional offices, which in turn fax the telexes to district offices, which in turn telephone the message to the various stores, which in turn copy down the information and type it up for photocopying and distribution to employees. Each of these is a source of delay, cost, and possible error (not to mention frustration).

- *Controlled access to source information will be provided.*   Source information is managed for integrity and timeliness. It is stored in one or more locations to provide cost-effective access. Unofficial copies lose integrity and increase information-handling costs.

- *Information relays will be reduced.*   This involves ensuring that systems are established to collect information once and to provide direct access to this information throughout the enterprise as needed. A key aspect of this is the replacement of document handoffs by shared database access.

- *Coordination of work processes will be automated.*   This involves automating "bring forward," tickler, and other process management systems. It also involves electronic communications tools that can be used to coordinate work processes.

- *Backup resources of people and information will be established.*   This involves avoiding structuring work so that only one person has the ability or knowledge to perform an activity. Technologies such as expert systems can aid in this regard.

- *Any individual will be able to communicate with any other through participation in the corporate network.* More structured support for "unstructured" knowledge flows will be established through technology tools such as voice mail, Email, facsimile, and teleconferencing facilities throughout the enterprise.

- *Systems required for high performance work will be available to users.* Designated work-group tools will be supplied to the desktop and access to information necessary to perform job functions will be provided.

- *Jobs will be clearly defined.* The work to be eliminated, the work to be done in a different way, the new things to be done with time saved, the service level and performance expectations, career plans, and compensation programs will be identified.

- *Focused job training and knowledge-based systems support will be provided creating a working-learning environment.* Education and ongoing technological tools to enable workers to meet both local and corporate objectives will be supplied. Activities that are inappropriate to the knowledge base of the individual or group (unless that base can be changed) will not be assigned.

- *Compensation will be linked to competency and to accomplishment rather than to position in a hierarchy.* A proportion of all compensation will be variable. It will be directly linked to the achievement of team-oriented performance goals. As there is no limit to individual contribution, there is no limit on professional compensation. At certain levels of accomplishment, contributors have the option of acquiring equity in the enterprise.

- *There will be no layoffs.* People are a company's primary asset — one that is appreciating. Their ownership of the vision and their personal commitment are critical to success. Every contributor must be worked with to ensure job security and the continuous learning required to grow and add value. No one need abstain from participating or fully supporting work reengineering efforts for fear of being designed out of a job. There may be reductions in staff through voluntary programs, attrition, retirement, or spinouts. Commitment to job security is bilateral. It requires active participation and job assignment flexibility on the part of the employee.

- *The old will not be eliminated until a suitable new alternative has been forged.* Vestiges of hierarchy will remain for a considerable period.

The first steps have been to establish matrix structures, with a strong emphasis on project teams. However, there are many cultural and other changes to understand in moving to an open networked enterprise. While appreciating the urgency of change, caution will be exercised, for example, in the elimination of traditional management controls and accountabilities. There will also be refinements in traditional structures that make sense in the interim.

- *The protocols for client/server organizational structures will be continuously defined and redefined.* These are the rules and ways of operating that constitute an accountability framework. They enable individuals and teams to manage the relationships with other individuals and teams on which they are dependent. This new process will produce a period of continuous improvement.

Are We Just Rehashing Total Quality Management?

If there are "50 ways to leave your lover," there are at least 50 methods, recently developed by 50 consultants, regarding how best to reengineer work. Some of these date back as far as the late 1970s and have gone through considerable testing and refinement.[12] Others are described in considerable detail in books[13] or prestigious academic journals.[14] Still others have been developed or adapted in-house by enterprises developing a reengineering program. Some high-profile companies with reengineering programs include General Electric (with its famous "workout" program), Westinghouse, Cigna Corp., Hallmark, Steelcase, Canadian Workers' Compensation Boards, American Airlines, Tupperware, IBM, Digital Equipment Corporation, Hewlett-Packard, General Motors, and Ford, to name a few.

Many have equated work reengineering with *total quality management* (TQM). While there are overlaps in philosophy and thrust, our experience indicates that TQM techniques are inadequate for the task of redesigning knowledge and service work for productivity and quality. One problem with TQM approaches is that, similar to industrial engineering, they typically do not appreciate the paradigm shift in technology and the enabling role that technology plays. Another problem is that, like industrial engineering, TQM approaches were developed for manufacturing environments. They rely on statistical process control systems—the class of systems that conduct measures needed for a quality management program. Such measures do not exist in most offices. Consequently it is necessary to develop new levels and measures of performance, a task involving some effort and rigor.

Engineering is an applied science. Unfortunately, however, the challenge of redesigning work systems is more of an applied art than science at this point. "A science," as they say, "this ain't." This is not to say that we should throw up our hands and "wing it." There has been considerable progress in applying some scientific discipline to the challenge, especially in the areas of opportunity measurement, work-flow analysis, and impact assessment. TQM is also historically suited to more structural processes and often has weaknesses in improving knowledge work. And TQM is a long-term process. Reengineering seeks shorter-term, nonincremental, radical change. As a result, it makes sense to kick-start a TQM process with a reengineering effort that can get shorter-term benefits.

Eight Guidelines for Work Reengineering Programs

When undertaking the job of redesigning your process, consider the following guidelines:

1. *Remember that business people, not IS professionals, must own and control the work-system redesign program.* Work reengineering is not something that the IS department can do for you (or *to* you). Reengineering does have a high-technology and systems content. Hangover approaches from the first era, in which the IS department conducts or even leads a systems analysis, are inappropriately applied to the second-era challenge. The new reengineering is essentially a learning program that must be undertaken by those who will learn to work together differently.

2. *Throughout a program, go for the quick hits.* Quick hits are fast changes that can be made before the implementation of a new work system. In the first week of a program you may discover some obvious problems with the business process which can be changed immediately. Do it. Quick hits provide momentum, encouragement, and credibility for the program.

3. *Keep in mind that communications with those involved can make it or break it.* You need consistent and clear communications among the various stakeholders. New work systems are one of those rare things that are best designed by committee. Workshops, presentations, position sheets, and informal collaboration are essential to avoid the minefields of misunderstanding, insecurity, and disengagement from the program.

4. *Acquire a methodology and outside expertise.* One of the problems with many TQM programs is that they establish the long-term, gradual incremental change process and all employees are oriented and trained to change the way they work. Typically the techniques used are not rigorous and complete. Because TQM practitioners often lack experience with the enabling role of information technology in the reengineering of work, new work systems are often suboptimal.

5. *Involve the IS people.* The flip side of the mistake of leaving all the work to the IS people is to not involve them. We have seen this mistake made numerous times, typically with unhappy consequences. Without IS know-how, the technology role in enabling new work systems is not conceived.

6. *Focus on benefits.* Every change that is identified can have a set of corresponding benefits. Each change should also be linked with specific individuals who are accountable for these benefits when the implementation begins.

7. *Measure.* As the law goes, "You can't change what you can't measure"—and make sure you measure the right things. Rethink how you measure business success. If you have an objective to improve service quality, then you need to establish new service levels and corresponding measures. The Federal Express case study in Chap. 3 is a great example of a work system based on clear measures of the desired performance levels.

8. *Think big. Start small.* It makes sense to iteratively redesign work systems through various releases of bundled changes. Some have described this as creating prototypes or developing pilots. The approach outlined below uses the concept of phased releases of change.

Plateaus for Work Reengineering

As with the other two thrusts of transition (retooling technology and realigning the IS function), reengineering the business is achieved through four plateaus:

1. Achieve a New Vision

In the absence of conducting a full strategic plan for the business, the visioning exercise described in the previous chapter can be undertaken.

This involves defining the context, identifying strategic drivers, developing a high-level business model, establishing principles for the new work system, and packaging for commitment and action.

As part of this visioning exercise, key questions for work reengineering need to be explored: What is your business value network? What are the key functions (logical service units) that are closest to delivering value to the customer? What are the key factors that will drive the change? For example, is the organization downsizing? Is it looking to expand markets? Is customer service a key element in the next period? Where are the key areas for focus? What are the key result areas? These should be examined from an outside-in, market-oriented viewpoint.

The visioning plateau should provide a platform for change. This includes a rationale for change. People need to know why they and the organization need to change, how the change will affect them, and what will be their role in the change process (everyone has a role). It should also include a definition of the change management process itself. This is the process by which change is introduced. Such a process will be unique to the organization. It should be considered a business program outside of the normal business functions, and not just a project. A program can include many projects involving changes to jobs, performance management, technology implementations. It can also involve many different disciplines.

2. Structure a New Work System

The work system is another area where architectural approaches can be a great assistance. There is a need to move beyond the high-level "architecture of the business" (described in the previous chapter) to the work architecture. This different but supporting view involves a different set of architectural components and their primary relationship to work-systems redesign. Each logical service unit can be modeled to determine the most appropriate business processes and related manual and automated work activities. This is shown in Fig. 9-2.

This architectural framework helps us understand the job of the work-system redesign team. The context is provided by the functional component under study. In an effectively reengineered business, this would be a logical service unit derived from the business architecture model with its associated services, clients, and suppliers.

Any functional component or service unit can be decomposed into a number of interrelated processes and work activities. For knowledge and service workers, these activities typically include:

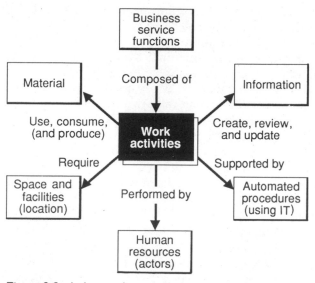

Figure 9-2. Architectural components and relationships for work-system redesign.

- *Collecting information,* particularly receiving work requests, monitoring the work environment, and accessing reference and file information
- *Processing information,* performing calculations and comparisons and applying rules (ranging from simple arithmetic and Boolean logic to complex mathematical and statistical analysis)
- *Making decisions* based on information, knowledge, experience, and intuition
- *Creating documents* to capture information and communicate ideas (ranging from simple forms to sophisticated documents incorporating stylized print, graphics, and color pictures)
- *Copying or printing documents*
- *Making recordings,* a living form of documents involving sound and possibly video composition and recording
- *Filing information* in many possible forms and media
- *Sending or distributing information* in many possible forms and media via many means (ranging from hand delivery to courier to fax to Email to EDI)
- *Interacting with others* to extract or convey information, exchange

ideas, resolve problems, and gain commitment (either in direct contact or via electronic conferencing facilities)

- *Monitoring, controlling, and maintaining facilities and equipment,* such as office equipment, security controls, computer equipment, or vehicles for transportation
- *Learning,* the acquisition of new skills and knowledge to advance the capabilities of the "actors"

These eleven types of work activities can be combined to model most of what goes on in an office or other typical work space for knowledge or service workers. The above list can be expanded to include materials handling, tools and plant equipment operation, assembly, and other related activities in nonoffice work environments particular to any type of industry.

These work activities are the center of the work architecture. They link the work to required resources, including raw materials, consumable supplies, tools, equipment, space facilities (link to work location), and, most importantly, the person or persons performing the activity. It is hard to conceive of an activity that does not require information in some form and that also does not generate information (at a minimum to record the status of the activity if not the results). In this way, information is regarded as a resource, just like all the other resources.

What is fundamental to the work architecture in era II is to determine the extent to which information technology can positively impact the work activities. Activities are themselves composed of tasks and procedures that are subject to mechanization or automation, in whole or in part. By supporting activities through automation, their nature and entire set of relationships described above can change. It is the job of the work-systems redesign team to uncover these opportunities.

Redesigning a new work system to take advantage of information technology involves a number of steps:

1. *Establish performance targets.* Quantifiable targets can drive the work architecture effort. They are derived from an analysis of the baseline of existing costs, performance levels, interview findings, and planning sessions. Measures should be taken in the areas that have the greatest impact on the customer. Typically these are areas such as finance, customer (external and/or internal) satisfaction, performance of internal processes, and organizational learning (the ability of the organization to continually learn, innovate, and improve). Federal Express developed 10 measures of customer satisfaction and from this developed performance targets for delivery of packages.

2. *Identify business opportunities and benefit areas.* An assessment of opportunities and benefits for each business area investigated can be developed through interviews, work-flow modeling, time measurement, and workshops. Because this step typically identifies so many benefits, they must be prioritized.

3. *Conduct initial redesign.* The process of iteratively redesigning the system is undertaken. The redesign is shaped by the reengineering principles and by establishing performance targets. At Citibank, members of the Corporate Real Estate group met in workshops to examine how the existing process could be improved. In examining a work-flow model, a discussion something like this could ensue:

> FACILITATOR: We know that this activity will be eliminated by technology, saving the two of you a total of 14 hours per week. How should we reinvest that time?
>
> TEAM MEMBER 1: Well, we could undertake an activity that could be delegated to us, or we could send customer correspondence at this point in the process, and still have time left over.
>
> TEAM MEMBER 2: I'd rather do the correspondence, as I think that would be really useful. It also fits with my career objectives of becoming more of a writer.

After days of such workshops an initial redesign was forged.

4. *Conduct initial redesign of jobs and organizational structures.* The implications of a new work system on the broader organization should be considered.

5. *Complete initial design opportunity assessment of technology applications and tools. Groupware packages should also be identified and selected.* This is a key point of alignment with the IT architecture effort (described in Chap. 10).

6. *Develop migration strategy.* Determine how the changes will be implemented.

3. Implement Your Programs

Once you have determined your migration strategy for each program, you will have identified a range of business programs. Each program must have a mandate, a business case, funding, resources, role definitions, accountabilities, measures of success, and business milestones (bundled releases of change). An important notion here is the *benefits register*. The register defines the planned project deliverables, identifies the relevant benefits from the business case, and establishes the individual management accountabilities for benefit attainment.

4. Extend the Implementation; Continuously Improve

You need continuous measurement in order to continuously improve. That is, you need to continually monitor how the change is working by collecting data from the embedded measures in the new work system. Build accountabilities for leading and implementing improvements into every job. This involves a culture change. Figure 9-3 illustrates a continuous improvement leadership cycle in which a business redesign program is established and various releases of the new work system are implemented, measured, and improved.

Continuous improvement cannot be an afterthought. It must be considered from the beginning through questions such as: "What are the things we need to continuously improve?" "How will we be able to monitor how we are doing?" Continuous improvement measures should also be built into the system design. For example, if the system includes a process management tool, helping in the collaborative production of

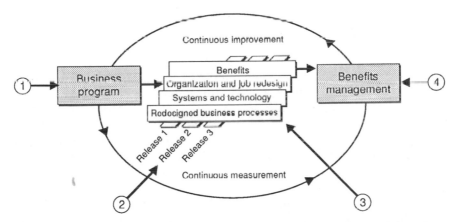

Figure 9-3. Continuous improvement cycle. (1) Business program is established to drive business and benefit objectives, business milestones, program and benefit accountabilities, and performance improvement targets and measures. (2) Delivery by release provides early deliverables and benefits and smooth transition. (3) Bundled sets of change are organized by release and managed by change owners. (4) Benefits register is maintained to manage benefit realization throughout implementation releases and continuous improvement process. (*From: DMR Group—Worksystems Redesign Consulting.*)

work products, then that tool should collect data regarding the performance of the process. (Needless to say, this should be done with the support of team members to avoid any unnecessary "big brother" fears.)

Continuous improvement is really continuous learning as well. According to Del Henderson-Langdon, who leads DMR's work-systems redesign consulting practice:

> When people get the tools they need, become involved in changing their own work processes, and have access to data regarding how they are doing, the light bulbs start to go on. They enter into a world where they and their teams can continually learn to do things better and develop themselves as contributors and professionals.

Building a Team Structure: The Shell Brockville Plant

One of the most far-reaching implementations of the open networked organization is the Shell Lubricants plant in Brockville, Ontario. The new plant that began operation in mid-1992 is based on collaborating, self-managed work teams, enabled by information technology. In addition, the fundamental responsibility of management has been redefined to support the self-sufficiency of the operating teams. The plant vision, which is "setting the standard, cost effectively and safely by people using technology in a fulfilling, self-managed team environment," serves as a daily reminder around which all operations are conducted and systems are measured.[15]

The new plant was established following a strategic review of lubricants production in which the company concluded that it had a problem. The lubricants operation was not competitive. It was not meeting its own quality standards, which were derived from an assessment of customer requirements. As well, the company anticipated that it would be unable to meet forthcoming environmental regulations regarding the production of lubricants. Shell concluded that it should consolidate all its lubricants plants into a new state-of-the-art facility, using radical new approaches to technology, organizational structure, and people.

Second-era *technology* provides the technical foundation for the plant. A strong theme is integration (i.e., integration of all control and information systems). For example, everyone has access to customer information. A forklift driver on the plant floor can directly access the latest sales data. An integrated technology infrastructure provides the basis for new forms of organization and work.

The *organization* is based on three self-managed teams — bulk handling, packaging, and warehousing. These teams, or *job families,* work together in a partnering relationship. The company believes that such a structure best promotes accurate, integrated scheduling and planning; enables control of key production variances; makes use of the technical support resources; promotes a sense of identification with the plant objectives; and promotes accountability for results.

People in a team rotate — becoming skilled in all aspects of work in that area. Once fully competent in the work existing in their own family, team members (*operators*) spend time in the remaining two job families, becoming qualified in at least one skill in each. Salaries are based on the level of competence a team member can demonstrate. There is also high-level integration of operational and administrative work. So a given team member may conduct traditional operational tasks such as operating in-line and automated batch blenders, conducting lab tests, operating packaging lines, working in shipping and receiving, and maintaining safety and security. Team members may also participate in a range of administrative functions such as stock balancing and control, telemarketing, vacation scheduling, training, scheduling, hiring, skill testing, and coaching. One of the goals is to ensure that every employee understands the goals of the business and his or her role in achieving these goals. Rather than think about putting a label on a drum, the employee should be thinking about drums, in perfect shape, going out on time to customers — and as such needing to be accurately and appropriately labeled. The work design ensures that at various points in the process the team members have some customer contact. The overall structure of the plant is depicted in Fig. 9-4.

The process of designing the new organization was highly participative, involving key employees and other stakeholders. Future team operators were (and continue to be) involved with most aspects of the design, including the system selection for the plant. According to the internal organizational design consultant, Alex Lowy, the process was also highly iterative: "To promote ownership and optimize the design, we adopted an approach of doing a piece, implementing, and cycling back to refine it, rather than trying to design it all 'right' the first time."

The starting point was a vision of a highly flexible, human-scale, technology-enabled organization. Due to the task complexity and high interdependence of different functions coexisting within the plant, a team-based organization design was chosen as most appropriate. From this a number of *core values* were developed. These are reflected in the following statements:

- Trust, honesty and responsibility are the foundations of our organization.
- Variety, challenge and feedback provide opportunities for learning and personal growth.
- In partnership with customers, requirements are mutually defined and met.
- A team-based organization is the most effective way to meet our business objectives.
- Our success is directly linked to shared goals and personal commitment.

A number of principles of the new organization were then developed. A key principle was the integration of business functions at the team level. According to Lowy, "A problem in many manufacturing sites is the emergence of class differences and distinctions which arise through the separation of office, managerial, and operational staff." A design goal was to minimize such distinctions. Resulting from this, the breadth of an operator's job was expanded to include the balancing of books, customer contact, stock control, and telemarketing. "Such an approach

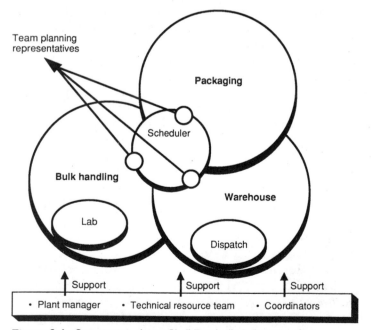

Figure 9-4. Organization chart—Shell Brockville Lubricants plant.

creates a resource with considerable understanding and commitment; it minimizes class differences and encourages partnering; it makes work interesting, lowering turnover, and over time contributes to lower over-all personnel costs," Lowy says.

Another principle was the notion of self-management. The goal is to minimize the need for and cost of supervision (i.e., an "accountability bureaucracy"). It was also judged essential to maintain "ongoing business awareness," ensuring that plant employees see clearly how they fit in with the rest of the value network of sales, promotion, and research. If individuals and teams understand the impact of what they do on co-workers and customers, then performance, motivation, quality, and the operation as a whole benefit.

Boring, repetitive work was systematically designed-out with the goal of making jobs meaningful, interesting, and full of variety. As well, compensation was tied to competency level, reflecting the belief that an organization gets what it rewards.

The result is that technology eliminated most of the old-style boring jobs and enabled the construction of a new, flatter, cooperative, net-worked structure focusing on self-managed teams. Warehoused goods are being reduced as they move to the real-time plant, through technologies such as the storage of goods for random access (based on computer models of optimized movements, availability of space, availability of forklifts, and frequency of access). The dream of cooperation is a reality, as all team members are dependent on others and knowledgeable about others' jobs and problems. Costs are lower, turnaround times are improved, and waste is reduced (with environmental implications). For example, reblend (the leftover oil in the lines at the end of a run) was reduced eightfold, resulting in significant savings.

Recasting External Relationships: Opening the Enterprise

The same four-platform approach can be applied to forging IT-enabled relationships with suppliers, customers, affinity groups, and even competitors. Most of the major efforts to establish new cooperative networks involved the creation of a common vision, and the architecting and deployment of a solution. More and more we have noticed programs to measure effectiveness and implement continuous improvement programs.

Interestingly, external reach to competitors often seems at first to be an unnatural act. Consider the experience in establishing the THISCO network in which 17 competing hotel chains have banded together to agree on an integrated reservations network. According to Gordon Kerr, vice president of MIS for Hyatt Hotels Corp., it took about a year "to understand that it was in our customers' and therefore our best interest to do this." Each hotel chain had to avoid temptations to tilt the system slightly in its favor. "Each of us had to shut out the 'compete at all costs' part of our brains to work for the common good."

10
Retooling Information Technology

When it comes to the technology transition, there is a big problem. The *irresistible force* of the new paradigm is meeting up with the *immovable object* of a $3 trillion installed base of first-era technology.[1]

Your organization has considerable legacy investments in information, software applications, and technology. If you are a Fortune 500 company, large insurance company, or bank, this investment is likely hundreds of millions or even billions of dollars. Some of the organizations we work with or studied have a staggering first-era installed base that grows larger daily. Consider the challenge facing Paul Strassmann at the Department of Defense which, including embedded systems, has *annually* invested in the tens of billions of dollars.

Max Hopper told us that American Airlines spends around $50 million per year maintaining and enhancing its host-oriented Sabre reservations system. The system has 100,000 terminals, uses multiple mainframe hosts, and consumes 1000 programmers developing applications in the extremely low-level language called *Assembler*. Moreover, it is based on an old-style 6-bit network, which, for example, only handles uppercase letters. According to Terry Jones, American's vice president of applications development, "It's about as far from open, client/server systems as you can get."[2]

Hopper says that the biggest barrier to the paradigm shift is the "legacy systems" which exist in every enterprise. He told us, "If you were starting from scratch, you would be doing it all differently. You've got to bring all that forward and make changes in the way you do things that your people resist. The IS community will have to spend time thinking this through."

In the last chapter we discussed reengineering the *business*. What is involved in retooling your organization's *technology* infrastructure? How do you fund such a change? How do you create a situation where past investments in systems are protected, yet where new investments contribute to the desired future rather than perpetuating the past. As with the transformation of the business organization, the retooling of technology requires reimaging, reshaping, realization, and renewal. This is depicted in Fig. 10-1.

Once you have forged a business vision, the first key to retooling technology is to know where you are going. To quote Lewis Carroll, "If you don't know where you're going, any road will take you there." When it comes to information technology, if you don't know where you're going, you'll end up perpetuating your installed base of era I systems.

To break the cycle, your organization needs to define a *target* information technology architecture that embraces the new paradigm—that is, an architecture based on standards, not vendor products, and oriented to network, not host computing. Such architectures are not de-

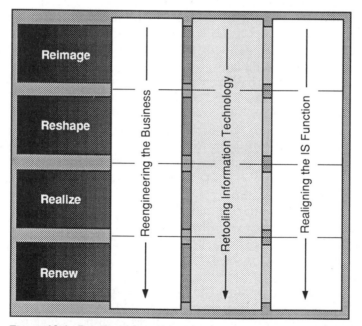

Figure 10-1. Retooling information technology.

signed simply to meet the specific application needs of a short-term business strategy. Rather, they must be dynamic and flexible, enabling the pursuit of unforeseen business opportunities and imperatives that the new business environment will assuredly bring. If you can model such a target architecture and compare it with a model of your current situation, it should be possible to begin to plan a migration route.

As explained in Chap. 6, this challenge is fundamentally different from implementing the "productectures," or specific system designs, which, in the first era, were misleadingly called "architectures." A new approach to architecture is required to embrace the new technology paradigm and to deliver required information and software applications that cross and help melt organizational boundaries. Such an approach is needed to enable evolution of information technology over time, and to encompass new business requirements and new innovations in technology which may come from unpredictable vendor sources. Through standard components and interfaces, organizations can create a dynamic technology infrastructure that can address constantly changing requirements. Standards enable architectures to be modular, vendor-independent, and loosely coupled with interchangeable parts. Yet at the same time standards can enable the construction and evolution of coherent, integrated technology environments as an enterprise backbone and as a basis for computer interaction with the external value chain of suppliers, consumers, stakeholders, and business partners.

Such an architecture can also enable the temporary preservation of the installed base, as appropriate, while enabling new applications to be implemented using client/server environments. Legacy systems can exist in the network computing environment by treating their proprietary hosts as servers on the network until such time as the applications can be redesigned to take full advantage of client/server concepts. Also many computer platforms, which still retain residual value, can be converted to support open systems environments. This avoids a disruptive and costly initial total conversion to second-era technology.

Once you know where you are going, a second, closely related requirement is to know how to get there. Walter De Backer, former director of informatics for the Commission of European Communities, made considerable progress in moving the CEC to a standards-based architecture. One conclusion the commission reached is that strategy and migration are both unique propositions. De Backer told us: "No two organizations which adopt open systems will have the same migration path."

As with travel, knowing the ultimate destination is a beginning. Knowing the route is as essential. One's starting point, preferences, travel objectives, available funds, attitudes, time available, and knowledge, along with the culture of the passengers and drivers, will determine the route. For a complex journey it is likely that no two routes will be the same.

A fundamental barrier to adoption of standards-based architectures has been the lack of a *process* whereby organizations can assess the merits of a new paradigm and then proceed to its definition and implementation. The old approaches are inadequate for the task of the new. Examples of comments received are: "We don't have a language for discussing architecture so we can't even get started talking to each other." "We don't really know what questions to ask ourselves." "Who should be involved in this process?" "How can we determine where standards make sense?" "What does a target architecture look like?" The researchers spend over $1 million in attempting to answer such questions. Below are some of the conclusions.

Toward the Standards-Based Architecture

Organizations need a process by which they can create and maintain a standards-based architecture. Architecture planning was nonexistent in era I and therefore requires some fresh thinking and new approaches. To begin, you need a framework that supports the many views and interests involved in the creation of an effective IT architecture. This framework provides the means to link concepts to reality.

The following outlines such a process and framework based on our research and consulting experience.

Retooling IT—The Architecture Process

The architecture planning process addresses the second layer, restructuring, in our transition framework for retooling information technology. It provides the critical linkages to the vision of the reengineered business and supports the realignment of IT resources. It leads to the formulation of well-conceived plans for developing and deploying era II technologies and staging the migration from existing systems.

The process for establishing a standards-based architecture consists of five basic steps, as shown in Fig. 10-2. Note that the process is cyclical to reflect the need for an evolutionary and ongoing approach. The intent is to focus on key areas of the business, drive out quick hits, and provide specific direction to near-term development projects. Later iterations can broaden the scope and increase the level of architectural detail.

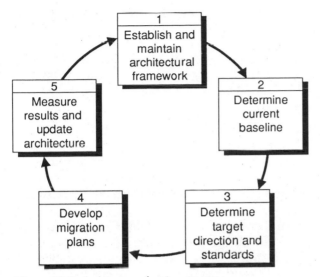

Figure 10-2. Architecture planning process.

The first step is to establish an architecture framework. The framework defines the various components and sets the context for organizing and managing the process of developing the architecture. This framework is described in the subsequent section.

In the second step, the framework is used as a basis for describing the current (or baseline) architecture. This allows for assessing the risks and opportunities associated with the installed applications and technologies.

The third step involves modeling the desired or target architecture to set the direction for change. Principles are established to guide the development of architecture models. These models provide the basis for describing the capabilities and benefits of the target architecture to different interest groups, including the business executive, the users, the developers, and the technology providers. Guidelines and standards associated with the architectural models are produced to further assist the developers and implementers.

The gap between the current and target architectures must be closed by a migration plan. This fourth step typically involves a series of plateaus that provide effective staging of the desired architecture and allow for benefits and costs to be accrued on a gradual basis. In the final step, the architecture must be assessed and updated on a regular basis to accommodate experience, changes in the business, and changes in technology.

This process should result in an ongoing approach to managing the evolution of the architecture. All associated delivery projects are driven from the resulting architecture plans and their results used to update the baseline and target architectures.

The Architecture Framework

What is an IT *architecture?* To help understand how architecture applies to information technology, it is useful to explore the more conventional use of the word. According to the dictionary *architecture* means "the structure of anything." Architecture "creates an image that suggests [the] function" of whatever you are trying to create.[3] You can tell when something has been wrongly architected—it's usually "back to the drawing board."

Good architecture combines creativity and applied science. The most common applications of architecture—the creation of buildings, campuses, shopping centers, and entire towns—have long since established standard practices involving naming conventions, principles, frameworks, and methods. These enable the transfer of knowledge among practitioners and students, allow integration of their work with other disciplines, and provide the basis for advancing their practice areas.

Whatever their field of endeavor, there are some common characteristics of the work of an "architect." Figure 10-3 illustrates the meaning of architecture.

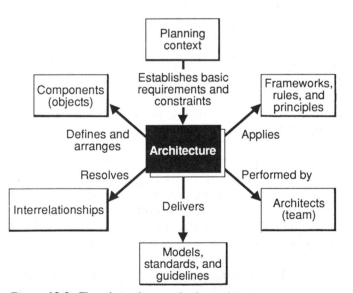

Figure 10-3. The relationships involved in architecture.

As shown in the figure, for any type of architecture, there must be a well-defined planning context. Most often this is some form of a plan which conveys basic requirements, associated guidelines, and constraints and which itself may be the deliverable of some higher-level architecture.

There must be a commonly accepted set of components (or objects) that provide the building blocks of the architecture. One or more classes of components might exist, each with unique types of members and with associated qualities or attributes. These building blocks and their attributes are defined at the appropriate level of detail to suit the needs of the planning decisions being made.

For example, the architect of a town is concerned with classes of residential, commercial, industrial, educational, and recreational properties and the various transportation and utility infrastructure components that they share. Key attributes for residential zones are type of structure, lot size, and expected number of occupants. At the next level, the building architect is concerned with the architecture pertaining to the structure and use of the individual buildings in the context of the subdivision model.

After identifying components, there is a need to understand the relationships among them. This usually involves some form of modeling to evaluate different placement options to best resolve the interconnecting components. The town planner evaluates various options for laying out communities to determine the allocation of available space to various types of properties, their use of common access and arterial highways, and their need for utility services.

In delivering models to the follow-on designers or contractors, architects indicate the requirements for using standard components or interfaces, and provide guidelines for the development of more detailed plans. The town planner applies zoning bylaws and building codes to ensure conformity with accepted principles and standards of construction.

Architects must also consider esthetics. Designing pleasing architectures is the artistic side of architectural planning. Thus the considerations of the town planner for laying out streetscapes that are attractive and that discourage through traffic, hide utility services from view, and impose certain structural restrictions on builders to ensure diversity of housing designs are all key elements of residential neighborhood design. It is these elements that will gain the accolades of the eventual home buyer.

Architects turn visions into reality. They are the link between the conceptualization of a need or opportunity and the creation of implementable plans. In particular, they must meet the needs of the in-

tended users of the planned facility. Users are often not directly involved in architectural planning. Architects communicate with the spon-
sors of the endeavor, with business and financial interests, and with the
subsequent contractors.

Architectural planning is often multilayered. Each succeeding layer
uses the same overall approach but with more detailed components. Architectures can move from the *conceptual* to the *logical* to the *physical* as
more detail is added. For *physical* construction plans, the word *design* is
usually substituted for architecture.

There is an analogous scenario associated with IT architecture. The
state of era I information technology planning can be compared with
the formative days of community living, where planning centered on
the needs of individual families and enterprises. Family or business
units developed specific solutions to their needs, with little regard for
long-term impacts or potential sharing of resources. In just three short
decades, organizations have passed through the pioneer days of IT.
They now recognize the need to function as interdependent societies.
Accordingly, there is a need to develop the master plan and the associated management processes to guide the next phases of this fast-paced
evolution.

Five Views of the New
IT Architecture

An IT architecture comprises five interrelated architectural models.
Each of these represents a different view or perspective of the way IT
will provide the desired business results. These five views are shown in
Fig. 10-4.

Business View

The *business architecture* (Chap. 8) models the future enterprise using
logical service units to represent the *reengineered* (or more precisely,
rearchitected) business. This view supports the principle that businesses
should first be reengineered, before work processes are redesigned and
new IT applications developed.

The business model is presented as a network of service functions
linking internal and external clients and servers. Business transactions
(i.e., information flows) move along defined communication paths between these service functions to trigger business activity and further in-

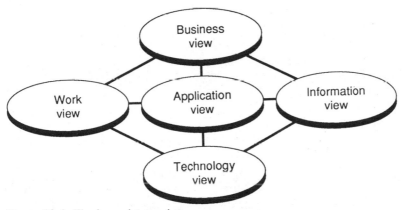

Figure 10-4. The five architectural views.

teractions. In this way, a very dynamic network model of the re-engineered business can be created.

Work View

The *work architecture* (Chap. 9) is the second view of the architecture. The reengineered service functions are modeled using work activities, associated human resources (classes of users), work locations, and associated resources, including information. The goal of the modeling is to determine the most effective means of supporting these activities with information technology.

Work architecture results in the creation of business process models that are very useful to convey the impact of IT on the changing nature of work, including who does what, where, and when, and with what IT tools. Before and after scenarios are useful techniques for building understanding and pointing out key opportunities for improvement. This work view is particularly useful in building the architectural requirements with business managers and intended users. It also provides an excellent basis for assessing business impacts and resulting financial benefits and costs.

Information View

Just as the work view is derived from the reengineered business model, so is the enterprise information model. This *information view* provides the information engineering perspective on the architecture. By understanding the basic service functions of the business, information architects determine fundamental information resource requirements and represent these as an information model.

Application View

The business process models and information models are linked by the *application view*. The goal is to have as much of the enterprise information as possible maintained in computer-accessible form. These automated information bases must be created, updated, accessed, and deleted using applications. These applications support the work activities of business processes by providing automated procedures and managing information storage and retrieval in support of integrated business service functions and associated users.

Technology View

The final view is the *technology view*. The technology view links up with the work model by providing the required technology platforms to meet the needs of various user classes at identified work locations. The work architects and technology architects resolve the basic requirements for workstations and servers, including functionality, associated peripherals, portability, etc.

The technology view also links with the application and information models. The many types of IT applications require different technologies to be integrated to support multifunction applications in both operational and developmental situations. The technology architect must not only place these applications on appropriate platforms, but also resolve their use of various information bases.

The resolution of all these various architectural links and technology choices is the challenge of building the technology architecture model. It is around this model that the standards-based IT infrastructure is defined.

Each of these five views can typically be assigned to a specialized architecture team. However, these teams must work together to achieve a coherent overall IT architecture. Each view represents a different client base for the architect. For example, the business model must appeal to business executives and strategic planners. This community is looking to the architect to identify and structure the strategic business opportunities involving information technology.

Once a new vision of the business is established, the work-system architects have a context. Their clients are managers of business units and the key users of the technology, the people who are most affected by automation and business transformation.

As with building architects, IT architects work with contractors. IT contractors are various technology specialists. *Application* developers build and maintain the resulting applications. *Information* managers organize and protect the information assets of the enterprise. *Technology* designers configure, install, and integrate the technology platforms and communication facilities that constitute the IT infrastructure.

These five views provide the architectural framework that can then be utilized to support the architecture process. In the early stages, the resulting models are highly conceptual. They become more logical and eventually physical as the architectural process links with the development and delivery processes.

Using this framework, architectural principles can be developed to guide the various architectural teams.

IT Architectural Principles

Architectural principles are *statements of preferred architectural direction or practice*. They help establish a context for architectural design decisions by using business criteria to rationalize basic architectural choices. Principles eliminate the need for evaluating endless alternatives in the modeling stages by agreeing up front on preferred directions. In combination with an architectural framework, they form the starting point for the development of target architectures.

One of the first organizations to adopt the new approaches to IT architecture was Chemical Bank in New York. In the late 1980s, the bank launched a major initiative to establish an enterprise architecture. Earlier attempts at choosing technology standards had not gained wide acceptance from a well-entrenched and very dispersed IT community, which included other acquired regional banking operations. Bruce Hasenyager, senior vice president, faced the challenge of helping Chemical make the transition.

Hasenyager described his planning dilemma, saying "I know we need an enterprise architecture for information technology. Is it possible to create an architecture when we haven't completed our strategic business and re-organization planning?" It was agreed that the best situation for Chemical would be "to be ready to support any conceivable change in business direction that the executive could throw our way."

The use of principles as a planning technique had gained exposure in a *Harvard Business Review* article.[4] DMR's integration study had developed proven techniques for modeling technology, particularly the migration from host to client/server computing. It was decided to marry these two techniques: develop architectural principles covering the different architectural views and build generic technology models as a framework for establishing technology standards.

However, the exercise required buy-in from the entire IT community at Chemical. This meant executive sponsorship, starting with Barbara Capsalis, chief technology officer, and with active leadership from a steering committee of senior vice presidents. Four task forces composed of senior managers and professionals were formed, each meeting approximately 1 day a week over a 3-month period. What was initially grudging participation became enthusiastic support. The task force members began to feel the lifting of resistance to change barriers and the ability to communicate their thoughts and ideas using the established principles and models.

One of the early outputs of this process was a list of 26 principles which had been produced and agreed upon by the task force members and steering committee. These became a powerful transition management tool in their own right. As reinforced by Barbara Capsalis, in her cover letter in the published principles brochure, "I intend to manage by these principles; I trust you will too."

Guidelines for Principles

The following are characteristics of good architectural principles:

- Each principle clearly states a fundamental belief of the organization.
- No motherhood! Each principle should have a counterargument. For example, "Information is an asset" is not a good principle because it is hard to disagree with it.
- Principles should be simply stated and understandable to both business and IT managers.
- Principles need to be rationalized. State, using business-related factors where possible, why this statement of principle is preferred.
- The implications of adopting a principle should also be identified. Show that you considered the types of impacts adopting the principle will have on the organization.

Figure 10-5 shows an example of a principle, complete with statement, rationale, and implications.

Principle

Our IT architecture should utilize standard, shareable, and reusable components across the enterprise

Rationale

- It is critical that the IS organization improve its responsiveness to business needs and deliver solutions faster and cheaper and with better quality. Our organization is going through substantial change, and IS must be better able to build flexibility into its systems and allow them to adapt to changing business requirements.

- Using standard components as the basis for defining and building the architecture and delivered application systems can improve our productivity through using previously defined and built modules. Rather than building new components each time, developers can concentrate on new business requirements.

- Using standard components will also improve the ability of our systems to adapt to changing requirements, as changes can be isolated to only those modules that are affected.

Implications

- Adoption of this principle will require attention to a number of key management and organizational requirements.

- A means of identifying, defining, and communicating the necessary standard components will need to be developed.

- Areas where standard components will apply include work processes, applications, information, and technology. A management process will be required to track the generation and usage of these common components and applicable standards. This further implies the need for a well-implemented, common system delivery methodology.

- A library of terms, definitions, access rules, characteristics, and interrelationships of each of the standard components needs to be implemented to support corporatewide requirements.

Figure 10-5. Sample principle.

Categories of Architectural Principles

Five categories of architectural principles should be developed, corresponding to the five architectural views. There are typically three to six principles in each category. Some sample topics and themes are presented below for each of the five categories:

1. General architectural principles
   - *Customer focus.* All architectural decisions will support the delivery of customer-oriented systems, i.e., systems that are responsive to customer demands, adaptable to changing markets, promote high quality, and are easy to use.
   - *Consistency.* Wherever we have common requirements, we will treat them in a consistent way.
   - *Modularity.* We will develop architectures based on modular components with standardized interfaces to support flexibility and reusability.
   - *Openness.* We will choose components and associated standards to increase the possibility of using industry standards with a preference for vendor-neutral implementations.
   - *Buy versus make.* We prefer architectural solutions that support the incorporation of purchasable and integratable components over building solutions from scratch.
   - *Cost of compliance.* Compliance with architectural standards may incur higher up-front costs than noncompliant solutions, but will pay off in the medium to long term.
   - *Measurement.* Measuring the use and performance of the architectural components will be included as part of the requirements.

2. Work organization IT principles
   - *Accessibility.* We will provide the necessary accessibility to authorized users to meet their requirements for various functions at different work locations.
   - *Information capture.* Information should be captured in computer-readable form as close to the source of origin as possible, including external sources.
   - *Information exchange.* Once captured, information should be stored and exchanged using electronic means such that manual transcription and reentry are avoided.
   - *Common user interface.* Wherever possible, the various applications and tools should present a common look and feel to avoid confusion and reduce or eliminate user training.

3. Application architecture principles

- *Simplicity*. We will avoid developing applications that are overly complex by separating functionality into basic and optional modules and by managing information rather than process.
- *Reusability*. We will support the sharing and reuse of common application modules or components across development projects and use common environments to increase reusability.
- *Distribution*. We will place the applications (tools) and associated information as close as possible to the point of use to address the required level of sharing.
- *Replication*. Where distribution results in replication of common applications in multiple work locations on local technology platforms, we will manage the compatibility of these software "packages" to maintain integrity and support a common architecture.
- *Methodology*. We will use a common development methodology to manage the application portfolio and development environment, including the means of providing shareable components.

4. Information architecture principles

- *Security*. Protection of confidentiality and privacy of information will be included in all architectural considerations.
- *Multiform*. We will develop architectures and resulting systems to manage information in all its forms (data, text, sound, image, and video).
- *Data definitions*. All information will be subject to data administration to ensure common definitions and provide for consistency of use.
- *Stewardship*. Responsibility for data integrity of various information subjects will be assigned to particular business units, and they will assume obligations for making this information available to other authorized users.

5. Technology architecture principles

- *Diversity*. We will use the best type of technology platforms for the intended purpose while reducing the diversity of different technologies within a single type of platform, in preference to one common standard per platform type.
- *Interchangeability*. We will choose and implement technology components such that we have the option of interchanging vendor products for functional, performance, or cost reasons with no or minimal disruption to the technology service.

- *Workstation orientation.* We will utilize intelligent multifunctional workstations as the exclusive or primary means of delivering functionality to end users.
- *Network orientation.* We will attach all workstations directly to the network, either locally or through wide area networks (wired or wireless) with secure communications linkages to all required servers.

These are examples of possible principles to support the transition to era II. It is most important to gain consensus on the choice of principles among the members of the various architectural teams before proceeding with building the associated architectural models. These principles will become embodied in the subsequent architectural models.

It is not uncommon or alarming, when conducting the baseline assessment, to discover that the newly agreed principles are not well reflected in the existing systems. This finding can be a useful grounding for the senior IT resources to agree that it's time to get serious about architecture.

Because of the importance of establishing an enabling technology infrastructure, we will concentrate the remainder of this chapter on this topic.

Technology Architecture

Although we stress the importance of aligning the IT plans with a reengineered view of the business (Chaps. 8 and 9), it is possible to begin retooling the IT architecture in advance of firmly established business requirements, as Chemical Bank was pleased to discover. By using a generic set of requirements and solutions, it is possible to develop a conceptual-level architecture that can be used to both foster understanding about the enabling effects of IT and begin the migration of the technology infrastructure itself.

Figure 10-6 shows the positioning of the technology view as the enabling infrastructure for work, applications, and information. It also shows the three types of technology components that make up a technology view.

There are three central components to the technology architecture. Applications provide automated functionality and manage information by using *application environments* to build or develop specific functionality. These application environments are composed of different types of *technology environments* which support the internal operations (known as *system software components*). These technology environments

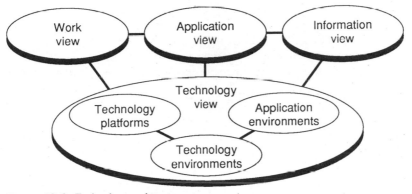

Figure 10-6. Technology architecture components.

are placed on or distributed across various *technology platforms,* which represent the physical computer and communications hardware.

Application Environments

Application environments are making it easier and easier to provide standard or customized types of applications using purchased software packages. Application environments are prepackaged groupings of procedures, often with customizable features, which have a natural affinity. Often the software that corresponds to these environments can be purchased shrink-wrapped—illustrating a high degree of applicability across different work environments and types of users.

The PC revolution popularized shrink-wrapped application environments in a big way. Many of these have set, de facto industry standards, such as document processing, spreadsheet, and graphic presentation tools. But the concept of application environments extends beyond PCs and beyond tools to provide an increasingly rich set of software functions that can be combined to build and customize applications for work automation. You should seek to take full advantage of shrink-wrapped, function-rich application environments to greatly reduce software development effort.

The concept of application environments is critical to gaining the productivity and flexibility that are so necessary in providing second-era applications. As we reviewed in Chap. 7, application development is shifting from being a craft to a production activity.

In early era I, the concept of application environments did not exist. Applications were developed using programming languages that linked through compilers (which enable computers to understand programming languages) to the technology environments on which they ran. The programmers created all of the functionality—even how the data were organized. The closest thing to reusability was something called program *subroutines* which were shared within a program.

Although the techniques for programming have been improved, the fact remains that organizations are burdened by large monolithic applications, often involving millions of lines of code that have been crafted, patched, converted, retrofitted, and cursed over several years of evolution.

As with any area of IT architecture, it is important to separate software requirements that are unique to one part of an organization and those that are common across several parts or across the entire enterprise.

Consider the generic list of work activities developed for knowledge and service workers in Chap. 9. Not surprisingly, a number of application environments directly support one or more of these activities.

We have identified 20 different types of application environments available today. Note that these are often combined to create even higher-level environments and are used by both end users and developers to create business applications.

1. *Data entry.* These environments provide data capture for collection or logging purposes. They support simple hand-held portable units and often incorporate various types of scanners to speed up data collection and improve accuracy.

2. *Transaction processing.* Transaction processing supports capture, processing, and storage of information. It could involve on-line interactive exchange with the user or batch processing of previously captured data.

3. *Inquiry processing.* Inquiry processing supports business activities requiring interactive selection, extraction, and presentation of stored information from files and databases.

4. *Decision support.* Decision support provides interactive modeling and simulation tools that allow the user to analyze the effects of alternative decisions.

5. *Expert systems.* Expert systems use a type of artificial intelligence that takes or recommends actions based on presented situations and past "experience." They are used to augment human decision-making processes where the expertise or thought processes of the decision maker can be described using rules, such as risk assessment.

6. *Real-time control.* Real-time control supports event-driven processing for monitoring and actuating physical processes, for example,

process control and robotics. For this reason they are often referred to as *sensor-based* systems.

7. *Document processing.* Document processing now includes text and graphics composition capabilities to produce high-quality documents and presentations, with advanced formatting, styling, and spell-checking features. Color production is becoming common.

8. *Electronic publishing.* Electronic publishing extends document creation and production tools to provide formal publishing capabilities. These include incorporation of photographic-quality images and color graphics and very advanced formatting and style features.

9. *Document storage and retrieval.* Document storage and retrieval is used to retain large volumes of stored information in document formats. Optical storage technologies allow for storage of scanned or computer-produced documents using digital storage techniques similar to those of audio CD players.

10. *Graphics processing.* Graphics processing supports the creation and manipulation of complex drawing applications such as computer-aided drafting and design (CADD). They often include the ability to derive different views of three-dimensional objects using rotation (visualization).

11. *Image processing.* Image processing allows for the manipulation of information in image (i.e., pictorial) format. This kind of processing is based on advance pattern recognition techniques. Image processing environments are at the heart of CAT scanning technology for medical applications and are also widely used to analyze aerial photographs, identify fingerprints, and age facial photographs.

12. *Sound processing.* Sound processing environments include voice recognition, interactive voice response, and speech or sound synthesis. They are used for voice-based computer interaction as well as production and editing of audio outputs and recordings.

13. *Video processing.* Video processing is used to create video productions for TV or workstation display incorporating video images, graphics, animation, and simulation. Interactive video will increasingly be applied in training and learning situations.

14. *Hypermedia processing.* These environments are the ultimate in combining multiple forms of information into a workstation context. Users "navigate" through the information displayed in the most appropriate form and follow whatever relationship best suits their need. This technique throws off the constraints of presenting information in the form of a document or recording.

15. *Electronic mail.* These environments distribute messages, docu-

ments, and files electronically among user's mailboxes. Some now integrate with facsimile equipment. Electronic mail systems are also used to route preformatted forms to or between transaction processing environments to support EDI.

16. *Voice mail.* Voice messaging environments capture messages from callers unable to connect. Ideally voice mail should be integrated with Email, at least to the extent of alerting the user through a common workstation.

17. *Enhanced telephony.* The plain old telephone system has been replaced by its computer-based cousin, which now delivers a wide range of features, including caller identification, call waiting, and call forwarding. The universality of the telephone resulted from standardization in the communications industry and will continue to improve its usefulness in era II. Improved mobility, beyond cellular, is just around the corner.

18. *Shared-screen conferencing.* Shared-screen conferencing environments allow for the connection of workstations over communications facilities providing concurrent display of information and interaction between two or more users. Combined with a voice conference, this kind of conferencing provides for low-cost "presentation" conferencing. This is an environment poised for rapid growth with the arrival of high-bandwidth dial-up services.

19. *Videoconferencing.* These environments provide limited or full-motion videoconferencing between worksites. This kind of conferencing allows for personal interaction on a video face-to-face basis. New workstation technologies incorporating CCD cameras (just like the camcorders) are bringing this technology to the professional or management workstation, rather than requiring studio environments.

20. *Broadcasting.* Broadcasting environments are now allowing private-use television for broadcasting to selected audiences. These systems are becoming popular for making announcements and providing education to those within corporations and to invited client audiences. The technology often incorporates broadcast video with audioconferencing for question-and-answer sessions.

Obviously, today's application architect has a lot more to work with than his or her predecessor in era I. These 20 application environments present a basis for tracking advances in functional capability and the feasibility of automating business procedures. They represent that critical link for aligning work-system redesign with IT—for connecting what is desirable with what is possible.

A useful technique is to determine the potential application for each of these environments with the logical service units in the business, to provide a high-level opportunity assessment. Similarly, it is useful to classify the various types of users and determine their need for these application environments. The empowered employee in an era II organization will have a high or medium attraction to a wide range of these environments. Realizing this fact can help the application architect package these environments into an appropriate workbench of tools and related applications for each class of user.

For example, integrated packages of various application environments could enable a sales manager to automate the entire production of a weekly sales report. Consider the following scenario:

The sales manager invokes a software "assistant" in his workstation which "remembers" the sequence of actions taken. He then selects his "information manager" tool and opens the customer sales database (which, unbeknown to him, happens to reside on the division's mainframe computer) and using the query language he selects the current week's sales results by region and by product line. He requests that this information be displayed in a spreadsheet tool (which resides on a local server), where he sets up a table both to compare this week's results with last week's and to compare the year-to-date results with plan objectives.

Next he selects the graph generator feature of the spreadsheet to display the comparisons using line graphs. He moves the graph over to his document-processing tool where he has set up a standard format and distribution list for the weekly sales report. He then places the electronic document in an out-tray on his screen, which requests the name of the recipient. He enters a distribution list but requests a "hold" on sending until personally released. He reviews the document, and a messaging capability (located on another server) sends the report. He enters an annotation into his tickler file to follow up in 2 days.

He then returns to the software "assistant" in his workstation who has been dutifully recording this process. He tells the assistant to store this sequence of activities under the label of *weekly sales report* and to perform those same activities every Monday morning at 6 a.m. From then on, he only need review the results already in his screen out-tray each Monday morning (which he can do from his home or portable PC while on the road) and add any comments or observations to the report before releasing it. Better still, he can spot the competitive price war emerging in the western region and get right to work along with the regional sales manager to develop a counterstrategy.

This is not science fiction. This is the reality of era II technology. This is achievable by having the application and technology architects set up the appropriate mix of application environments for this type of user, by defining the sales management application around a standard database also supported by the query language, and by teaching the sales manager to use the various tools, made easier by the common user interface. This is the second-era approach to building software applications. Combined with work system reengineering, the result is high productivity and effectiveness, flexible use of information, and tightly controlled corporate information.

Technology Environments

Technology environments are "services" required to support an application environment, as described above. These are most often implemented through various types of systems software. Where possible, technology environments should be based on industry standards. It is at this level of the technology architecture where the majority of standards exist or are under development.

Common technology environments include services in the areas of:

- User interface management
- Information management
- Transaction management
- Operating systems
- Communications management

Technology environments are of prime importance in achieving integration and enabling the migration to client/server computing. They can be used to compare and contrast the key industry standardization thrusts, called *open systems environments*, being proposed by various consortia, standards bodies, and vendors. They are primarily used to evaluate and select appropriate technology models for choice of component and interface standards. They are also tightly linked to the choice of technology platforms and specific vendor offerings.

Technology Platforms

Technology platforms refer to the client/server hardware required to support IT applications. They constitute the hardware model of the architecture. Technology platforms include the following classes:

- Intelligent workstations
- Work-group servers
- Departmental servers
- Enterprise servers
- External servers

They are interconnected by:

- Local area networks
- Local switching systems
- Value-added wide area networks

A typical second-era conceptual technology architecture is shown in Fig. 10-7. In Chap. 5, we examined the shift from host computing to network computing. It is the job of the technology architect to match the technology components shown in Fig. 10-7 to the work, application, and information views and provide the most flexible and efficient technology infra-

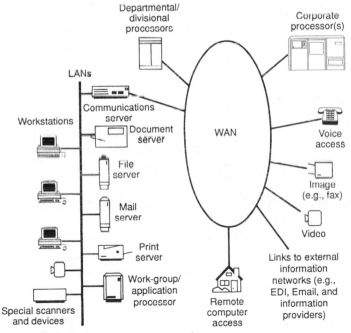

Figure 10-7. Conceptual technology architecture.

structure possible. The architecture must define roles, set standards, and establish guidelines for the use and placement of application environments, technology environments, and technology platforms.

Ten Guidelines for Achieving an Era II IT Architecture

To summarize, the process of retooling the IT architecture is key to making the transition. The following 10 guidelines should be followed:

1. Emphasize the *process* of architecture planning, not the plan. Experience has shown that architecture projects are first and foremost challenges of organizational change, not technology. Typically inherent in the new approach to architecture is a new culture and a new vision of how technology can support the business. The process should seek to achieve organizational change around a shared, participative process.

2. Ensure that the architectural vision is owned *jointly* by the IS function and the business units. With the dispersion of many IT responsibilities, business unit professionals are stakeholders in the IT architecture and need to have joint ownership for it and be central to its creation. We recommend that if you are not going to involve key business stakeholders in the process, don't bother undertaking the process. The result will be an interesting document, rather than a real change in the enterprise and its capacity to compete.

3. Ensure that architecture planning is *business-*, *not technology-*, *driven*. The process is oriented to aligning IS with the business: linking with key business drivers through architectural principles and key architectural models on the one hand and involving business practitioners on the other.

4. Focus on *migration*, not just on the issue of target architecture. Research shows that the issue of "how do we get from here to there" is as important as defining the ultimate destination.

5. Design for *continuous change*. Through principles, generic models and adoption of standards, and continual iteration, seek to create a systems environment that evolves and changes continuously rather than being cast in concrete.

6. While the planning horizon may be longer term, *emphasize action and delivery of short-term results* that can be of immediate benefit to the organization. An architectural process can only be sustained through successes that affect the performance of the enterprise. As such, it should in-

vestigate opportunities to implement new paradigm systems and/or standards before the completion of the broader architectural process.

7. Create a *fast-path process*. The goal is to iteratively define and develop architecture quickly in cycle times of weeks and months rather than years. Major enterprisewide modeling activities, which were on the critical path of traditional architecture efforts, should be background activities if conducted at all.

8. *Drive down to the actual delivery of systems,* end-user tools, and facilities. A key problem of traditional architectures was often the big "so what?" By failing to link with the actual acquisition of technology and construction of systems, the raison d'être of an architectural process broader than a specific application design is typically undermined.

9. *Use the five architectural views as a framework for architecture.* They provide the basis for linking the new vision to effective development and deployment of a supporting technology infrastructure.

10. *Just do it!* This slogan has been dubbed the "Nike law" by DMR. Walter De Backer argues that the need for enterprises to begin a migration process is urgent. "The longer an enterprise waits, the greater the inertia and investment in its legacy systems—in turn demanding conversions to the new platform rather than orderly migration." It is recommended that organizations undertake a process to define and migrate to a standards-based architecture as soon as is possible.

11

Realigning
the IS Function

The walls between the traditional IS department and the business units in enterprises are crumbling in ways that few anticipated.

In the early days of computing, the mantle of leadership was held by the professionals and managers in the IS department. This organization grew out of the needs and constraints of the first era of information technology. The demands of the second era are causing IS management, their superiors, and the internal customers of IS to rethink the nature, purpose, structure, and management of the IS function. Senior management is coming to the conclusion that the old organization is inappropriate to meeting the needs of the new environment. As is the case with the technologies themselves, the walls of the first era are falling as system resources migrate into business units and as information technology and business goals converge. Growing numbers of IS stakeholders in every organization are taking on important responsibilities for IS strategy, implementation, and leadership—beginning with their own personal use and that of their work groups, enterprises, and external partnerships.

What are the implications of the new paradigm for the nature and structure of the IS function and the relationship between the IS and business? What does the new era demand regarding strategies for aligning the IS organization with the business organization?

Essentially, there is a need to realign the IS function with the business as it and supporting technology go through their corresponding paradigm shifts. As depicted in Fig. 11-1, this involves forging a new vision of the function, reshaping its structure, implementing the new, and establishing an ongoing renewal process.

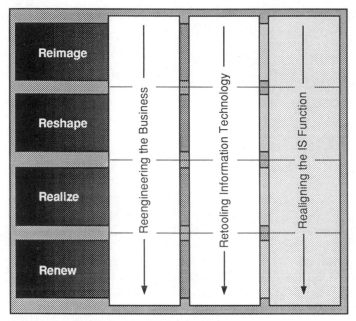

Figure 11-1. Realigning the IS function.

The Stereotypical Era I
IS Organization

The IS organization has been stereotyped as the "embattled fortress."[1]
While this stereotype does have some valid historical roots, many IS organizations today do not fit into the old mold.

However, an embattled fortress it often was. Over the three decades of its existence, IS data-processing (DP) or management information system (MIS) departments grew to be formidable entities within a heavily controlled and secure environment. They also happened to consume significant financial and other resources of a corporation. The data center, referred to as the "glass house," was protected by a glass wall that preserved the air-conditioned climate for the corporate mainframes, while at the same time displaying the mystical technology. Like the technology, the IS function was centralized, reporting to an IS executive, who typically reported to the chief financial officer. Corporate systems were almost exclusively mainframe processors that were expensive not only to purchase but also to maintain. The proprietary systems that dominated the first two decades of enterprise computing left the department subject to the pricing and technology of the computer supplier. As computers grew in importance to the enterprise, so did the price tag. The centralized keepers of the keys expanded their role and power into what often appeared to others as an empire.

Alignment of IS resources with business needs was not a problem in the early days, as there was only one computer and it did mostly corporate accounting. Except for payroll, the computer was not critical for running the day-to-day business. Information services was run as a service bureau, and the emerging IS culture celebrated a mystery and exclusivity that created walls between IS and the rest of the enterprise.

Among other things, this resulted in an image problem for the IS manager. During the advent of data processing, few business executives could imagine how much information technology was going to cost. The DP (as they were often called) departments created isolated systems that depended on programmers and systems experts. Because of their general lack of experience in day-to-day business operations and limited awareness of overall corporate strategies and objectives, systems professionals often operated in a vacuum, essentially cut off from the rest of the organization. As demand for computer applications grew, so did contention for the centralized resources. User departments had to submit their applications to the central queue and lobby, plead, or fight for attention and priority.

The attitude of people outside the data-processing function often ranged from indifference, to hostility, to passive resignation. As increasing numbers of people in divisions throughout the enterprise began to better understand technology and some of its potential benefits, they often became more critical of their systems departments. Some complained about the inadequacy of the existing software applications, while others were often left hoping that this would be the year when their application requests would float to the top of the development backlog. In either instance, they generally felt isolated from the development and implementation of systems functions and applications. The data-processing department was viewed as a department, located off in a corner, that didn't really understand or care about the real needs and objectives of the corporation.

The attitude of IS personnel and their approach to systems development did nothing to diminish this user perspective. IS either owned everything and dictated what was going to be done (and when), or acted like a service bureau detached from the enterprise it served. IS managers were perceived as being technocrats speaking an arcane language and of not understanding the "real" business.

According to Tom Lodahl, of Cognitech Services Corporation (the company that partnered with DMR on the multiclient investigation *Aligning IS with the Business*), the old stereotype has become less applicable for most organizations.[2]

The stereotype of the IS function, trapped forever in the amber of its own early history and ground assumptions, is fading. In fact, IS takes on many different roles and shapes today, based partly on technological history, partly on the momentum of outdated impressions, partly on its legacy of conflict with business people, and most recently on its demonstrated ability to make a difference in the competitive struggle. One organization perceives IS (and assigns it a role as) the guardian of the back room, dealing only with labour displacement. Another perceives it as an essential partner in strategic forays. Right now I think what shapes the IS function mostly is the extent to which business management gives a strategic role to IS; whether IS can handle this role or not; and whether IS can deliver.[3]

The New Strains on the IS Organization

Such new roles for IS have been fostered by the new business environment and demands on IS for effective systems. Business pressures and the new role for information systems have placed considerable strains on the IS organization to change. As we have explained, information technology is moving from the back rooms to the front lines as it becomes part of mission-critical business functions. Users need systems that integrate tools at the desktop, bridge applications across the enterprise, and reach externally. Users need systems next week, not next year. Waiting 18 months for a central IS function to develop an application is no longer acceptable in the new business context.

By the late 1980s the demands for mission-critical applications were a major factor causing dispersion of IS responsibilities. Because IS often couldn't deliver, organizations took steps to remove the walls that isolated data processing from the rest of the organization by redeploying IS resources in their own business units. In an important study conducted by Cognitech Services Corporation for the Society of Information Management, researchers Lodahl and Redditt found that pressure for competitive advantage systems was causing organizations to disperse their IS resources. Over and over the researchers heard "We had to do it, because centralized IS couldn't get out the applications fast enough."[4]

Other factors are causing dispersion pressures on the IS function. The recessions of the early 1980s and 1990s brought about massive pressures for cutbacks in central IS expenditures. Whereas IS costs in the typical first-era organization grew at a rate of well over 15 percent per year, the 1990s enterprise has a priority of reducing IS costs, often by a similar proportion. The 1980s also heralded the emergence of the lean and mean, decentralized organizations that achieved "excellence" through tight control over their corporate missions and objectives and highly decentralized entrepreneurial and autonomous business units.[5]

At the same time, the technology paradigm shift *made it possible* to disperse. In the first era, IS was centralized because the technology required this approach. As explained in Chap. 5, Grosch's law dominated thinking—the more applications that could be combined on a computer, the cheaper the cost of processing. This "bigger is better" mind-set led to centralized systems that required a centralized IS function.

The rise of the personal computer and later the rise of the powerful workstation of the early 1990s, together with standards and network computing, have enabled organizations to take a fundamentally different view of how to deploy IS resources. In the extreme point of view, some have argued that there is no longer a need for *any* central IS function, as IS professionals in the various business units can work together to achieve any common goals they may have. For example, the *Sloan Management Review* stimulated the debate with two controversial articles. One was entitled "Whither the IT Organization?"[6] The other went further, predicting through its title "The Withering *Away* of the IS Organization"[7] (italics added).

But ironically, while numerous market and industry factors have encouraged more decentralized organizations, the need for strong, enterprisewide capabilities has also stormed into the picture.

To begin, a critical business unit is the enterprise itself. As discussed in Chap. 3, enterprisewide systems are becoming critical to success and survival. Executive information systems and management support systems that consolidate information from across the enterprise, technologies such as EDI which link the enterprise with suppliers and consumers, corporatewide office communication systems, enterprise applications such as the reservation systems or courier company tracking systems—all argue for the creation of strong enterprise capabilities.

The focus of information systems is now changing from reducing costs and improving internal operating procedures and administrative efficiency to a multifaceted mechanism for uniting an enterprise and directly delivering products and services to the customer. It is precisely because information technology is a tool to reshape and revitalize divisions and operations throughout the enterprise that an enterprise architecture is required. As explained in Chap. 10 such an architecture is not a monolithic system, but a commonly agreed-upon set of principles, models, and standards that enable autonomous organizational units to work together through a shared network, a common information architecture, and a standardized technology environment.

Initially, this tension between dispersion forces and needs for enterprise capabilities has often unfolded as a turf battle. However, it is something far more profound. The issue is one of alignment—bringing IS into synchronization with the business. The business pull and technology push are causing an alignment problem. To fix this problem, a realignment of the IS organization with the business is required. This challenge was the topic of the syndicated research Aligning IS with the Business.

Building the High-Performance IS Function: What Is Involved?

As with reengineering the business (Chap. 9) and retooling information technology (Chap. 10), realigning the IS organization for high performance has four main dimensions or plateaus:

1. *Reimaging.*   This involves setting a vision and overall strategy for the IS function. It begins with a diagnosis of the IS function and its contribution to the business as well as a set of goals and/or principles for IS which will drive realignment.

2. *Reshaping.*   How should IS resources be deployed; in what organizational structure and in what locations? The main structural alignment approaches are dispersion of IS resources, (re)centralizing IS resources, decentralizing IS resources, converting IS to a profit center or establishing the IS function as a separate company, and "outsourcing" IS or parts to a third-party contractor. Although many organizations adopt a hybrid of these, there is typically a main thrust that can be identified.

3. *Realizing.*   The research found evidence that differing approaches to IS work processes and the way people are hired, promoted, and developed affect IS contribution to the business. These include policies and programs in the areas of recruitment, promotion, career development, training, rewards, motivation, and quality management. To be effective, such approaches were found to require a high degree of planning, management commitment, and often cultural change.

4. *Renewal.*   An ongoing measurement program can evaluate performance of the IS function and enable ongoing feedback and refinement. Measures include the performance of the utility (for example, network downtime), rapidity of software development (for example, the reusability of code), user satisfaction (for example, perceived IS contri-

bution to the business), organizational readiness (for example, for further change), and user support (for example, service-level management response or hotline turnaround time).

Because this book is designed for non-IS executives and professionals, we focus below on the first two of the levels: reimaging and reshaping. Before we discuss these two levels, however, we turn our attention briefly to identifying symptoms that indicate that an organizational alignment problem exists.

Eight Symptoms of an Organizational Alignment Problem

Signs that IS is not organizationally aligned with the business include:

1. *Ongoing internal conflicts.*   The corporation faces ongoing organizational conflicts between the traditional IS function and user departments over roles, responsibilities, and control of system planning, development, and operations.

2. *Complaints about the performance of the IS function.*   In this situation, IS faces ongoing and substantial complaints from users about slow IS delivery and excessive chargebacks, and from senior management about high costs and questionable contributions. These problems may arise because of a fundamental inability of IS to demonstrate contribution to the business on the one extreme or a communication gap between users and IS on the other.

3. *Lack of an enterprisewide vision.*   Here, IS has been dispersed to the business units, but the requisite coordination to achieve an appropriate cross-organizational vision and architecture does not exist. Rather than a strategy of dispersion with coordination, the IS function has been balkanized, resulting in an inability of the enterprise to respond to enterprise-level opportunities.

4. *Competitive decline.*   Business unit managers see competitors leapfrog them through the innovative use of IT. The organization is unable to marshal the right business and IS resources to identify new opportunities and quickly deliver appropriate systems.

5. *Lack of business unit or senior management interest in the effective use of IT.*   In this situation there is little conflict between IS and the business units. There is the peace of the grave. All thinking, planning, and implementation of systems is controlled and conducted by a central

IS group. The typical result is the decline of organizational competitiveness and effectiveness.

6. *Inappropriate or deficient skill base.*   Lacking effective organizational alignment, the skill and knowledge base of IS professionals remains unchanged (first era) in face of new (second era) requirements. Typical deficiencies are lack of support for local area networks due to a mainframe-oriented skill set and lack of expertise to assist with business reengineering.

7. *High turnover of IS professionals.*   High turnover can be due to many factors, but typically the cause boils down to an IS alignment problem. IS professionals lack a clear strategy, role, and career program that can enable them to work effectively, grow as professionals, and share in the success they create.

8. *Redundancies in systems development.*   Similar systems or components of systems are developed in different parts of the enterprise on similar or different technology platforms. The unnecessary cost can be considerable. There is little reuse of information. The problems of gaps and overlap discussed in Part 1 can be significant.

Reimaging: Twelve Principles of IS Alignment

A solid business foundation should drive realignment, rather than the purely technological, turf, or personality considerations that often loom large. Our clients have found it useful to develop, through workshops, an overall set of principles that will determine the structure of the IS function, programs for the development of IS people and processes, and a program for continuous improvement. Below is a listing of sample principles. These can serve as a basis for discussion and development of the customized set of principles that are right to help your organization realign itself. Principles, in turn, can serve as a basis for a decision analysis to select from alternative alignment strategies.

1. *The requisite IS structure will enable rapid development of systems.*   The "applications queue" of yore is unacceptable. The solution to this problem not only is technological, but requires a strategy for the deployment of IS professional resources. The new structure must enable IS professionals to be responsive to user requirements. It must be fleet of foot — enabling fast translation of business requirements into

systems. Minimal bureaucracy should encumber it. IS should not be viewed by users as a constraint, but as an enabler.

2. *The IS function and the business operation should work in harmony.* The requisite IS structure must facilitate partnership. It will break down cultural walls, enabling IS professionals to better understand the business, and business professionals to better understand IS-enabled opportunities and important related issues. We must minimize turf issues, unnecessary conflict, and the human effort and turmoil they create. We must eliminate cultural walls between IS and the business. By encouraging closer contact between IS and the user community we must break down the IS stereotypes and their role in the organization.

3. *The structure will enable a tailored service to clients.* The days of one size fits all are gone. Within our enterprise there are vastly different systems planning, development, and management needs in business units serving very different markets. IS should deliver the appropriate, differentiated types and levels of system functions to users throughout the organization.

4. *The structure will be cost-effective.* This does not mean it must be the lowest-cost structure, but rather one that appropriately balances the tradeoffs between the need for cost control on the one hand and the need for fast, effective systems on the other.

5. *The structure will facilitate the moves by our enterprise to have an IT architecture.* It must enable our enterprise to move beyond our islands of information, applications, and technology to the kind of coherent infrastructure required to succeed as a corporation.

6. *The structure will enable a clear division of labor and responsibilities among IS professionals and between IS and the business.* The new era raises needs for new IS functions including the measurement of the IS contribution, the reengineering of work processes, the tracking of technology directions (the technology "gatekeeper"), and the management of the IT "utility," service levels, and softwarehouse repositories. The structure must enable ongoing execution of these functions with minimal redundancy, on the one hand, and minimal oversight or neglect, on the other.

7. *The approach will enable linking of staff goals and rewards to business success.* By tying IS success to business success, enterprises can help to ensure that IS and other business units move in the same direction. Strong links to business success are required to ensure that IS has a vested interest in understanding and fulfilling enterprise objectives.

8. *The structure will optimize user participation in the process of change.*   The reengineering of work processes and jobs can only be led and accomplished by those in the work group or business unit. Only business personnel can understand the change required. It is only through their complete ownership of the problem that transformation can be achieved.

9. *The approach will enable development of a leading-edge IS professional resource.*   It will facilitate the attraction of a higher-caliber professional resource than that of our main competitors. It will enable retention of our best talent. It will facilitate low turnover of IS professionals.

10. *We will have IS human resource standards in the areas of compensation, career development, training, and education.*   Employees will be compensated equally for work of equal value. Consistent with our corporate mission, commitment to social responsibility, and need to comply with government procurement restrictions, we will launch and maintain an affirmative action program.

11. *The structure will facilitate the shift in software development from IS professionals to end users.*   We will work with object-oriented software and our internal softwarehouse with a strategy of purchasing software parts. Rather than building software, we will encourage the user-driven construction of software.

12. *The structure must enable the measurement of IS costs.*   The main thrust of our enterprise is on investing in IT for competitive advantage and productivity, as opposed to displacing clerical and administrative costs. It is also critical that we don't lose a handle on the cost of that investment.

Five Structures for Aligning IS with the Business

There are five main structural approaches to aligning the IS organization with the business. Some clear themes have emerged from the DMR-Cognitech research on the issue of alignment.

Structure I: Dispersion of IS Resources

The dominant realignment theme is the movement of IS resources and influence away from central management and outward toward operat-

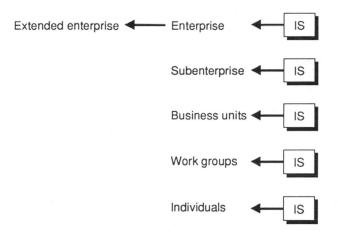

Extended enterprise ◄──── Enterprise ◄── IS

Subenterprise ◄── IS

Business units ◄── IS

Work groups ◄── IS

Individuals ◄── IS

Figure 11-2. The dispersed IS function.

ing units, work groups, and end users. A dispersion strategy places IS resources at each level of the enterprise, including the individual, work-group, enterprise (or subenterprise), and extended enterprise levels. All or part of the functions of IS may be dispersed. Typically IS resources are controlled by the user at the appropriate level where they gain a better understanding of operations and opportunities and are directed according to the business needs of the organizational unit involved. This is depicted in Fig. 11-2.

The alignment research cited the case of Merrill Lynch (ML) as a striking example of a corporation that has made an abrupt decision to disperse IS resources:

> Early in 1990 Merrill Lynch and Company announced its plan to de-centralize most of its 12,000 IS staff to the main business units of the company. Their move is astounding in more ways than one. Aside from being one of the very largest IS organizations in the country, Merrill Lynch's IS function was responsible—in the early 1980s—for one of the great preemptive competitive strikes of all time—the CMA (Cash Management Account). CMA literally drained savings institutions of their main source of funds, making this money available to brokerage account managers and giving Merrill Lynch at lease a five-year head start against competing financial management institutions.
>
> What happened? The CMA system integrated information from a wide variety of sources, built a comprehensive customer-relationship file and brought it to a terminal on the account manager's desk. Such a project could only be done with the support of a visionary champion, an integrated systems and communications architecture, inspired link-age between IS and business planning, a centralized development function, and very deep pockets. Preemptive strikes (especially

planned ones) are very rare, and the Merrill Lynch IS functions prospered — and grew.

By 1989, the seams started to show. Competing institutions now had their own versions of CMA. ML's profit center and business unit managers, seeing business opportunity in further developments of the core information system, demanded faster and more flexible development. The IS function was by now a prisoner of its own success; projects needed multiple levels of approval, structured project lifecycles stretched delivery times, and the competition started beating ML at its own game. ML believes that decentralizing the development function — to business units — will improve their competitive ability.[8]

Dispersion is different from the concept of decentralization, which takes the centralized functions and replicates them in smaller multiple locations — typically reporting up through an IS stovepipe. Dispersion is also different from the technical term *distributed computing,* which locates computing resources out in departments but generally maintains strong central control over systems operations and development. Instead, dispersion recognizes the necessary redefinition of roles and responsibilities which must occur if information technology is to support the business needs of the era II organization. For example, one of the key objectives of dispersion is to make IS more responsive to business strategies and needs. Yet there are huge benefits in integrating systems and cooperating with others in the organization. Coordination, in many areas ranging from technology architecture to IS compensation programs, should therefore accompany dispersion as an enterprise-level strategy.

Dispersion to business units does not mean that an organization has created the islands of automation that were often typical in the proprietary environment of the first technology of era I. While the applications are resident on the desktop and work-group server, they can also be integrated with other functions and operations of the enterprise. In a dispersed organization, the information technology tools and resources are located where they are needed to enable individuals or work groups to perform all of the necessary functions to meet both local and enterprise needs. By dispersing computing resources in a real estate company, for example, a customer's prearranged home mortgage and personal insurance arrangements can be more easily made by one division of the same organization. The technology is there to support the business objective of providing the most cost-effective and efficient customer service. With technology resources available at one source, the inappropriate internal barriers that separated the insurance operations from the mortgage operations disappear.

The developments enabling and encouraging dispersion correspond to the main themes of the paradigm shift:

- The arrival of the microprocessor that enables massive computing power to reside on the desktop rather than in a centralized computer center. It can also provide local access to the information resources of the entire enterprise.

- The growth in networking standards that support network computing and that enable dispersed computing environments to communicate.

- The increased interest and knowledge of line executives in using information technology to achieve business objectives.

- The need for business unit autonomy enabling responsiveness, flexibility, and the ability to sell off organizational components.

- The growing pressures on the centralized IS department to control costs. By dispersing the resources to the individual business units, the technology costs are spread across the organization and can be more closely measured against the business unit productivity.

The major driving force behind the dispersion trend is the need for IS to get closer to its customers — to deliver systems faster in response to competitive pressures. In their efforts to be more competitive, organizations are asking how they can better integrate the IS functions with overall business operations. Organizations are also recognizing that as information systems become central to business operations, they must change as rapidly as business demands, which means that the organizations have to be flexible and more closely aligned with specific enterprise operations. Financial institutions, for example, that want to bring new investment instruments to the market often have to act quickly to take full advantage of volatile market conditions. The window of opportunity for these competitive offerings may be days instead of weeks, months, or years as in the past. What this means is that information systems and support infrastructures have to be highly responsive. In a dispersed environment, technology has a greater capacity to change the nature of business operations quickly to meet sudden changes in market demand.

Dispersion is not a strategy that is necessarily forced onto a reluctant IS department. The concept of dispersion is sometimes introduced by enlightened IS executives who appreciate the need for the line organization to get involved in systems planning and implementation.

However, "central" IS disappears — replaced by an IS function that addresses the needs of the enterprise-level business unit. The new enterprise-level IS department can take the lead in planning, implementing, and operating the utility and may disperse its operation across multiple locations. The IS department also provides, supports, and coordinates network management facilities. Once the role of technology in supporting enterprise objectives and strategies is established and the utility is in place, IS may assist in expanding the business unit's role in application planning, development, and implementation. There is also a need for coordination in the establishment of project management standards, systems controls, software development environments, security, auditing, backup and recovery procedures, and standards. Of particular importance are the standards for the establishment of the storage and reuse of software parts in the enterprise softwarehouse. Another key area is *network management* — the establishment of enterprise-level standards, procedures, and technologies to manage a complex enterprise network consisting of components under the control of business units.

The enterprise-level IS department can assist a dispersed IS organization in other ways. Although dispersing the responsibilities for training, implementation, and management of change will make the transition to an automated environment easier, there is still a role for central coordination and planning. A centralized IS department, for example, can help to determine how the organization manages the change to a new way of conducting systems planning and implementation and can serve as an ongoing source of knowledge and expertise to the individual business units.

Dispersion is only one of many approaches to achieving an effective organizational alignment between IS and the business enterprise. However, our research has found it to be effective in a wide range of circumstances. Even when not combined with overall coordination, dispersion of IS correlated with high IS contribution to the business. Inversely, when IS reports through an IS stovepipe, IS contribution to the business tends to be lower.[9]

Structure II: Centralization
of IS Resources

One reaction to the centrifugal dispersion of IS technology and resources of the 1980s has been to regroup the forces under a tightly centralized IS organization. In its extreme, all IS functions are provided by a single concentrated group of IS resources to all levels of the organization (regardless of where they may be located). This is depicted in Fig. 11-3.

Centralization can enable effective control over many aspects of systems planning, implementation, and use. It is an effective way to achieve an information technology architecture — for example, with consistent data definitions and elements across the enterprise. It is often efficient, as there can be good planning and economies of scale in projects. The

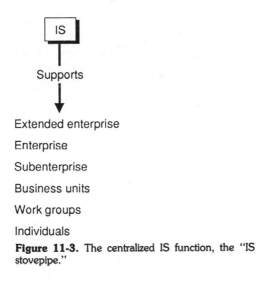

Figure 11-3. The centralized IS function, the "IS stovepipe."

massive pool of resources can increase the probability that highly spe-cialized resources can be found.

However, our conclusion regarding centralization is that, overall, it is an ineffective alignment strategy. To begin with, it is correlated with low overall IS contribution to the business.

Highly centralized organizations often build, rather than reduce, cul-tural walls between IS and its clients. IS professionals are typically re-mote from the people they support. One group must provide differen-tiated support to clients, which is often difficult. Costs can be high due to the necessity of a considerable bureaucracy. This is ironic, as central-ization is sometimes undertaken as an approach to get runaway costs under control. Additionally, centralized costs tend to be more visible be-cause they are easier to measure and have a higher profile to senior management. The visibility of these costs can sometimes be a liability.

Most important, centralized strategies often have an Achilles' heel — they can make the rapid development of many mission-critical systems difficult. Centralized IS resources are often too out of touch with the business op-portunities and requirements to use information technology for competi-tive or strategic advantage. Their culture is also often one of the first era — ranging from traditional mainframe expertise to a lack of appreciation of the dynamic, volatile competitive nature of the user's marketplace and ex-ternal environment. We have often found that centralized organizational strategies go hand in hand with the highly centralized, host-based technol-ogy architectures of the first era of information technology. Horse and cart — the two go together and which comes first is not particularly rele-vant, especially in the era of the automobile.

Further, centralization confuses the need for architecture (which can be achieved through cooperation in a dispersed environment) with the need for central ownership of technology resources. While many organizations have recentralized their IS operations to get control over architecture, others have attempted to achieve the same control by setting architectural standards—while at the same time delegating many IS responsibilities in a dispersed business environment. The goal is to have the architectural cake and eat it too—dispersed, entrepreneurial development and implementation of systems at the same time as a standardized enterprise platform that can maintain the integrity of the enterprise technology infrastructure.

Finally, centralization confuses the notion of a *central IS* department with the notion of an IS function that has an *enterprise level*. In a dispersed IS function every appropriate organizational level from the individual to the extended enterprise has corresponding IS resources—including the business unit called *the enterprise*. The enterprise-level IS function can address enterprise-level IS needs—as with any other business unit. Such needs could include enterprise applications, the enterprise softwarehouse, and enterprise approaches to career management for IS professionals. However, because the enterprise-level IS function sits on top of an IS stovepipe, it is obliged to work in a collaborative way with business units at other levels, in the spirit of forging agreements for shared needs.

Structure III: Decentralization of IS Resources

Another strategy is to *decentralize*, as opposed to *disperse*, IS resources (see Fig. 11-4). Here there are various IS groups throughout the organization that support two or more levels of the organization or two or more geographic locations. All IS functions (or a subset) may be provided at each location. For example, operations and development may be decentralized to a regional location, while planning and architecture functions remain centralized.

Arguably, centralization and decentralization are similar strategies, differentiated primarily by the physical location of the IS group. They are similar in that the IS professionals, though decentralized, usually report through a central IS stovepipe. That is, a dedicated IS group is still supporting multiple clientele and is usually managed by IS professionals. Unlike dispersion, a decentralized IS structure brings IS closer to the users but still retains walls between the IS group and the business organization. The main objective of decentralization is to get IS resources closer to the users.

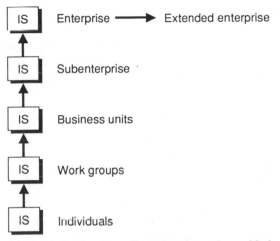

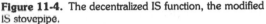

Figure 11-4. The decentralized IS function, the modified
IS stovepipe.

While colocation of IS people with business people was found to improve IS contribution, decentralization has a number of problems. Consultants Lodahl and Redditt have argued that instead of one big problem, a decentralized IS function simply creates many small ones.[10] The decentralized group often continues to operate like a centralized IS group providing multiple functions to a mixed clientele. Often, they argue, despite being moved out of the physical location of centralized IS, systems are still developed and services provided in the traditional ways, leaving the cultural walls between IS and the user intact. Further, IS usually continues to plan and motivate its professionals in exactly the same manner as does a centralized IS function.

The result can be a pendulum swing every few years between a centralized and decentralized IS structure, as in the case of American Express. The company reorganized its IS function several times through the decade of the 1980s, moving from centralization to decentralization and back again. IS professionals' career needs are not interrupted by decentralization, as the career paths between central IS and its outlying units usually remain intact. But, socially, IS groups relocated to business units can sometimes be isolated or even ostracized.

There is evidence that dispersion, as opposed to decentralization, can avoid these problems, through the complete integration of IS resources into each business unit. IS resources can be dispersed throughout the organization at the structural levels and to different geographic locations based on need. So, for example, there can be an enterprise-level IS function and other functions at the division, department, work-group, and other levels.

Structure IV: Establishing a Profit
Center or Separate Company

Another alignment strategy is to convert the IS function into a separate profit center that contracts with and services internal clients on a profit or break-even basis. The objective is usually to provide motivation for IS to break out beyond the traditional, unresponsive glass house culture and mentality to an entrepreneurial, innovative, cost-conscious, responsive organization. The pressure for this comes from free-market pressures, since a user organization can seek assistance or even technology from other external or internal sources.

A variant of the profit center strategy is the spin-off. Creating a separate company to develop systems, and possibly compete in the external marketplace for IS, has worked well in a number of situations.

A good example is Qantas Airlines. In the late 1980s Qantas management had concluded it had a poorly aligned IS function. IS was contributing poorly to business strategies and goals — in particular, in providing core business systems for critical functions such as reservations and aircraft maintenance. Systems delivery was terrible, with long lead times, high costs, and a lack of service orientation to its users. In an unusual move Qantas management also identified a lack of accountability by IS users for the resources they used.

An investigation of the problem raised additional alignment requirements. The alignment strategy had to attract and retain staff with the necessary skills and experience and establish a businesslike environment for providing information services. Since information was considered a strategic resource, the company realized that it should remain largely self-sufficient in providing information services. This was a critical consideration that precluded outsourcing the problem to a third party.

From a range of possible alignment strategies, Qantas adopted an approach based on a wholly owned autonomous business unit (QANTEK) with a 3-year contract for injection of specialist IT skills from an external supplier. A key feature of the arrangement was that the external supplier and QANTEK management and staff were required to enter into a partnership relationship with Qantas. In fact, this partnership included a contractual obligation for a measured annual improvement in the performance of the IS function.

An additional objective was to create software products and services that could be sold to the airline and travel industries in the Pacific region. A separate corporate entity provided the business, organizational, and legal context to undertake such a venture.

QANTEK was a success story — surpassing the contractual performance improvements at each of the audit reviews held to date. The company was able to quickly reorient its IS function so as to become a responsive, entrepreneurial, service organization. The story is evidence that a spinout alignment strategy can make sense if severe management, skill, and cultural changes are required — especially if there is an external market for the software products and services of the new enterprise.

A similar story, coincidentally Australian, involved a public-sector organization — the Melbourne and Metropolitan Board of Works. In addition to the need for a separate company to pursue business opportunities (similar to Qantas), the board concluded that a spinout enabled easier access to funding for such a venture.

Structure V: "Outsourcing" IS to an Outside Contractor

The decision by Eastman Kodak Company at the end of the decade of the 1980s to outsource significant portions of its IS operations to IBM and Digital Equipment Corporation coupled with the economic downturn of the early 1990s brought significant attention to outsourcing as a strategy for achieving good alignment between IS and the business.

Often, companies investigate or pursue outsourcing of IS to reduce or contain both fixed and variable IS costs. However, there is evidence that this does not occur. As a result, we have noted a shift in rationale for outsourcing which includes the following:

- Achieve innovative use of IS and mission-critical systems without increasing head count; achieve and maintain unique IS expertise or adequate levels of staff.

- Deliver systems quickly given competitive pressures; continue to develop critical systems during organizational turmoil such as during or after an acquisition or merger.

- Meet departmental demands for applications development or shift the costs of development to departments.

- Apply the best in-house talents and resources to focus on key areas of the business rather than on delivery or operation of data-processing systems.

- Avoid the capital costs of equipment, which are provided on an expensed basis by the contractor, or get big capital items off the balance sheet.

Outsourcing has many variants. Various IS functions can also be transferred, including systems planning, development, and even operations of a network, data centers, or other activities. Sometimes IS personnel (ranging from a handful to all) may be transferred to the contractor. In some cases the subcontractor purchases or otherwise acquires technology such as hardware processors and then leases it back to the enterprise.

Software development and maintenance is a case in point. It has become a massive, complex, and costly undertaking for organizations. Hundreds of billions of dollars have been invested in the United States alone during the first era of information technology. Over time, these applications — many of which already are old enough to vote and drink — will require reengineering. There is still a huge, and often growing, application development backlog problem, typically over 2 years long. Often IS organizations, using first-era software development methods and tools, have productivity levels far below what they could be.

Moreover, there is a huge budgetary requirement for the maintenance and upgrade of existing systems — often estimated by DMR to exceed one-half of the costs of MIS personnel in a typical large organization. IBM itself estimates that in 1 year its customers spent $109 billion (36 percent of all IS expenditures) on operations and support, $132 billion (44 percent) on products and technology, and $59 billion (20 percent) on planning and application development. If current trends continue (they could get worse), the cost of operations and support will grow to $152 billion per year! IBM argues that a key challenge facing organizations will be to reduce this component of the IS dollar to achieve a shift in proportion toward the value-added areas of new technology acquisition and new application development, and to achieve an overall reduction in projected IS costs.[11]

More and more organizations are turning to external professional support organizations to address these problems. As one CEO of a large department store chain told us: "We're in the retail business, not the computer business. Our unique expertise is in the area of retail, not software."

As organizations adopt the new technology paradigm and begin to retool their entire technology infrastructure, an issue is raised: By what means will this occur? As we make the transition to the second era, new complex, integrated, network-based applications must be constructed. Unfortunately, large organizations typically have an era I culture, knowledge base, skill set, and tool environment.

It was concerns such as these that led Kodak to consider outsourcing much of its IS function. For Kodak it was a "question of value."[12] Senior management perceived that the company was spending too much on IS compared with the value it was receiving. As well, management wanted to ensure that IS personnel were focused on the areas where they could add the most value. Management examined the information technology value chain to determine the points at which Kodak personnel could make the greatest contribution. It concluded that IS personnel were best at solving business problems as well as creating new business opportunities to use information technology to achieve the company's objectives.

Eastman Kodak adopted a strategy of "infrastructure services via strategic alliances," seeking to maximize leverage of Kodak personnel for increased scope without increased internal size. It concluded that by outsourcing the data centers and SNA network (to IBM), the telecommunications infrastructure (to DEC), and the PC support services (to Businessland), it could increase the quality of service, increase shareholder value, improve quality of work life for Kodak personnel, and position itself well for the future.

Among the key advantages identified in the Kodak business case for outsourcing was the transfer of fixed costs to variable costs. Substantial parts of the IT payroll became variable, depending on the conjunctural need, rather than being fixed, based on head count. Parenthetically, this has become a fundamental rationale for outsourcing in many countries where labor laws make laying off underutilized resources extremely difficult and costly.

Kodak also believed that it could achieve greater creativity in the use of IT by freeing up its own precious resources to focus on business problems. This was facilitated through the synergy and creative interchange achieved by working with an external partner. Another important advantage was the increased discipline that could be marshaled on a wide range of IS challenges through a contractual relationship with a highly professional and well-tooled organization.

Outsourcing is not without its problems. Some of these are identified through the program *Aligning IS with the Business*. The issue of which functions (if any) to outsource is complex, and there is no broadly accepted body of knowledge regarding what works best under what conditions. Experience is anecdotal and mixed. One general theme is that there may be considerable risks in outsourcing strategic resources, especially in the early days of a relationship.

Further, many question the wisdom of becoming highly dependent on an external provider. The vendor may have a singular focus on profit rather than service, delivering to the letter of the contract rather than to changing business needs. Both the relationship and the contract require scrupulous attention. There are also tricky human resource issues regarding outsourcing. For example, challenges include the shifting of existing IS personnel to an external contractor and the management of this external resource. Many have found that during the process they have lost important IS resources, for example, those employees who identified strongly with the enterprise.

For Travelers' President Brophy, outsourcing of IS and other functions will become more important. He told us:

> You are going to see a trend toward outsourcing. We are going to do the things that we do well. Why do I need a mailroom? Why do I need a data capture unit? Outsourcing can provide us with highly motivated people at good cost. I think outsourcing is ready to take off. Let's concentrate on the things that we need to do well, and oursource the rest.

Max Hopper, American Airlines senior vice president, still has some reservations, believing that many companies with weak IS leadership are looking to outsourcing as a way of washing their hands of IS leadership problems:

> For us outsourcing makes sense. For example, today, I buy a tremendous number of applications, rather than build them. I'd like to buy more—where there are economies of scale and it makes sense. My fear is that some companies which are looking at outsourcing are really still in era I. They still don't really understand information systems, and they don't know what is required to run IS. For them outsourcing is a cop-out.

In balance, where outsourcing makes sense, the effectiveness of the strategy is largely contingent on the partner selected and the relationship established.

Making the Transition to the Second-Era IS Organization

In a well-aligned organization, IS goals and rewards are often tied to business success. This helps to create an environment where IS and business operations are in sync and headed in the same direction. The holdover first-era IS culture and its service bureau mentality are not suited to today's environment. They must be replaced with an IS group that is an equal partner, motivated by the same performance needs as its business clients.

Overall, the shift in the influence over information systems decisions away from the centralized data-processing function to individual business units and users of the technology has brought many changes. Systems expertise and personnel are being located where the technology is being used. Companies are moving their IS professionals into business areas to serve specific uses and through these initiatives establishing a true partnership between IS and business. As well, they are increasingly using external resources to achieve the benefits discussed above.

An organizational alignment strategy should flow from an overall strategy for the use of IT within the enterprise and for the transition to the new paradigm. A good starting point is a program to evaluate the

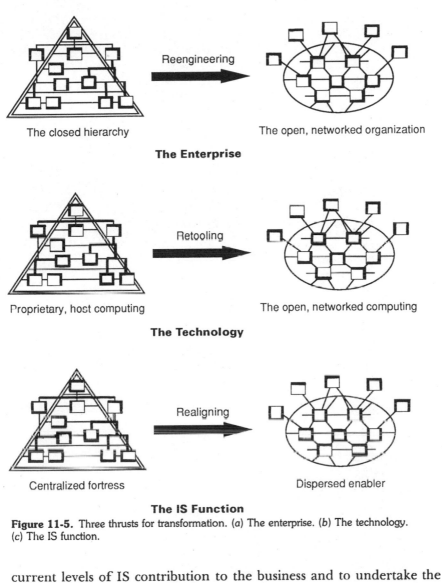

Figure 11-5. Three thrusts for transformation. (a) The enterprise. (b) The technology. (c) The IS function.

current levels of IS contribution to the business and to undertake the transition process discussed in this chapter.

However, organizational realignment is part of a broader issue, the challenge of leadership for transformation. Figure 11-5 illustrates and summarizes the three thrusts described so far in the book. How can the requisite leadership for the three transformations in the figure be achieved? This is the topic of the next chapter.

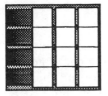

12

Leadership for the Transition

The Leadership Crisis

Old paradigms die hard. Whether they regard the flat world, Newtonian physics, or the first era of information technology, old paradigms and their corresponding attitudes, institutions, and cultures have built-in resistance to their own self-destruction. But they also contain the seeds of their own creative transformation. An outmoded paradigm in its death agony calls forth leaders for the new.[1]

However, if your organization calls forth its leaders a decade from now (or maybe even a couple of years from now), it will be too late. The winners will be those who can first comprehend the new promise of information technology and undertake a transformation process. There is an urgent need for leadership in every enterprise to make this transition. This presents you, not just your organization, with a personal challenge.

The experience with the first era of information technology was a prerequisite for progress. However, it fostered organizational learning disabilities regarding just about everything to do with information technology and its use.

It created structures that inhibit individual and team involvement in systems. It created a view of the technology and its application in business which is fundamentally outmoded. It created approaches to systems planning, software development, implementation, and change management which are becoming obstacles to making the shift. Through massive investments, it created legacy systems that have caused inertia that boggles even the most progressive executive mind.

Moreover, years of relying on traditional approaches to operating and managing traditional corporate bureaucracies have made many organizations almost incapable of using the new technology paradigm to creatively respond to the market and industry changes around them.

Failure to overcome the era I learning disabilities will be fatal. It is only through individuals rising up to break from the old paradigm and allying themselves with like thinkers in team action (and thereby team learning) that dramatic progress is possible.[2]

Leadership for the paradigm shift is required on four dimensions, corresponding to the four plateaus discussed earlier. This is depicted in Fig. 12-1.

Leadership, Not Just Management

Back in 1985, discussing the trend away from traditional computing environments, we argued:

> The term "leadership" rather than "management" better describes the key requirement for successful change. To begin, this change involves more than good management of a routine process where approaches are well documented with outcomes that are fairly predictable because of prior experience with the degree of change that these systems bring about. Instead we are dealing with innovation on a wide scale with which only a handful of enterprises and individuals have had actual experience....We are breaking new ground; forging new concepts of what works best.[3]

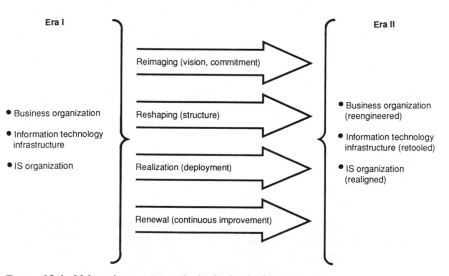

Figure 12-1. Making the transition—the leadership bridge.

Later, the same year, Bennis and Nanus published a widely accepted book on the issue, asserting that you should lead others and manage yourself: "The problem with many organizations, and especially the ones that are failing, is that they tend to be over-managed and under-led."[4] This theme grew strong as the business environment became more volatile. It is all the more applicable as the transition to era II becomes full-blown for growing numbers of organizations. As Jack Welch, chairman of General Electric, put it: "Call people managers and they are going to start managing things, getting in the way."[5]

But Not the Old-Style Leadership

The old-style, brilliant-visionary, take-charge, rally-the-troops Alfred Sloan or Tom Watson style of leadership is not adequate for the transformation that is required. For one thing, the old days when a great leader could learn *for* the organization are gone. As Peter Senge points out: "In an increasingly dynamic, interdependent and unpredictable world, it is simply no longer possible for anyone to 'figure it all out at the top.' The old model, 'the top thinks and the local acts,' must now give way to integrating thinking and acting at all levels."[6] For Senge, "In a learning organization, leaders are designers, stewards and teachers. They are responsible for building organizations where people continually expand their capacities to understand complexity, clarify vision and improve shared mental models—that is they are responsible for learning."[7]

When you think about the level of transformation enabled by the technology paradigm shift, Senge's words (written as a general theory of organizations) ring true. The old approaches of the great strategist developing a vision and "selling" it to the enterprise are inadequate for the challenges of reengineering, retooling, and realigning described in this book.

Individuals will *comply* out of fear or desire for material rewards. They will only set out to transform themselves and their organizations, however, through *personal commitment* based on deeply felt understanding. Such understanding cannot be achieved solely through listening to a great visionary. Rather, it comes from collaborating with others and learning through the experience. It comes from struggling to understand common interests. It comes from the confidence that a new tomorrow is possible and achievable—confidence that grows through the sleeves-rolled-work of teams and of successes in implementing plans.

Leadership Can Come
from Anywhere

One of the striking findings of our investigation is that leadership can come from anywhere in an enterprise. We have worked with CEOs who understand the paradigm shift and are providing top-down leadership for change. This is obviously a desirable scenario as power is the basic energy needed to initiate and maintain action. Power is required to bring new concepts and new intentions into being.

On the other hand, we have found people who started out at the bottom of the hierarchy—such as a secretary—who have become key leaders in the transformation. Consider the case of Audrey Howe.

Leadership for the Work Group: Eight Lessons from Audrey Howe

Reengineering of work systems became popular in the 1990s. But it was 1981 when Audrey Howe, who had previously been on the clerical staff at Citibank Canada, was moved into the Corporate Real Estate division as its new manager of administration. One of her first responsibilities was to determine a strategy for word processing. As she pursued the issue of how documents were produced and managed, she began to conclude that there were some significant problems in the overall process of marketing and negotiating large corporate loans. She ended up being a key leader in the implementation of a high-performance team and the IT-enabled transformation of the division. As discussed earlier, everyone in the division received networked workstations, and the business process, jobs, and organizational structure were reengineered, resulting in spectacular improvements in productivity, revenue, and profit.

Through this experience Howe grew professionally and personally. Three years later she became the vice president in charge of customer/market support for Corporate Real Estate and the work-group system approach was adopted in Citibank in locations across North America.

This is a case of someone at the lower end of a hierarchy grasping the need for change, taking some risks, and rising to the leadership challenge. The result was success for her organization and for herself. We asked Audrey Howe to describe the factors that led to success.

- "The critical success factor for us was senior management commitment," she says. "We were lucky to have a new executive in charge who was not hung up on the old ways of working. He wanted to fix the performance of the group and he wanted to make a name for himself in doing so." In this case, a new senior executive was brought in to do something about the poor profits and success of the group. He had 2 years to turn the situation around, and he was open to any ideas from team members on how to do so. He was one of the first to accept a workstation on his desk. Back in 1982, this was an unusual and seemingly unnatural act for a senior vice president.

- On the other hand, the senior executive empowered his staff to make the far-reaching changes they had formulated. According to Howe, "The leadership team must have the actual authority and power to make changes. This was a good part of our culture, which was oriented to giving people authority at even low levels to get things done."

- A third factor was to "communicate, communicate, communicate"— appropriate to a real estate group where what's important is location, location, and location. Throughout the project every employee in Corporate Real Estate was involved in the process of reengineering. Howe recommends that you provide meaningful and ongoing input. "This is where the best ideas come from anyway—from the people who do the work and will be changing."

- Developing group ownership of the program was essential. Initially, the tracking of work flow and measurement of time looked to some people like a Machiavellian program to cut heads. Over time a real sense of trust and team accountability was developed. In contradiction to the praisers of hierarchy discussed earlier who believe that only individuals can be accountable, Howe notes that "we all had a real sense that we, as a group, were on the line to make the thing work." The leadership also ensured that everyone shared in the overall success of the project. "Another important factor was the support of the central IS group. Initially we just asked for their opinions regarding vendors. Eventually, we concluded that they should be full partners in the implementation."

- They learned to question everything. Initially they found themselves examining relatively conservative opportunities for improvement. However, a mind set developed in which the team began to question virtually every aspect of the business process. "We started to get radical, think radically. Some sacred cows remained unscathed, but not many. And for those that survived, we now understand much more deeply why they should be sacred."

- To establish a reputation for reliability, it was important to "manage expectations and always deliver when you say you will." One of the initial problems was that the IS department overcommitted, even on things for which it had no control. This undermined initial credibility in the program.

- Another factor was the role of an external consulting company. "They were instrumental in helping us through this thing, helping us understand the factors which we needed to consider in moving forward and providing us with methods and tools to redesign the workflow." Clearly the organization needs to own the transformation process. However, an outside facilitator or change agent can make a significant difference.

- Finally, it was important to "manage enthusiasm and keep it focused on business results." Ironically, one of the problems was the over-enthusiastic user overly enamored with the technology. One manager would go home at night and come back with reams of new automated forms that didn't necessarily make sense for the business. Others would try and do everything by the system when it may have made sense to use old approaches (such as a face-to-face discussion) for certain tasks.

Jack Hoffman and the Transformation of the IS Executive

Leadership can also come from the progressive IS executive. Initially Jack Hoffman, Citibank's senior vice president in charge of information systems, had little idea about the significance of the change on which he and his group were embarking. He told us:

> We were a traditional IS group doing traditional IS things. In the 1970s we had a pretty elitist view—we saw users as an unfortunate, but necessary, element in the systems equation. We even had jokes about it, like complaining that we couldn't have "contract users"—users for hire. Users were generally pretty submissive and accepted our directives. We really did have a technology fortress.

However, through the experience their view of the role of IS changed. By participating as part of a team investigating opportunities in the Corporate Real Estate division, they learned about the far-reaching opportunities to reengineer the business and dramatically improve productivity. They also began to rethink the division of responsibilities between IS and the business unit and further to change their thinking regarding the importance of the users. As Howe indicated, they quickly became a critical element in the implementation. Members of the IS group found themselves doing technology integration, client/server computing, and work-group applications which were easily 5 years ahead of their time.

To begin, the group decided that users were its customers. Hoffman told us:

> We now view our customers as the reason for our existence. Our customers are our in-house users and also customers of the bank. We want our external customers to see and believe in some advantage of doing business with Citibank because of the technology-based services we provide. On the other hand we have to earn the trust of our internal customers as well.

The customer focus led the IS group into some very innovative technologies which it would not have otherwise considered. The internal customer needed a work-group application that would manage the new team process of marketing, negotiating, and contracting large corporate loans. The work-group environment required intelligent workstations, local networks, and integration with the corporate mainframe world. To meet the needs of its newly found customer, IS had to implement groupware and client/server computing before the terms were invented.

Rather than determining what technology the users would acquire, the group came to understand the need to establish mutually agreed-upon standards. "We became a facilitator as opposed to a provider. We all work to agree on standards, which enables users to acquire whatever technology they need while at the same time it enables the company to have a coherent IT infrastructure."

Hoffman also decided that the entire structure of the IS department was wrong for the new paradigm. "We learned that we needed a more responsive organizational structure to respond to these new needs. This was facilitated by the technologies. Distributed technologies require a less rigid support structure." This included dispersion and colocation of IS resources out to the business unit as well as the acquisition of second-era technology skills.

Hoffman's view of his role changed as well. "We started to view ourselves as business executives, not technology executives. We needed to convince ourselves that we were first and foremost executives of our corporation looking for ways to improve corporate performance. Holding on to the old view would have entombed us in our fortress walls."

Hoffman is a good example of the new kind of leadership required for the shift. Rather than leading the troops forward in a bravado charge, he let go of the old view, shifting power to his customers. His actions were designed to help his customers succeed. He became a facilitator. And through the process he succeeded.

Hoffman believes that further changes are in store for the IS executive:

> IT considerations become part of our business strategy. IS today is playing an important role in helping create the technology knowledge and corporate culture required for the paradigm shift. As technology and business lines continue to blur, I believe the notion of the IS leader will go away. There will be different skill sets in the business unit re-

quired for competitive success. I view this as a positive thing. Instead of sitting in the back rooms being a technocrat, we are becoming business people with some special knowledge to bring to the table.

The experience is insightful because it is a good example of team learning for the new paradigm. Through the joint project team, Hoffman and his people and Howe and the people from the Corporate Real Estate division were transformed. The process of working together on initial, limited objectives became a new shared vision of what was possible and an organization that could learn and change.

The Chief Information Officer and the Gorbachev Syndrome

How is the role of the senior IS executive changing? In the 1980s, many organizations created the position of the chief information officer to help them achieve the leadership required to quickly move the ball forward on the strategic use of IT. All had some form of chief financial officer responsible for the management of the financial resources to achieve the objectives of the organization. As information systems moved to the center of business success, it seemed reasonable to many that such a senior-level officer was required to manage the information resource. For many the strategy worked. At a minimum it raised the profile of IS in the business, and at best provided important impetus for transformation.

As enterprises move to a complete era II environment, however, the role of the CIO becomes less clear. Will the CIO fall victim to something we call the *Gorbachev syndrome* — initial leaders for paradigm shifts are often swept away by the tide they initiated — being bypassed or becoming irrelevant in the process?

The challenge of today's CIO is typically to serve as a bridge between IS, senior management, and users. The CIO may also work to encourage joint problem solving. The CIO's most important role is often to provide vision and leadership to accelerate the delivery of new competitive or business-critical systems. The CIO is often a full member of the senior management team, reports to the chief executive officer, and is part of managing the business. Membership on the management team gives the CIO role credibility — more than just a trendy new title for the same old job.

All CIOs are responsible for setting corporate strategies and policies for information technology. The CIO is supposed to be like Janus, looking simultaneously at the business and at technology. Her first responsibility is to contribute a technology perspective to the business direction. Then she must build the vision and strategies to ensure that information technology makes the maximum contribution to achieving corporate goals and objectives.

The CIO does not necessarily have responsibility for the IS function. Often, the job of managing IS resources and operating the IS infrastructure is left to IS managers who may report through a combination of business function executives and a central IS executive. Some CIOs have shed the responsibility for developing new applications and/or for ensuring that systems operate smoothly. This may be due to a desire to focus on the strategic planning issues, or it may be because of the dispersion of these functions to operating units. In either case, the CIO must retain control over corporate technology policy issues.

In some organizations, the term *information* is taken far beyond traditional IS boundaries. For example, the CIO for one major U.S. food manufacturer is also responsible for the market research function.

The CIO is a highly controversial position. Many have argued that without the authority of line responsibility for IS resources the CIO is powerless to implement a vision. Others have pointed to the unrealistic expectations placed on CIOs to have a big hit (i.e., a quick, mission-critical implementation success). This could be a major factor causing longevity or lack of longevity of the typical CIO. When systems are developed quickly and predictably, and when they operate with utmost reliability, the CIO has a great deal of influence with his peers. But if there are problems in either of these areas, the CIO's credibility as a member of the team may suffer, reducing his or her ability to influence business directions. It is now a standard joke that the letters *CIO* could stand for "career is over."

There was some consensus among the organizations investigated regarding what is required for the CIO to succeed. Most important, the CIO must have an excellent understanding of the business. Without it, a CIO cannot be a credible member of the management team. As a result, many CIOs are not longtime IS professionals, but have moved into the position from other parts of the business. Organizations will have to develop the same kind of cross-functional career development for CIOs that they already have for other senior executives.

The CIO must also be able to articulate and forge a vision of the role of technology in the company's future. She must work with others to transform the vision into pragmatic strategies, policies, and standards. That is, the CIO should be a leader—able to facilitate shared vision and action for transitioning. Dave Carlson, chief information officer at Kmart, views himself fundamentally as an agent of change. He describes the significant transformation under way at Kmart as a "paradigm shift." He told us, "All the issues of change are raised: who is the change agent, what is the change process, what will people's roles be after the change takes place."

In some ways, these are the requirements for any senior executive in this time of transformation. According to information management consultant Michael Anderson, the emerging role of the CIO is a sign that the information systems function is finally coming of age, and is ready to be an equal business partner with functions such as marketing, manufacturing, and finance.[8]

The CIO's role is not standardized and is still evolving. There have been many cases of both success and failure. The consensus, however, is that the establishment of a CIO is inadequate as the central strategy to achieving IS alignment with the business. Moreover, many question the long-term future of the role.

American Airlines' Max Hopper—probably the best known CIO in the United States—told us he believes that the CIO currently has two main roles. Some CIOs provide business leadership in the use of IT. Today, however, the main role of most CIOs is as the engineer responsible for the formation of IT infrastructure. Hopper wonders what will occur once most enterprises have put together such an infrastructure. "Once most of that is engineered, then I question the need for a CIO in this role. It will be relegated to a lower position in the hierarchy. In many cases it will be acquired externally," he says.

Hopper also believes that the role of the CIO as business strategist will also tend to disappear as IS becomes dispersed into the day-to-day activities of business units:

> If the marketing people understand their information needs, and if the engineering and finance people understand their information needs and so on, then it [IS] will become much looser—based on teams in the business units. As this emerges and as the information is engineered, what is the role of a CIO? I'm not sure that the CIO will become the strategic business planner. It [the CIO function] will become a normal part of each discipline, each business department.

One thing is certain. For the period of the transition to the new paradigm—going well into the next decade—there will be a strong need for both technology and business leadership for the transition. Whether or not a CIO role makes sense and what are the main functions of that role are probably only answerable within the specific context of each enterprise. Many variables determine the usefulness of the CIO role. They include the personalities of the key stakeholders, the IS history of the enterprise, the culture of the enterprise, and the state of maturity of the enterprise in making the transition.

One liberating approach is the establishment of a CIO who views himself as a kind of Gorbachev. One good example (given to us not for attribution) is the CIO of a large group of companies in the consumer products business. A former president of one of the companies, he was brought into the CIO position by the chairman to initiate some far-reaching changes in the enterprise's use of information and its technology infrastructure. He told us, "My mission is to provide leadership to move our companies toward era II. Our chairman believes we have fallen behind in information management and wants to see some big changes. I'm here to stir up the waters and facilitate the process." The changes envisaged include the corporatewide adoption of open systems and of a standards-based architecture, and the diffusion of IS thinking into every business unit.

He sees his role as creating a type of *perestroika* in the enterprise, in which the pent-up demand for change is released. It involves working more productively, thinking "infopreneurially," and exploiting new technologies. So far, the waters have certainly been stirred, and there is an energized (at times unwieldy) process of change under way. This situation is one of the most striking organizational learning processes we have witnessed. A key ingredient is the fact that this individual is supremely confident, and as a successful former president, he has considerable credibility and influence in the enterprise.

He also fully understands that when *glasnost* is under way, his role as CIO will have been completed and he can move on to other things. Having had the experience, he believes he will be better equipped to participate in whatever transformation challenges come his way.

Perhaps rather than "career is over," *CIO* may come to mean "career is opening."

Leadership for Learning

The leadership challenge is really a challenge of learning. The enterprise needs to learn about the new era. It must reimage itself to understand how tomorrow is going to be different from today and then translate that new vision into action. The learning challenge is one of conditioning the enterprise with the knowledge, attitudes, and skills required for success in the new era. When you stop and think about this, it is an enormous undertaking. For most organizations this involves a cultural transformation that includes changes in[9]:

- *Awareness and knowledge.* Achieving an awakening and understanding of the concepts of the new paradigm
- *Motivation and commitment.* Developing a new shared vision, orien-

tation, and confidence to pursue opportunities and undertake a transition

- *Skills and competencies.* Building the expertise necessary for business transformation and effective use of the new technology

A cultural transformation requires learning throughout the organization in all three arenas.

Most organizations tend to address these three arenas separately. For example, companies send a manager to a groupware course to learn the skills of work-group applications. Unfortunately, they don't couple that with knowledge development in the area of reengineered processes for the business team. As well, they often don't customize awareness programs to the organization or link them to the change program they are trying to manage. Often training and education personnel are buried in the information systems or human resources functions and go about their work outside any global change management considerations.

External considerations will also be raised, as external reach involves more suppliers, distributors, consumers, etc.

To make the transition to the new era, a strategy for learning is required.

In the era I organization there are three constituencies to which systems are relevant: senior management which is responsible for providing vision and sponsorship (directors), the IS function which is responsible for structuring and implementing technology (providers), and others throughout the organization who receive benefits (users).[10] Each has its own orientation, objectives, and needs. For each there are implications of not making the transition to era II. *Within* each there are learning gaps and a challenge of building understanding. *Between* each there are gaps and the challenge to build bridges — that is, common views. As these gaps are narrowed, the roles of the three constituencies converge. For example, users begin to take on many areas of responsibility such as vision, sponsorship, and provision of their own technology.

Senior management has a strategic orientation. Its focus on systems more and more includes the success of the enterprise as a whole. The IS function has typically been oriented to planning, providing, coordinating, and maximizing the effectiveness of technology. Its focus has been on architecture, vendor decisions, development, and delivery of centralized or corporate systems. The end-user department often has an operational orientation. System concerns focus on issues such as autonomy, self-control, and quick acquisition of technology to meet operational needs.

All three roles are in transition. Strategies for systems and for business are converging, forcing all three to strengthen their understanding of the relationship between technology and business objectives. All are becoming supported directly by a workstation, raising new awareness, commitment, and skill implications.

There is a need to build understanding so that each can be better equipped to assess and exploit ongoing opportunities and understand the changing roles. There is also a requirement for users to take responsibility for decisions and action in all three areas.

There are inherent historical conflicts between these three groups which have created a lot of "action" at the borders. Examples are:

- IS (with finite resources and limited technologies) versus users (with urgent operational needs and big expectations)

- Users (with unique departmental systems needs) versus senior management (with corporate information needs)

- Senior management (with a business orientation to systems) versus IS (with a technology orientation)

The action at the borders is exacerbated as organizations make the transition to the new paradigm and as the walls between these roles break down. The roles of each group and the requirements for interaction, collaboration, and common understanding between them began to change with the advent of new technologies (dating back to the personal computer), new opportunities, and new issues. Technology proliferation has created a proliferation of new issues. Now integration of systems has an organizational counterpart.

This points to the need for both *specialized* programs addressing historical group needs and *common* programs that can help build bridges and converge roles. The goal is that at every level of the enterprise down to the work group and individual user, the responsibilities for direction, provision of technology, and use of technology are integrated. Ultimately, you must personally accept responsibilities for all three challenges.

How People Learn the New Paradigm

Many factors influence awareness, commitment, and skills regarding the new technology and the new enterprise. Much is acquired informally through day-to-day life in a changing world. The *Business Week* cover story, the daughter showing her father how she uses her PC at college, and the discussion at the golf club about how technology is helping a company compete better are all part of the learning process. However, random events such as these are a poor foundation to build the culture for the future enterprise. Rather, it makes sense to be proactive. Plan and design a *working-learning environment* where participation in daily work and change goes hand in hand with integrated learning programs for training and education. This means initiating two related thrusts for learning:

- *Action learning.* Learning through *participation* in change. As the old Chinese proverb goes: "I hear and I forget; I see and I remember; I do and I understand." By *doing,* people achieve a concrete feeling of what is possible or what the change will mean. Participating in a modeling or principles workshop or sitting together in a room experimenting with an expert system application will tend to have a different impact on senior executives than, say, attending lectures on these topics. This approach can be extended to actual experience working with the new technology. For example, work-group implementation and reengineering can provide ongoing information regarding the effectiveness and performance of the business team. Our experience has shown that such information can rapidly accelerate organizational learning, as the team learns in real time, knowing performance is affected by the changes it makes and the actions it takes.

- *Formal learning.* Learning through a set of *training* and *education* programs that are linked to the changes sought. Formal education and training programs are also essential to a change of this type. Integration of these formal programs with experience in action has proved to be very effective.

The impact of learning programs on awareness, commitment, and skill competency is illustrated in Fig. 12-2.

An Organizational Learning Program for the Shift

When Kmart CIO Dave Carlson set out to lead the shift, he anticipated losing 25 percent of his IS staff due to skill discontinuity and fallout from a change of this magnitude. In anticipation of this, a program was introduced to help staff members make the transition in their knowledge, skills, and orientation. He told us that staff members were given the message: "You're world experts in something that the rest of the world doesn't care about. Give us a chance to retrain you in something

Change arena	To acquire the	To	Through formal learning programs such as	And action learning— participation in team action for
Cognitive	Awareness, knowledge	Understand, identify the new	Information sharing	
Affective	Commitment, motivation	Pursue the new	Workshops	Reimaging Reshaping Realizing Renewing
Behavioral	Skills, competencies	Exploit the new	Skill-building programs	

Figure 12-2. Learning programs.

which will bring you into the mainstream." The result of the program was that Kmart had very little turnover during the transition.

How can your organization create a comprehensive program to overcome the organizational learning disabilities created by the first era. A program should have several components.

1. Adoption of learning principles and definition of the knowledge, motivation, and generic skills required in each community over the transition horizon of, say, 5 to 10 years.

2. Definition of the programs required to achieve the target learning levels. These include (1) training and education programs and (2) participation in team action to achieve the knowledge, attitudes, and skills required for reimaging, reshaping, realizing, and renewing.

3. Definition of the vehicles that will be used to implement the learning programs. Vehicles include techniques such as workshops, video courses, seminars, computer-assisted instruction, on-site visits to other companies, and classroom courses. They include materials such as newsletters, research reports, quick reference guides, books, and posters. They may also include project teams, task forces, employee computer purchase programs, an in-house computer store, an information center, technology incentive programs, and numerous other techniques designed to change the knowledge, motivation, and skill base.

For each of these three definitional activities it is possible to construct a *learning architecture* that maps the target community by learning type and strategy area (generic requirements, programs, or vehicles). One such matrix, showing example training and education programs, is presented in Fig. 12-3.

A similar matrix could be constructed showing how education and training regarding the new paradigm will be integrated into other formal education programs throughout the enterprise. The Royal Bank of Canada integrates technology education into its banking and management education. For example, the general manager's course has modules on information technology, and technology training has been integrated into the bank's credit courses.

Another effective approach has been to hold high-profile learning events—especially ones in which customers are involved. Jim Grant, former CIO at Royal Bank, told us of the huge success the bank had with its 3-day senior management symposium. Banking managers are

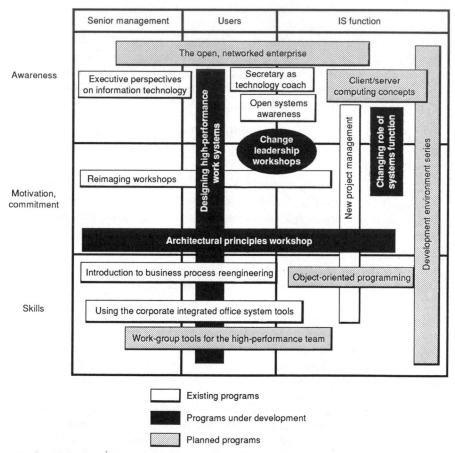

Figure 12-3. Partial learning architecture—example formal programs.

invited to attend a discussion on the integration of technology in business, also attended by some of the bank's best customers who are flown in for the event. Everyone gets hands-on use of technology. The themes of the first session were "technology means business" and "in partnership we can do it together." The session was opened by the president of the bank and closed by the chairman. At a recent session the press was invited, and the event made prime-time television news. Grant told us that "these sessions changed the profile of IS in the bank and opened up the eyes of bank executives and customers alike to what is becoming possible."

The need for a program can be triggered by various inputs. These include the ongoing tracking of technology trends and uses, problems identified in getting consensus in an opportunity analysis, an upcoming system implementation, organizational difficulties in building bridges between technology stakeholders, the launching of a strategic initiative toward integrated systems, and demands from user communities. There are a number of elements to an awareness program.

1. Reimaging

The starting point is to formulate a picture of the learning principles and future learning objectives of the organization.

- *Learning principles.* Examples include: "All employees must understand the centrality of the new information technology to achieving our business objectives." "All employees will develop a strong commitment to reengineering their business units for high performance." "All employees will develop the basic competencies to function in a work-group computing environment." "We will invest the equivalent of 8 percent of each employee's salary in formal education and training, per year." "Education requirements will be developed cooperatively by the self-managed teams in the plant."

- *Program definition.* What is the desired result of the program? Who is the target group? What are the objectives? What do we want people to do differently (behavioral changes)? What new knowledge should they have (cognitive changes)? How should they feel differently as a result of the program (motivational changes)?

2. Reshaping

- *Current awareness assessment.* What is the existing awareness level? What are the current skills, knowledge, and motivation of the target population? What have other organizations done given comparable conditions? What worked? What didn't work? What risks are associated with the proposed program? How easily will the target group grasp the knowledge, skills, or motivation? What is the climate for learning and change? How supportive are key influencers, such as senior management?

- *Definition of learning architecture.* What general approach will we use: should the program stress information sharing (knowledge), attitude changing (motivation), or skill building (expertise); and/or should the program focus on the creation of action (learning through change)? What awareness architectures do we need? What are our architectures? Who will be the educators and trainers?

- *Creation.* Joint brainstorming sessions with the educator and client have proved effective in creating a program, project plans, implementation schedules, resources, and budgeting. Individual program elements need a clear set of behavior objectives, main messages, an architecture of the course seminar, etc.

3. Realizing

- *Integration.* Formal programs need to be integrated with *action learning*. For example, a seminar on reengineering techniques should be implemented as part of a reengineering program. Executive briefings on the new paradigm can be integrated with strategic planning activities.

- *Purchase.* Many excellent programs can be purchased. Make sure not to buy era II education or training from an era I consulting company.

- *Construction.* Customized or otherwise unavailable formal programs should be constructed interactively with the internal clients.

- *Operation.* How will we operate the program? How will we handle user contact, course registration, pre-preparation, resourcing, etc.? How will we maintain program integrity—control of the content and quality of instruction?

- *Delivery.* Formal programs should sizzle, generating excitement and commitment.

4. Renewal

- *Monitoring/impact evaluation.* How will we measure the success of the program and its impact on the organization? How will we feed this back to senior management, course designers, other stakeholders?

- *Trial/feedback.* How will we pilot elements of the program? What are our evaluation criteria? What evaluation techniques will be used? Interviews? Questionnaires? Workshops?

- *Proliferation.* How will we extend the program throughout the target organization while maintaining the content? What "train-the-trainer" programs do we need?

- *Expansion/evolution.* How will we set up a network for sharing new ideas that arise as a result of the new learning achieved? For example, how can we incorporate new ideas that result from a completed work-group reengineering program in our learning programs? How can we implement on-the-job reinforcement? How can we evolve to the working-learning environment where work processes and learning reinforce each other and go hand in hand?

Organizing for Learning

An entrepreneurial culture is required for success in the new era. The cultural values, attitudes, and behavior are such that opportunities for new ways of working spring up and are identified throughout the organization. Just as the objective is to diffuse this culture and learning throughout the organization, so learning programs should be initiated and, in a sense, owned throughout. Thus it is important for senior management, technology providers, and users each to play a role in initiating and participating in programs.

The role of the systems function is expanding to include systems beyond the domain of data processing. Systems that support users (such as the telephone system) or that interface directly with the physical world (such as a radar system for air traffic controllers) are becoming part of the integrated systems picture. Historically the providers of information systems took a leadership role in information systems awareness. Now as they become the providers, coproviders, coplanners, and more, the responsibility for learning is broadening.

As technology becomes central to the execution of business functions, the imperative for learning grows for users. Users who may have been satisfied to attend a spreadsheet course or attend an awareness seminar find that their need for learning is broader and shared across organizational boundaries.

As systems that manage information, people, and physical resources become integrated and more central to business strategy, the awareness ante is upped for senior management as well. The chips on the table represent the future of the enterprise. A strategy for learning can't be left to a little training group six levels down in the organization.

All of this points to the need for leadership to address the issue of changing the corporate culture. It also points to the need for joint efforts, multidepartmental steering committees, and cooperation. Integration of technologies has an organizational counterpart. Initially this is intensifying the action *at the borders*. But it holds out the potential for improved cooperation, based, ironically, on self-interest among converging stakeholders to achieve common goals.

Leadership and the IT Industry

The technology paradigm shift is causing a reinvention of the computer industry which has far-reaching implications for customer-vendor relations, leadership for IT, western economic growth, and national competitiveness.

The first era was a hardware era. Most customer expenditures for computing came from hardware, and major hardware companies dominated the picture. These companies received not only virtually all of the revenue from the industry but also all of the profit as they could charge high margins due to the proprietary nature of technology. Customers were locked in to their host computer manufacturer because software ran only on the computer of that manufacturer. In the 1950s, and 1960s the mainframe was king, as were companies that sold mainframes. These large hosts ran a vast array of applications — everything from accounting to text processing. IBM dominated the market, receiving some competition from "the BUNCH" — *B*urroughs, *U*nivac, *N*CR, *C*ontrol Data, and *H*oneywell. In the 1970s we witnessed the rise of minicomputer vendors such as Digital Equipment Corporation, Hewlett-Packard, Data General, Wang, and Tandem. IBM also entered the mid-range picture.

The transition to the new paradigm was initiated by the introduction of the personal computer, along with the rise of the microprocessor, clone makers, and an independent, shrink-wrapped software industry. During this period — the 1980s — we also saw a number of new forces complicate the picture. One was the *plug compatibles* such as Amdahl, Fujitsu, NEC, and Hitachi, which manufactured IBM-compatible mainframes and related equipment. Third-party software companies grew quickly, creating applications to run on various proprietary hardware platforms — mainframe and minicomputer. Local area networks came into the picture, as did the various value-added wide area network services discussed in Chap. 4. Even the telephone system got into the action as switches became computers capable of switching data as well as voice information. A new product category called workstations — powerful desktop systems that initially focused on the Unix operating system — appeared on the scene, led by the California start-up company Sun Microsystems. The industry was in transition.

By the early 1990s, it became clear that the industry was being turned on its head. Our work has led to the conclusion that the computer industry as we have known it is coming to a tumultuous end. A new industry is being born, and a historic battle for leadership is taking place. There are a number of central themes.

Nine Themes of the New IT Industry

1. Computers Are Becoming Commodities

Computer peripherals such as terminals and printers have behaved like commodities for some period. The personal computer has also had many characteristics of a commodity—you purchase the greatest quantity of power for the lowest cost—not completely unlike grain in the Chicago commodities market. Now all hardware is becoming based on microprocessors, and software standards enable portability of information and software applications. As discussed in Chap. 6, these factors free customers to switch suppliers of mainstream processors with minimal penalty. As a result, computer hardware is changing to become a low-cost, low-margin commodity product category.

This is not to say that all processor hardware is exactly the same. There are, and will continue to be, differences. However, because software is portable, differentiation in the industry will tend to move up the "food chain" into software and above in services.

There are many signs of such a "commoditization" occurring in software. For example, although different operating systems have different features and functions, more and more they are looking very similar with similar capabilities, running on the same hardware, and enabling the execution of the same or similar software applications. In fact, growing numbers of software applications, such as word-processing packages, have a similar look and feel, perform similar functions, and run on similar gear.

2. A Consolidation and Restructuring Is Occurring

Because of this, the computer industry is being restructured. Let's start with mainframes, looking at a case in point—Burroughs—the *B* in BUNCH.

Imagine it's back in 1987 and you own an independent software company that creates products that only work on Burroughs proprietary computers. You sit down with your management team to kick off your strategic planning session. Market research and intelligence tell you that in the future most people will want to purchase software that works on the emerging commodity hardware, not just the narrow Burroughs platforms. You develop a strategy to shift your company into these new markets. Over time, customers of Burroughs lose their main reason to purchase proprietary computers from the company—as fewer and fewer business solutions will be available.

The result? Burroughs realizes that the days of its proprietary systems are numbered and merges with the second BUNCH company, Sperry (formerly Univac), to form Unisys. It happens that Sperry has had a Unix offering for several years. The new company wisely develops a strategy to abandon all its proprietary architectures, and it embraces Unix and open systems. It then acquires Convergent Technologies (a hot open systems company) and reaches a distribution arrangement with Sequent (a manufacturer of high-end Unix-based multiprocessor systems). The new Unisys presents itself to customers as their best partner for open systems.

The *N* in BUNCH (NCR) saw the writing on the wall even earlier—in the mid-1980s—and reduced the emphasis on its proprietary products at that time. NCR was an early entrant in the new marketplace. It announced an elegant and innovative product strategy in 1991 and immediately became an attractive acquisition candidate. AT&T, which had laid but never hatched the golden Unix egg, snapped up NCR in a hostile acquisition, which so far has turned out well for both companies.

The *C* in BUNCH—Control Data—also abandoned its proprietary technologies. Honeywell Bull severed its relationship with Honeywell (the controls company) and became simply Bull, owned by the French government (with a partial stake held by NEC). Bull, too, has shifted to an open systems strategy.

Now that the dust has settled, only a handful of suppliers support proprietary operating systems on large, expensive mainframe computers. One group consists of IBM and plug-compatible suppliers like Amdahl. The other is Digital Equipment Corporation, which has built ever-larger processors for customers of its proprietary VMS offering. All these vendors also offer Unix on their large systems. They all face shrinking demand for these historic engines of success.

Open systems and the client/server model wreak havoc on the very product category offered by minicomputer companies like Digital Equipment Corporation, Hewlett-Packard, Wang, and Data General. The collapse of the proprietary minicomputer market has contributed significantly to the depressed state of the New England economy, since many of these companies are located in the Boston area.

Every minicomputer vendor has adopted the new paradigm and is working feverishly to deliver the new technologies. Some, in addition to offering Unix, are adding industry standards to their proprietary operating systems. One company that has followed the logic to a further conclusion is Wang—which is moving away from hardware manufacturing to become a software and services company whose main involvement in hardware is as a value-added reseller of other companies' gear. It has decided to become a "computerless computer company," in support of the thesis of a controversial *Harvard Business Review* article published in 1991.[11]

The battle for the desktop is equally volatile with:

- Microsoft consolidating its massive dominance despite the lack of robustness of MS-DOS and its windows enhancement, and despite the fact that these standards are essentially controlled by a single vendor

- IBM reinforcing its commitment to OS/2 with a new, well-crafted release in 1992

- A multiplicity of suppliers (Sun, Univel, and Santa Cruz Operation) offering shrink-wrapped implementations of Unix for conventional PCs

- Apple and IBM allying to create a new-generation personal and multiuser computing platform that promises an enhanced, object-oriented version of the Apple user environment combined with high-performance IBM hardware and operating system technology

- Unix and its variants dominating powerful desktop workstations that are dropping quickly in price

3. Account Control Is Dead

In the days of proprietary mainframes, customers had few alternatives. The presence of the "Amdahl coffee mug" on an MIS executive's desk was often surprisingly effective—but typically led to savings no greater than 10 percent. In the competitive world of open systems, large customers can exercise much wider freedom of choice, and they often do.

The hardware vendor no longer controls the account through proprietary software lock-in. Vendors must find other ways to win and maintain customer loyalty. One of the interesting findings of the research is that customers are not seeking promiscuous relationships with suppliers. Customers recognize the value of freedom of choice. But they do not wish to exercise this freedom unnecessarily. Frequently changing suppliers adds to costs, and there is a cost to diversity. Stable relationships can be in everyone's interest. The difference is that such relationships are based on free will and a more open market. It is therefore incumbent on vendors to deliver.

Some criteria for vendor selection have not changed. Customers still want good product features and functions, service and support, reliability, and serviceability. Interestingly, and seemingly paradoxically (given the freedom of the new paradigm), customers are also looking for vendor stability.

We noted several cases where a customer was shifting suppliers due to concerns about the supplier's viability and stability. However, in an open systems environment, a hardware vendor need only be viable for the duration of the projected useful life of the equipment. Innovative start-ups (like Stratus and Silicon Graphics) have a better chance in this sort of market.

New criteria are also emerging. Many customers focus on hardware price/performance and conduct "benchmarks" to test speed, capacity, and other features such as graphics quality. Benchmarks were difficult to compare in the first era, as applications often worked on only one computer family.

Standards compliance has become critical to supplier selection. In the first era, compatibility with existing products in the vendor's family was important. Now compliance with industry standards is key. Products must comply with the right set of standards, and enough of them, so that customers can avoid using vendor value-added functions that surreptitiously produce lock-in. During this transition period, customers want documented proof that the supplier truly embraces openness and standards.

Another factor is something we call *enterprise architecture*. As discussed in Chap. 10, every customer is struggling with the issues of getting from here to there. As a result, they are looking for suppliers who can help with making the transition, integrating open and traditional computing environments and so on.

Account control is history. The customer-supplier partnership based on free choice has arrived.

4. Revenues and Profits Are Shifting to Services

Hardware has declined dramatically as a vehicle for adding value; the action is shifting to software and services. Outside of the DMR reports, which are restricted to our clients, one interesting description of this phenomenon is in the previously cited *Harvard Business Review* article entitled "The Computerless Computer Company." Its authors argue that by the year 2000 the most successful computer companies will be those that buy computers rather than build them. "The leaders will leverage fabulously cheap and powerful hardware to create and deliver new applications, pioneer and control new computing paradigms, and assemble distribution and integration expertise that creates enduring influence with customers.... The future belongs to the computerless computer company."[12]

Evidence for the view that the action is shifting to software and services is shown in Fig. 12-4, which compares the growth of these sectors with hardware. When you consider that margins in the hardware component are declining, it is clear that most of the profit to be made in the industry will be in software and services. (At the same time, we do not agree with the authors' thesis that the decline in profitability justifies the abandonment of hardware fabrication by North American and European manufacturers.)

5. The Software Industry Is Becoming a Parts Industry

As explained in Chap. 7, the industrial revolution in software is creating a software products market based on standards. This enables independent software companies to create products that are like specialized Lego pieces. Rather than having to invest the tens of millions of dollars (or more) required to create a complete computing environment, companies can focus on a piece. It is not necessary to create a complete user interface (with windows and menus), networking software, full databases, or software for distributed computing environments. These com-

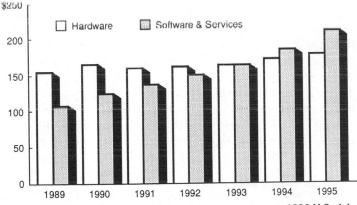

Figure 12-4. Worldwide information technology revenues in 1990 U.S. dollars (billions), 1989–1995.

ponents are already standardized and available, enabling the independent software vendor (ISV) to create software product "parts" that "plug and play" in a broader set of solutions. This is both good and bad news for ISVs. It reduces in many ways the development investment required to create innovative products. On the other hand, it increases the demands for state-of-the-art capabilities, familiarity with standards, knowledge of the availability of other parts, and sophisticated software development environments, to name a few challenges.

For the user, however, the news is basically good. The creative genius of a growing industry is being applied to the development of compatible, friendly components that can be combined creatively with others to create powerful business solutions. By the mid-1990s, customers will be able to build their own large-scale softwarehouses that contain preassembled building blocks of application code objects—some purchased and some constructed in-house.

6. The Playing Field Is Leveling

Many computer marketing personnel have been reluctant to introduce new paradigm concepts and products into their accounts for fear of opening a Pandora's box of competition. This, of course, is folly, as virtually no customer is immune to competition. Most large organizations will have adopted open systems by 1994. Vendors who appear hesitant to embrace the new paradigm are paying the price.[13] The playing field is leveling, causing many vendors to rethink their technology and marketing strategies, and to transform the attitudes, knowledge, skills, and culture of their sales and marketing forces.

This need is particularly acutely felt in companies that were most successful in the first era—specifically IBM and Digital Equipment Corporation. As we said, old paradigms die hard. Often success in the old becomes inertia in the new. Digital made considerable progress in 1992, fixing this problem with a multifaceted program supported by extensive advertising aimed at positioning the company as a leader in open systems. IBM, with an even greater need for reorientation (and opportunity), due to its weight in the market, has also taken bold steps. These include moves to restructure the entire corporation as a new paradigm enterprise, investments in RISC and Unix, the "opening" of proprietary offerings such as SAA, and internal education and training programs.

7. New Distribution Channels Are Moving to the Fore

Throughout the 1980s there was a shift from direct sales to the use of third-party distribution channels to sell and service technology. Our research indicates that this trend will continue, especially as manufacturers "spin out"[14] business units that can undertake various marketing and implementation activities effectively. Various categories of resellers have appeared on the scene in addition to the traditional distributors and dealers.

One such reseller is the VAR (value-added reseller), which adds unique value—such as specialized software and services for the retail industry—to a chosen hardware vendor's product line. The customer prefers to do business with the VAR because of its specialized know-how and ability to deliver business solutions, not just technology.

AVARs (affinity VARS) are established companies that enter the computer industry and sell to those for whom they have an affinity: the drugstore company that sells computers and specialized software to its store franchises; the auto manufacturer that sells to its dealers; the airline that sells to the transportation industry; the stock exchange that sells to the brokerage community.

SVARS (superVARS) are, ahem, VARS for VARS. They pass down large-volume discounts to smaller VARS and do training, education, and support for VARS. One even has a uniVARSity, called the Institute of Higher Earning.

Customers like one-stop shopping in which one company takes responsibility for ensuring that everything works. So they often turn to system integrators. The system integration distribution channel has grown rapidly, spawning newsletters, associations, magazines, conferences, trade shows, and related companies. The major hardware vendors have also entered the business, taking the lead in integration bids. Interestingly, IBM is the largest system integrator in the United States, with a multibillion dollar annual business.

All of this adds complexities to your relationship with technology suppliers. Not only do you need to select technology, but also you need to choose from among several categories of technology suppliers.

8. Power Is Shifting from Vendor to Customers

The research identified a power shift from producers to consumers. "Our investigation gave a striking portrait of the change in the relationship between vendors and customers. Among these is a stunning shift in power between the two. As vendors lose control of the account and the customer has new options, the account environment becomes more volatile."[15] Many customers were enamored with their new-found power, telling us of the huge leverage they were achieving by being able to play the field. Even when they kept their principal vendor, the relationship was changed forever by a customer recognition of the new paradigm, new options, and changing rules.

9. The Future of Technology Is Being Shaped Cooperatively

In the first era each producer made unilateral decisions about its products and product strategy. Each had its own user organization as a source of input and advice. For example, IBM's GUIDE and Digital's DECUS recommend product enhancements and new ideas. Some suppliers agree to respond formally to user requirements in statements of product direction, resulting in a level of accountability.

According to DMR's David Ticoll, this "many (customers) to one (supplier)" approach is inadequate in the second era. "Because of open systems, requirements need to be translated into widely accepted written specifications [such as standards] before they are turned into products." Because the goal is industrywide standards, a "many (customers) to many (suppliers)" model is needed, he says.

This takes many forms. One consists of formal standards bodies such as IEEE POSIX and the International Standards Organization's Open Systems Interconnect activities (discussed in Chap. 6). Another form produces government procurement standards such as the U.S. National Institute of Standards and Technology, the Treasury Board of Canada, or the European Working Group on Open Systems. However, although such formal standards bodies are necessary, they are not sufficient to address the problem. They tend to be slow-moving and do not design real products that companies can actually buy.

Two types of organizations fill this gap. One is a set of new product consortia. The Open Software Foundation (OSF) and Unix International, for example, collectively have more than 500 members who are funding the production of detailed specifications. This leads directly to the creation of products. OSF is in fact a not-for-profit software products company that receives seed funding from IBM, Digital, Hewlett-Packard, and other large suppliers. It creates software products and licenses them to systems manufacturers, software companies, and large user enterprises. These organizations in turn add features and resell or implement the newly packaged offerings.

A second type is best exemplified by the X/Open consortium, which has been building a many-to-many user requirements process since 1989. X/Open's membership includes influential users and suppliers, providing a forum for multilateral communications and multivendor accountability. Each year X/Open does an update of user requirements based on various research and workshop activities and designs or recommends standards specifications that meet user needs. Products that comply with these specifications may display the X/Open brand—a form of an open systems *Good Housekeeping* seal of approval.

Leadership for a Changing World

The transformation of the computer industry and the ensuing epic battles for leadership along with the IT-enabled transformation of the customers have far-reaching implications for the competitiveness of nations, national strategies, and ethics. This is a topic for another book. However, permit us to leave you with a few issues.

Whither the National Computer Industry?

It is widely held that the economic health of nations in the information age will be determined largely by national success in developing their information technology industries.[16] In fact the important battles for world leadership will more and more be fought in the global information technology marketplace, rather than the battlefield (military technology). Moreover, the IT and telecommunications infrastructure in any country constitute its information highway for economic renewal and wealth creation.

However, the information age is entering its second era, and a transformation of the industry is occurring. It follows that those nations that have industries that can make the technology paradigm shift will prosper. The task is not just to come out with better products and marketing strategies. The task for producers is to make the turn—to move as rapidly and effectively as possible from era I to era II—in terms of product strategy and merchandising. And the task for other stakeholders is not simply to develop an industry infrastructure that can compete internationally. The challenge is to make a national turn—in terms of industrial development and national policy.

Producers understand to varying degrees that a paradigm shift is occurring, and most are struggling to transform themselves. But how many governments and other influencers, stakeholders, and supporters of industry are even aware of the shift, let alone have developed national strategies to make the turn? How can the weight of R&D be shifted from military technology to the new information technology paradigm? What can be done about the sorry state of public networks in the United States in which first-era, balkanized, privately owned network fiefdoms have become a substitute for a national telecommunications highway? Will industrial development programs respond to the rising dominance of the software and service industries? Will nations that have fallen behind capitulate to protectionist pressures—causing a fatal, self-fulfilling prophecy?

Whither National Productivity?

There are big issues for national economic health beyond the computer industry itself. It is also widely held that the productivity of knowledge and service workers is becoming a critical factor in the competitiveness of companies and industrialized nations.[17] However, the critical factor in achieving productivity of knowledge and service workers is to embrace and implement the new organizational and technology paradigms we have explained. Continuation of era I approaches will result in, at best, marginal productivity improvements, and over time will become counterproductive.

National transitioning is a prerequisite for national productivity, improved living standards, and the quality of life. As a result, there is an urgent need to link the discussion of productivity and the new enterprise occurring everywhere—from boardrooms to classrooms—with an understanding of how the information age is entering its second era.

Whither Management?

The shift raises some far-reaching and sensitive issues about management prerogatives, management skills, and the future of management in general. Chances are, as a reader of this book, you are a manager or an executive high up (or moving up) the hierarchy. You are someone who is open to change and interested in new ideas. But what is your initial personal reaction to the idea of moving beyond the familiar hierarchy?

Skepticism and unease are understandable, especially given the lack of knowledge about the technology shift and its role in creating the new. However, the shift is catching up with era I organizations that face a glaring reality. That is, the most effective, competitive, and profitable enterprises will be those that have adopted and integrated the new organizational and technology paradigms, including the adoption of self-managed, team-based networked structures.

DMR has been working to make the turn in its own organization—both from the perspective of our consulting services and skills in the market and also in terms of our own structure and computing environments. One thrust has been the adoption of team structures, beginning in our U.S. division. Important decisions in the division have been shifted to teams of project, marketing, and practice professionals who must reach consensus. Another thrust is to shift the focus in the company from managers to professionals—those who create value for our clients. The professionals with the greatest expertise are members of the DMR Council who work with their counterparts in management to provide leadership for the company. Professionals can achieve similar levels of compensation, influence, and recognition without having to switch to management, as has been the case in our industry in the past.

However, the changes have not been without difficulty. A couple of years ago the two of us were sitting on a plane after a particularly difficult meeting loaded with political and turf issues. It occurred to us at the time that if DMR, the company that first conceptualized the shift, was having difficulties making the turn, the challenge would be considerable in the broader market.

The shift will require all managers to personally evaluate their relationships with others, their work goals, and the ways they can use their talents well. The shift raises far-reaching issues regarding personal and organizational power. Rather than power over people to achieve results, we are shifting to power with people for results.

Max Hopper put it well when telling us of the difficulties he is having in changing the attitudes of IS people to make the shift at American Airlines, saying "This is going to take a long time." Back in 1985, a book by Tapscott, Henderson, and Greenberg, described the challenge:

> The new technology has raised the need for a new kind of manager—a manager who sees no contradiction between productivity and the quality of work life; who can think and act strategically; who has the courage to lead change; who has the confidence to encourage innovation; who seeks joint-ownership of problems and system solutions; and who is willing by personal example to integrate technology into his or her job. In many ways the new technology is at the center of the transformation of yesterday's managers into tomorrow's leaders.[18]

Whither the Dark Side?

The paradigm shift brings a new promise of information technology. It also brings new dangers.

One of the biggest concerns in the first era was the danger of technology "deskilling"—eliminating jobs and causing massive unemployment. Both of us found ourselves on podiums, panels, and advisory committees debating the "job threat" that computers might cause. This was not surprising, as the main focus of technology was the elimination of clerical head count and the deskilling of secretaries to become word-processing operators.

Ironically, the paradigm shift has turned the discussion upside down. The big danger to unemployment in the second era (for both individual companies and nations) comes from the *failure* to proliferate and effectively use the new technology. Similarly, it is only through the enhancement of work and creation of whole jobs as part of team structures that the big gains in productivity can be achieved.

However, other very real issues are arising from this shift to integration. The balkanization of systems and networks did provide a degree of technology-necessitated privacy. Integration of information creates a new weapon that will be decisive in the competitive battles unfolding. It also creates a dark-side weapon that can be used by corporations and governments to the detriment of their stakeholders.

It is not only the protection of privacy for individuals but security issues for organizations that come to the fore. As we become more reliant on our networks, our vulnerability to system failure increases. In fact, in a 1991 survey of opinion leaders in North America, Europe, and the Far East, we discovered that security had moved up the priority list from nowhere as a technology issue to second place.[19]

Further, an issue of values is raised. That is, what will be the values and ethics driving the transformation? The need to improve quality of work life as part of a strategy for making the transition may not be apparent or even desirable to first-era planners and implementers. What will happen to the large numbers of people working from their homes? What will happen to the workweek? Will the new enterprise increase gaps between haves and have-nots, between north and south, between men and women, between skilled and unskilled, between knowledge workers and production workers, between knowers and know-nots? It is true that overall the shift will be central to the generation of wealth and prosperity, but what will happen to those who due to knowledge and skill gaps—or sheer redundancy—are dislocated in the process? These are issues that will be shaped largely by the values of individuals, corporations, and governments. Collectively we can determine the outcome, rather than abdicating responsibility and just letting things happen.

Leadership for the Transition Is Your Opportunity

We believe the paradigm shift raises some far-reaching issues regarding the social distribution of the benefits and wealth generated. Alvin Toffler touches the issue, explaining how Marx contended that workers would be powerless until they seized the means of production from the capitalist class that owned them.

It is one of the grand ironies of history that a new kind of autonomous employee is emerging who, in fact, does own the means of production. The new means of production, however, are not to be found in the artisan's toolbox, or in the massive machinery of the smokestack age. They are, instead, crackling inside the employee's cranium—where society will find the single most important source of future wealth and power.[20]

However, the owners of these crackling brains still have little or no ownership in the wealth they create, other than a salary and maybe a bonus plan. As the shift evolves, and as their power grows, the issue of ownership of wealth will, we believe, be posed. The shift to high-performance self-managed teams and the new integrated enterprise is a shift toward workplace democracy. The cultural attitude that someone else should decide everything that is important in one's work life is changing—to the benefit of organizations, economies, and society. It is an evolution from someone selling you a solution, to your participation in determining the solution, and finally to your joint ownership of team solutions and new ways of working. And more and more the question will be posed, Who should benefit from this transformation we are working to achieve?

Passive observation of tumultuous change breeds paralysis and cynicism. Your world is in transformation, and you have an opportunity to be an active participant in this change—to lead—not necessarily to give great oratory or call troops to arms, but to lead, helping your organization learn and be able to learn. Wherever you are in the hierarchy, whatever your job type, whatever your special competency, you have an opportunity to work with others in making the transition to the new.

We not only have an opportunity but a responsibility to ourselves to shape our own destiny—to create a productive, fulfilling life. As we enter the second era of the information age, the future doesn't just happen. It will be created by people, with values, aspirations, and growing expectations. It will be created by those who demand that the smaller, more open world we are living in must be a better one.

Notes

Notes to Preface

[1]Thomas Kuhn, *The Structure of Scientific Revolutions*, 2d ed., University of Chicago Press, Chicago, 1970.

[2]Marilyn Ferguson, *The Aquarian Conspiracy—Personal and Social Transformation in Our Time*, St. Martin's Press, New York, 1976.

[3]"Stage IV Report: The Integration of Data, Text, Voice and Image," DMR Group Inc., Toronto, 1987.

[4]Unix in Canada, Final Report, 1988. Thanks to Robin Macrae for his thoughts during this period on the technology paradigm shift.

Notes to Chapter 1

[1]*Newsweek*, January 9, 1992.

[2]Peter F. Drucker, "The New Productivity Challenge," *Harvard Business Review*, November–December 1991.

[3]Donald L. Barlett and James B. Steele, *America: What Went Wrong?*, Andrews & McMeel, Kansas City, 1992.

[4]Kenichi Ohmae, *The Borderless World, Power and Strategy in the Interlinked Economy*, Harper Collins Publishers, New York, 1990.

[5]Peter F. Drucker, *The New Realities in Government and Politics/in Economics and Business/in Society and World View*, Harper & Row, New York, 1989.

[6]Patricia Aburdene and John Naisbitt, *Megatrends 2000, Ten New Directions for the 1990s*, William Morrow and Company, New York, 1990.

[7]Jack Nadel, *Cracking the Global Market, How to Do Business around the Corner and around the World*, American Management Association, New York, 1987.

[8]Michael E. Porter, *The Competitive Advantage of Nations*, The Free Press, New York, 1990.

[9]Drucker, "The New Productivity Challenge."

[10]Jerry White, from a presentation describing research conducted by Ernst and Young. A longitudinal study of companies that had undertaken massive cost-cutting programs showed revenue erosion, marketplace decline, and ironically creeping cost increases necessary for survival.

[11]D. Quinn Mills, *Rebirth of the Corporation*, John Wiley & Sons, New York, 1991, pp. 34–36.

[12]Drucker, *The New Realities in Government and Politics/in Economics and Business/in Society and World View*, p. 209.

[13]Marilyn Ferguson, *The Aquarian Conspiracy — Personal and Social Transformation in Our Time*, St. Martin's Press, New York, 1976.

Notes to Chapter 2

[1]Peter F. Drucker, "The New Organization," *Harvard Business Review*, January–February 1988.

[2]Rosabeth Moss Kanter, *When Elephants Learn to Dance: Managing the Challenges of Strategy, Management and Careers in the 1990s*, Simon & Schuster, New York, 1989.

[3]Peter Keen, *Shaping the Future: Business Design through Information Technology*, Harvard Business School Press, Cambridge, Mass., 1991.

[4]Tom Peters, "The Boundaries of Business Partners — The Rhetoric and Reality," *Harvard Business Review*, September–October 1991.

[5]D. Quinn Mills, *Rebirth of the Corporation*, John Wiley & Sons, New York, 1991.

[6]Charles M. Savage, *5th Generation Management: Integrating Enterprises through Human Networking*, Digital Press, New York, 1990.

[7]Drucker, "The New Organization." For a more complete presentation of Drucker's views, see Peter F. Drucker, *The New Realities*, Harper & Row, New York, 1989.

[8]Robert Johansen, *Groupware: Computer Support for Business Teams*, The Free Press, New York, 1988. For an excellent more recent discussion of workgroup systems, see Robert Johansen et al., *Leading Business Teams*, Addison-Wesley, New York, 1991.

[9]James P. Womack, Daniel T. Jones, and Daniel Roos, *The Machine That Changed the World*, Rawson Associates, New York, 1990.

[10]Rosabeth Moss Kanter, "The New Managerial Work," *Harvard Business Review*, November–December 1989.

[11]Elliott Jacques, "In Praise of Hierarchy," *Harvard Business Review*, January–February 1990.

[12]The notion of designing for accomplishment rather than accountability was articulated to us by Toronto-based consultant and author, Joe Arbuckle.

[13]Art Caston and Don Tapscott, "Stage IV Report: The Integration of Data, Text, Voice and Image," DMR Group Inc., Toronto, 1987.

[14]Michael Hammer, "Reengineering Work: Don't Automate, Obliterate," *Harvard Business Review*, July–August 1990. The term *reengineering* as applied to business processes was later popularized by Hammer and is discussed in this article. Hammer also argued for this perspective as far back as the early 1980s, which is discussed further in the following article: Michael Hammer and Michael Zisman, "Design and Implementation of Office Information Systems," *Office Automation Infotech State of the Art Report*, series 8, no. 3, Infotech Limited, Maidenhead Berkshire, England, 1980.

[15]Don Tapscott, *Office Automation: A User-Driven Method*, Plenum Publishing Corporation, New York, 1982. This book contains the most comprehensive early presentation of the role of procedure, business process, job, and organizational redesign in office systems.

[16]Thomas H. Davenport and James E. Short, in "The New Industrial Engineering: Information Technology and Business Process Redesign," *Sloan Management Review*, Summer 1990, define a business process as "a set of logically related tasks performed to achieve a defined business outcome."

[17]For G. A. Pall, *Quality Process Management*, Prentice-Hall, Englewood Cliffs, N.J., 1987, a business process is "the logical organization of people, materials, energy, equipment and procedures into work activities designed to produce a specified end result (work product)."

[18]Marvin R. Weisbord, *Productive Workplaces: Organizing and Managing for Dignity, Meaning and Community*, Jossey-Bass Publishers, San Francisco, 1991. This is a thorough, contemporary assessment of Taylor and his contribution.

[19]Peter F. Drucker, "The New Productivity Challenge," *Harvard Business Review*, November–December 1991.

[20]Weisbord, *Productive Workplace*.

[21]Frederick Taylor, in F. B. Copley, *Frederick W. Taylor, the Father of Scientific Management*, 2 vols., Harper & Row, New York, 1923.

[22]Douglas Englebart, "Augmenting Human Intellect, a Conceptual Framework. Summary Report," Stanford Research Institute, Menlo Park, Calif., 1962, D. C. Englebart, R. W. Watson, and J. C. Norton, "The Augmented Knowledge Workshop," Proceedings of the National Computer Conference, New York.

[23]Christine V. Bullen and John L. Bennett, "Groupware in Practice: An Interpretation of Work Experience," *Centre for Information Systems Research* (CISR WP no. 205), Sloan School of Management, MIT.

Notes to Chapter 3

[1]John Naisbitt and Patricia Aburdene, *Re-inventing the Corporation*, Warner Books, New York, 1986.

[2]Paul Konstadt, "The Sharper Image," *CIO Magazine*, April 1991. An excellent article on the integration of image technology with enterprise computing.

[3]Pierre Goad, "Feeling Better—Canada Seems Satisfied with the Medical System That Covers Everyone," *Wall Street Journal*, December 3, 1991.

Notes to Chapter 4

[1]Benn R. Konsynski and F. Warren McFarlan, "Information Partnerships—Shared Data, Shared Scale," *Harvard Business Review*, September–October 1990.

[2]Tom Peters, "The Boundaries of Business Partners—The Rhetoric and Reality," *Harvard Business Review*, September–October 1991.

[3]Max D. Hopper, "Rattling Sabre—New Ways to Compete on Information," *Harvard Business Review*, May–June 1990.

[4]D. G. Copeland and J. L. Kenney, "Airline Reservation Systems: Lessons from History," *MIS Quarterly*, September 1985.

[5]Harvard Business School Case #9-186-005, American Hospital Supply Corporation (A) the ASAP System, Harvard Business School, Cambridge, Mass., 1985.

[6] Don Tapscott, "Open Systems—Managing the Transition," *Business Week,* October 14, 1991. The same issue, apparently coincidentally, had a 37-page advertising supplement on open systems.

[7] Art Caston and Don Tapscott, Stage IV Report, "The Integration of Data, Text, Voice and Image," DMR Group Inc., Toronto, 1987.

[8] As quoted in *Business Week,* November 12, 1990, in a special advertising supplement entitled "The Strategic Link between Business Partners."

[9] As discussed in "Point of Sale Systems," *CIO Magazine,* February 1991, p. 18.

[10] *Business Week,* May 8, 1989.

[11] As cited in Stephen A. Caswell, *E-MAIL,* Gage Educational Publishing Company, Toronto, 1988. Refer to this book for the best general discussion on electronic mail issues.

[12] Starr Roxanne Hiltz and M. Turoff, *The Network Nation,* Addison-Wesley, Reading Mass., 1978. Computer conferencing is a powerful technology that has been slow to take off due to the huge change in human communication it requires.

[13] Soft·Switch Inc., "Electronic Mail: Technology, Applications and Infrastructure," Wayne, Pa., 1989. A stimulating paper authored by and available from Soft·Switch Inc.

[14] For a good early discussion of this, see Peter G. W. Keen, *Competing in Time: Using Telecommunications for Competitive Advantage,* Ballinger Publishing Company, New York, 1988.

Notes to Chapter 6

[1] X/Open is an independent, worldwide, open systems organization supported by most of the world's largest information systems suppliers, user organizations, and software companies. Its mission is to bring greater value to users through the practical implementation of open systems.

[2] Don Tapscott, "Open Systems—Managing the Transition," *Business Week,* October 14, 1991. These findings of the Strategies for Open Systems program were reported in this article.

[3] Adapted with permission from "Throughout History with Standards: Speaking of Standards," a document of the American Standards Association (now the American National Standards Institute), Cahners Publishing Co., Des Plaines, Ill., 1972.

Notes to Chapter 7

[1] A. S. Rappaport and S. Halevi, "The Computerless Computer Company," *Harvard Business Review,* July–August 1991. This article provides a provocative discussion of the growing importance of software in the computer industry.

[2] Bertrand Meyer, "The New Culture of Software Development," *Journal of Object-Oriented Programming,* November/December 1990.

[3] Kathleen Melymuka, "The 4,000-Pound Gorilla," *CIO Magazine,* March 1991.

[4] Frederick P. Brooks, *The Mythical Man-Month: An Essay on Software Engineering,* Addison-Wesley, New York, 1975.

[5]Frederick P. Brooks, "No Silver Bullet: Essence and Accidents of Software Engineering," *IEEE Computer*, April 1987.
[6]Peter F. Drucker, *Managing for Results*, Harper & Row, New York, 1964.
[7]Meyer, "The New Culture of Software Development."
[8]John W. Verity and Evan I. Schwartz, "Software Made Simple: Will Object-Oriented Programming Transform the Computer Industry?" *Business Week*, September 30, 1991. This article provides a readable explanation of object-oriented programming written for a business audience.
[9]Tony Baer, "The Mighty Pen," *Information Week*, December 30, 1991. This article provides a good discussion of pen-based systems.
[10]Stan Rolland, director, DMR Group Inc., is responsible for the company's research and development of software development tools. His comment is quoted from personal correspondence, February 1992.
[11]Brad J. Cox, "There *Is* a Silver Bullet," *Byte*, October 1990. This article provides a good discussion of the software industrial revolution. Cox was the first writer we are aware of to introduce the concept of a "standard parts marketplace" for software. He argues that "the software crisis is not an immovable obstacle but an irresistible force—a vast economic incentive that will grow toward infinity as the global economy moves into the information age."

Notes to Chapter 8

[1]Michael Hammer, "Re-engineering Work: Don't Automate, Obliterate," *Harvard Business Review*, July–August 1990.
[2]We are indebted to Joe Arbuckle for his suggestion of the terms *reimage, reshape*, and *renew*.
[3]Although this may seem like motherhood, our experience indicates that it is still exceptional line managers who have embraced IT thinking into their jobs. Expect articles, speakers, and even prestigious business journals to continue to argue for change. For example, as put forth by Kim Clark, "Technical questions cannot be the concern of only the technical community. General managers must know the value and advantage of the company's own processes and methods and know how to match their potential technical capabilities with opportunities to serve customer needs." Clark, "What Strategy Can Do for Technology," *Harvard Business Review*, November–December 1989.
[4]Aligning IS with the Business, Stage II–III Report. A program of DMR Group Inc. and Cognitech Services Corporation, 1991. Executive summary, p. 7.
[5]A. P. deGeus, "Planning as Learning," *Harvard Business Review*, March–April 1988, pp. 70–74. Arie deGeus contended some time ago that *planning is learning*, arguing that the most important results of planning are not the strategies and goals adopted but the learning that has occurred. So if learning is a legitimate goal, then you will organize and structure a planning process differently than if a document is the goal. His thinking is all the more relevant considering the significance of the transformation enabled by the paradigm shift.
[6]Joe Arbuckle, from an interview of January 1992.

[7]Ray Stata, "Organizational Learning—The Key to Management Innovation," *Sloan Management Review*, Spring 1989. According to Ray Stata, "I would in fact argue that the rate at which individuals and organizations learn may become the only sustainable competitive advantage, especially in knowledge intensive industries."

[8]Peter M. Senge, *The Fifth Discipline: The Art and Practice of the Learning Organization*, Doubleday, New York, 1990, p. 9.

[9]James Martin, *An Information Systems Manifesto*, Prentice-Hall, Englewood Cliffs, N.J., 1984.

[10]See Paul A. Strassman, *The Business Value of Computers*, Information Economics Press, New Canaan, Conn., 1990.

[11]Senge, *The Fifth Discipline*, p. 9.

Notes to Chapter 9

[1]Peter M. Senge, *The Fifth Discipline: The Art and Practice of the Learning Organization*, Doubleday, New York, 1990, p. 274. "Without a genuine sense of common vision and values there is nothing to motivate people beyond self-interest....But a non-political climate also demands 'openness'—both the norm of speaking openly and honestly about important issues and the capacity continually to challenge one's own thinking. The first might be called participative openness, the second reflective openness. Without openness it is generally impossible to break down the game playing that is deeply embedded in most organizations. Together vision and openness are the antidotes to internal politics and game playing."

[2]Stan Davis and Bill Davidson, *2020 Vision: Transform Your Business Today to Succeed in Tomorrow's Economy*, Simon and Schuster, New York, 1991. According to Davis and Davidson, the real-time organization does not yet exist. A good popularization of the concept.

[3]Peter G. W. Keen, *Competing in Time: Using Telecommunications for Competitive Advantage*, Ballinger Publishing Company, New York, 1988.

[4]Based on a personal interview with Joe Arbuckle, independent consultant, author, and visionary, conducted in January 1992 in Toronto, Canada.

[5]John Naisbitt and Patricia Aburdene, *Re-inventing the Corporation: Transforming Your Job and Your Company for the New Information Society*, Warner Books, New York, 1985, p. 72. According to Naisbitt and Aburdene, the top-down authoritarian management style of traditional industrial organizations must yield "to a networking style of management where people learn from one another horizontally, where everyone is a resource for everyone else, and where each person gets support and assistance from many different directions."

[6]D. Quinn Mills, *Rebirth of the Corporation*, John Wiley & Sons, New York, 1991, p. 3. According to Mills, who popularized the cluster concept, "The main obstacle to the rebirth of the corporation is the hierarchy. A cluster organization breaks down the artificial walls that stifle creativity, innovation, communication and productivity."

[7]Peter F. Drucker, "The New Organization," *Harvard Business Review*, January–February 1988. For a more complete presentation of Drucker's views see Peter Drucker, *The New Realities*, Harper & Row, New York, 1989.

[8]Naisbitt and Aburdene, *Re-inventing the Corporation*, p. 41. "In thousands of American corporations, career ladders have traditionally been set up so that competent technical people and other specialists must abandon the area they have— and in which they excel—in order to land a high level job with more power, influence and money."

[9]Davis and Davidson, *2020 Vision*.

[10]Senge, *The Fifth Discipline*, p. 206.

[11]Michael Hammer, "Reengineering Work: Don't Automate, Obliterate," *Harvard Business Review*, July–August 1990, p. 110. Hammer tells the story of Hewlett-Packard, which had 50 manufacturing units each with its own purchasing department. The arrangement provided excellent responsiveness and service to the plants but prevented Hewlett-Packard from realizing economies of scale. The company decided to introduce a corporate purchasing unit to coordinate the others—each having access to central databases with, for example, information to help with negotiating discounts. The results included lower costs, reduction in lead times, and reduced failures.

[12]The methods used in the Citibank work-group implementations described earlier were developed in the late 1970s under the leadership of Del Henderson-Langdon at Bell Northern Research. A multimillion dollar research project established methods for determining opportunities for and implementing office information communication systems involving the redesign of office work. These methods were further developed by the BNR spin-off Trigon Systems Group Inc. and further by DMR Group, which acquired the consulting practice of Trigon.

[13]H. James Harrington, *Business Process Improvement: The Breakthrough Strategy for Total Quality, Productivity and Competitiveness*, McGraw-Hill, New York, 1991. This book provides a detailed method to process redesign. Harrington's approach, endorsed by the American Society for Quality Control, is a modern extension of industrial engineering approaches, but does not examine the enabling role of information technology in creating new work processes. For a good discussion of the issue, focusing on the role of IT, see Peter Keen, *Shaping the Future: Business Design through Information Technology*, Harvard Business School Press, Cambridge, Mass., 1991.

[14]Peter F. Drucker, "The New Productivity Challenge," *Harvard Business Review*, November–December 1991. Peter Drucker has entered the fray with his own four-step approach to improving performance. Also see Hammer, ibid., and Thomas H. Davenport and James E. Short, "The New Industrial Engineering: Information Technology and Business Process Redesign," *Sloan Management Review*, Summer 1990.

[15]From the Shell Brockville Lubricants Plant "Information Booklet for Team Operator Recruitment Process," Shell Canada, Toronto, 1991.

Notes to Chapter 10

[1]To paraphrase our colleague George Shaffner of X/Open, who, at the World Congress on Open Systems in November 1991, said: "The irresistible force of

open systems has met up with the immovable object of a trillion dollar installed base." Shaffner's trillion dollars refers to the nondepreciated base of hardware and packaged software, but excludes services and all the in-house costs of developing and maintaining systems. When all costs are considered, our figure of $3 trillion is likely underestimated. Whatever the case, the legacy investment is a big number.

[2]Speech to the UniForum, San Francisco, January 1992.

[3]Random House Dictionary of the English Language, unabridged edition, Random House, New York, 1990.

[4]Thomas Davenport, Michael Hammer, and Tauno Metsisto, "How Executives Can Shape Their Company's Information Systems," *Harvard Business Review*, March–April 1989, p. 130.

Notes to Chapter 11

[1]Joe Izzo, *The Embattled Fortress*, Jossey-Bass Publishing Co., San Francisco, 1987.

[2]Aligning IS with the Business. A program of DMR Group Inc. and Cognitech Services Corporation. Available through DMR Group Inc., 1991.

[3]Thomas M. Lodahl, from personal correspondence on the issue of the changing role of the IS function, November 1991.

[4]Thomas M. Lodahl and Kay Lewis Redditt, "Aiming IS at Business Targets," *Datamation*, February 15, 1989.

[5]Thomas J. Peters and Robert H. Waterman, *In Search of Excellence*, Harper & Row, New York, 1982.

[6]Antoinette La Belle and H. Edward Nyce, "Whither the IT Organization," *Sloan Management Review*, Summer 1987.

[7]John Dearden, "The Withering Away of the IS Organization," *Sloan Management Review*, Summer 1987.

[8]Aligning IS with the Business, Stage I Report.

[9]Aligning IS with the Business, Stages II–III Report.

[10]Lodahl and Redditt, "Aiming IS at Business Targets."

[11]Thomas V. Esposito, "Services Outsourcing: IBM Directions," from a presentation to the Yankee Group Conference, "Insourcing versus Outsourcing," held July 31–August 1, 1990, in Atlantic City, N.J.

[12]As cited by Katherine M. Hudson, vice president and director, Corporate Information Systems, Eastman Kodak Company, in a presentation to the Yankee Group Conference, "Insourcing versus Outsourcing," held July 31–August 1, 1990, in Atlantic City, N.J.

Notes to Chapter 12

[1]As Warren Bennis and Burt Nanus, in *Leaders, the Strategies for Taking Charge*, Harper & Row, New York, 1985, state, "Effective leadership can move organizations from current to future states, create conditions of potential opportunities for organizations, instill within employees commitment to change and instill new cultures and strategies in organizations that mobilize and focus energy and resources. These leaders are not born. They emerge when organizations face new problems and complexities that cannot be solved by unguided evolution" (p. 18).

[2]Peter M. Senge, *The Fifth Discipline: The Art and Practice of the Learning Organization,* Doubleday, New York, 1990, p. 10. Peter Senge argues that "team learning is vital because teams, not individuals are the fundamental learning unit in modern organizations. This is where 'the rubber meets the road': unless teams can learn, the organization cannot learn."

[3]Don Tapscott, Del Henderson, and Morley Greenberg, *Planning for Integrated Office Systems: A Strategic Approach,* Holt, Rinehart and Winston, Toronto, 1985, p. 200.

[4]Bennis and Nanus, *Leaders, the Strategies for Taking Charge,* p. 21.

[5]Stratford P. Sherman, "Inside the Mind of Jack Welch," *Fortune,* March 27, 1989.

[6]Peter M. Senge, "The Leader's New Work: Building Learning Organizations," *Sloan Management Review,* Fall 1990. Senge has been instrumental in the change of thinking on leadership. His book, *The Fifth Discipline,* is the best single source on the topic.

[7]Senge, *The Fifth Discipline,* p. 340.

[8]From discussions held in 1991.

[9]Art Caston and Don Tapscott, "Stage IV Report: The Integration of Data, Text, Voice and Image," DMR Group Inc., Toronto, 1987, chap. 3.

[10]Many thanks to R. E. McCulloch, whom we consider a leader in changing organizational cultures to exploit the new technology.

[11]Andrew S. Rappaport and Shmuel Halevi, "The Computerless Computer Company," *Harvard Business Review,* July–August 1991.

[12]Ibid. The article set off a torrent of controversy in subsequent issues, in which many argued that what is true for corporate strategy is not necessarily true for national policy and the United States would be ill-advised to withdraw from the manufacturing of hardware.

[13]By 1995, 78 percent of sites of greater than 50 people will have adopted open systems standards.

[14]John Sculley, *Odyssey,* Fitzhenry & Whitside, Toronto, 1987, pp. 391–395. For a discussion of the spinout, refer to this novel.

[15]Strategies for Open Systems, Stage II Report, DMR Group Inc., 1990.

[16]Stan Davis and Bill Davidson, *2020 Vision: Transform Your Business Today to Succeed in Tomorrow's Economy,* Simon and Schuster, New York, 1991. Davis and Davidson argue, "Sustained dominance of core information technologies and industries is the critical platform for future world leadership" (p. 147).

[17]See the discussion on productivity in Chap. 1.

[18]Tapscott, Henderson, and Greenberg, *Planning for Integrated Office Systems,* p. 220.

[19]From the X/Open World Survey, conducted by DMR Group Inc. Available through X/Open Corporation.

[20]Alvin Toffler, *Powershift: Knowledge, Wealth and Violence at the Edge of the 21st Century,* Bantam Books, New York, 1991, pp. 216, 217.

Index

About the Authors

Don Tapscott is vice-president technology for DMR.
Employing more than 2200 professionals in Canada, the
United States, Australia, and Europe, DMR offers services
including information technology planning, architecture and
management, technology transfer, outsourcing, and systems
integration. An internationally sought speaker and
consultant on the topic of information technology, Mr.
Tapscott has advised and given executive briefings to
leading enterprises and governments around the world.
Paradigm Shift is his third book.

Art Caston is vice-president architectural consulting for
DMR. His work in developing business reengineering
methods and in leading major transformational change
assignments has been instrumental in building DMR's
reputation in this area. He was the principal author of
DMR's 1986 syndicated study, The Integration of Data,
Text, Voice and Image—the formative study that first
explained the paradigm shift.